COMPUTERS AND THE LAW

LAW IN CONTEXT
Editors: Robert Stevens (Professor in Law in Yale University)
and William Twining (Professor of Law in the University of
Warwick)

Already published:

Accidents, Compensation and the Law, P. S. Atiyah
Company Law and Capitalism, Tom Hadden
Karl Llewellyn and the Realist Movement, William Twining
Cases and Materials on the English Legal System, Michael Zander

Computers and the Law

COLIN TAPPER

Tutor in Law at Magdalen College, Oxford

DISTRIBUTED IN U. S. A.
EXCLUSIVELY BY

Fred B. Rothman & Co.

SOUTH HACKENSACK, N. J. 07606

WEIDENFELD AND NICOLSON
London

ISBN 0 297 76571 X
Printed in Great Britain by
Willmer Brothers Limited
Birkenhead

CONTENTS

CASES

ENGLISH

AMERICAN

AUSTRALIAN

NEW ZEALAND

STATUTES

BRITISH

REPORTS

FOREWORD

One of the objectives of the Law in Context series is to publish scholarly works on new or neglected subjects which cut across orthodox classifications of legal fields. The interaction of computers and the law is such a subject.

The development of the computer has widespread and fundamental implications for law and for lawyers. But, as Tapper points out, few of us have passed beyond the stage of uncomfortable jokes about the subject, thereby exhibiting a mixture of ignorance, irrational fear and exaggerated awe. Yet, even after more than two decades of 'the computer age', such attitudes still predominate in many circles; and only a small minority of law students in the United Kingdom and elsewhere are given even an elementary introduction to the subject as part of their formal legal education.

This book sets out in a sober and cautious way to counter this ignorance and remedy this neglect. *Computers and the Law* should establish beyond a reasonable doubt that far from being an esoteric subject, of concern only to a few specialists, it has important practical and theoretical implications for lawyers, teachers, students, researchers, as well as law reformers and publishers. It also has broader implications as a case study of the interaction between law and technology.

Colin Tapper has already established a reputation in England and the United States as a teacher and scholar. His special interests in jurisprudence and evidence have a direct bearing on the present work. Throughout his career he has worked extensively with computers, both as a researcher and as a consultant, and he is recognized to be one of the leading pioneers of the study of computer applications to law in the United Kingdom. It is particularly appropriate that he should be the author of the first substantial book on this subject by an English lawyer.

R.B.S.
W.L.T.

PREFACE

The invention of the computer is the greatest contribution to the quality of human life since the development of language. And for the same reason. Its effect has been to magnify the power of our greatest natural resource, the human brain, by making its use more efficient. Although computing is still in its infancy, it is not too early to consider its impact upon our lives and institutions. The more attention that is devoted now to starting in the right way, the faster we shall be able to reap the benefits which lie ahead.

The computer will condition every facet of human life in the future, and so far as law is used to regulate that life, it will affect the development of the law. The impact of the computer upon the existing pattern of rules forms part of this book. As yet, relatively few areas of law have done more than extend and adapt rules devised for other circumstances and technologies. Soon this will not be enough, and more specific responses will have to be made. It is already clear that some parts of the law are beginning to feel the strain. As more and more records are being handled by computer, for example, the law of evidence has had to make specific provision for the admissibility of such records as evidence of the transactions they record. The same phenomenon has led to pressure for new ways to be devised to protect individual human beings from the misuse of such records by way of invasion of privacy. Both topics are accordingly dealt with here.

Over and above such responses the computer will have a direct effect upon the quality of law as a human institution. The greater part of this book examines some of the various ways in which the law can benefit from the invention of the computer. Here the emphasis is on the tasks with which the computer can help, such as the preparation of documents, the retrieval of information, the prediction of decisions, the compilation of statistics and the organization of procedure. These functions vary with the context in which they are applied, legislation, litigation and registration for example.

In some of these areas aspiration has so far exceeded achievement. An attempt is made here to separate the fact from the science fiction. A conservative approach has been adopted, based on the desirability of personal verification, with the result that some achievements may indeed have been understated. Most of the work described has either been visited or at least discussed with its authors. My thanks are due to all those who have helped me by extending their cooperation in this way. The central chapters on the retrieval of case law largely reflect my own research experience.

It is already too late to hope to be able to provide complete documentation for the field covered by this book. It is however hoped that the short and highly selective bibliography will help newcomers.

This is not a technical book. It can be understood by anyone. I have tried to avoid using jargon, and where I have been aware that I have failed, have tried to explain it. A short background description of the computer is included at the beginning for those who are interested. It is hoped that this book will serve as an introduction for a newcomer to the area of interaction between computers and the law, and that it will also be suggestive for those who are already well established. It does not purport to be a comprehensive index to all that has been done, or is being done. Still less is it an exercise in prophecy.

I

The Computer

This book will suggest various ways in which lawyers may make use of computers. It is as unnecessary for the lawyer to understand the technical details and programming of the computer in order to make use of it as it is for him to understand the components and circuitry of his television set. If anything it is even less necessary since the computer is unlikely to be installed on his premises, is less likely to break down, and if it does, automatic procedures will come into play to prevent his knowing that anything has happened. It follows that this chapter is included merely for the sake of interest, or completeness. Nothing that it contains is essential for understanding the rest of the book.

1 THE NATURE OF A COMPUTER SYSTEM

A very short and untechnical description of a computer system will be given so as to indicate roughly what the constituent parts are, and how they can be made to operate. Some attempt will be made to translate computer jargon into ordinary English throughout. The chapter will end with an indication of possible lines for future development.

It is necessary to establish some major distinctions at the outset. The first, and most fundamental, is that between 'hardware' and 'software'. Hardware refers to the physical components of the system, the machines themselves; while software refers to the instructions which establish a pattern of operations, or the programmes. It is the combination of these features which distinguishes the computer from other machines. It is thus a device which operates on the basis of instructions which it has the capacity to store, and apply sequentially. The instructions may be extremely complicated, and together with the simplicity and generality of application of the hardware give the computer its characteristic versatility. None of these features should be too rigidly defined. There is room for argument about whether a given device is or is not a computer, and clearly many more distinctions may be drawn between different types of computer. Nor is the distinction between hardware and software by any means absolute. It is often a matter of indifference whether a particular facility is built into the device as a new component, or is merely achieved by a special set of instructions for the existing components.

It is helpful to explain these concepts of hardware and software in the light of two further distinctions, one for each. So far as hardware is concerned this is that between the Central Processing Unit (CPU) and the remainder of the devices which constitute the total system. The CPU is the most typical part of a computing system, and a system without a CPU is unimaginable. It is indeed what the ordinary person understands as a computer. In it, all the manipulation of the information entering the system takes place. When the computer system is used for calculating, it is the part in which all the calculations take place. In a system devoted to data processing, the retrieval of legal information for example, it is the part in which all the sorting and rearranging takes place. The remainder of the associated devices are regarded as peripheral to it. These may include devices for preparing and storing the data to be entered into the CPU, and devices for presenting or transmitting data. Since these devices are defined negatively by reference to the CPU, and since the concept of a computer system is vague, there is sometimes room for doubt as to whether a particular device is properly regarded as a peripheral part of the computer system or as being altogether separate from it.

In the case of software, or programmes, the important distinction is that between the operating system of the computer, and application systems. The essential feature of most CPUs is a collection of minute components capable of registering and transmitting an electrical charge which will be either positive or negative. These components are interconnected according to a geometric pattern characteristic of the particular CPU. All information which enters the system must be translated into the appropriate sequence of charges, distributed to the appropriate components, and at the output stage translated back into a comprehensible form. At its most basic level it is the operating system which enables this to take place. Its func-

tion is to provide a means by which sets of instructions, or programmes in conventional form, as described in programming
manuals, can be made to create the necessary physical states in the
component parts of the CPU. Such systems are provided by the
manufacturers and are of vital importance to them; they are of much
less interest to the average programmer, who writes programmes in
the conventional programming languages, which presuppose such
operating systems. Programmes of this type constitute the bulk of all
programming activity. They are, unlike operating systems, not so
exclusively geared to particular machines, but are often capable of
being run with a minimum of alteration on different models.

A computer is thus a general purpose device capable of storing
and operating upon a set of instructions. As part of a computing
system it embodies a central processor and peripheral devices. It
needs an operating system to enable it to transform instructions into
the appropriate pattern of physical states; and to enable it to accomplish specific tasks, sets of instructions orientated towards each such
task must be compiled.

2 CENTRAL PROCESSING UNITS

This section will discuss briefly both the nature of such units, that
is their characteristics as hardware, and also their mode of operation. There are two main types of computer: analogue computers,
which work on the basis of a set of continuously variable physical
states, and operate by comparative measurement and disposition of
such states; and digital computers, which work on the basis of a set
of discrete though connected elements which can be in one of two
states. Analogue computers are used extensively in design and
machinery control systems, but are unimportant in legal applications and will not be discussed further.

The CPUs of digital computers have developed rapidly in capacity
and speed since the change from thermionic valves to transistors
as their basic components, and have generally benefited from advances in micro-circuitry and large-scale integration of components.
Information is contained in the CPU as a pattern of positively or
negatively charged units of core, or bits. Any character which is a
member of a set, such as a letter of an alphabet, can be represented
by a group of bits, the minimum number of which is determined
by the number in the set. Thus if the set is the ten decimal digits,
the minimum length is four bits; if it is the twenty-six letters of the

alphabet, the minimum length is five bits. In practice a single character is often expressed by a group of eight bits, or word, to allow
for the appearance of letters in both upper and lower case, decimal
digits, punctuation and other symbols. This may well seem unwieldy
but it is compensated for by the capacity and speed of modern
CPUs which may well have a capacity in excess of a million bits, and
an access time of less than a millioneth of a second, or one microsecond.

Within the CPU these bits are manipulated in a separate space,
sometimes known as the arithmetic and logic unit, which can perform either arithmetic operations such as addition and subtraction
or logical operations such as those prescribed by Boolean algebra.

The efficiency of the CPU is determined by the operation of a
control unit which integrates the operation not only of the internal
memory and arithmetic and logic unit, but also the interaction of
the CPU with its various peripheral devices. In large modern systems
this unit has to perform extremely sophisticated tasks, and stands at
the borderline of hardware and software since it often consists of a
physical part of the CPU permanently occupied by a particular basic
programme which is its operating system. In large modern systems
this unit is necessary to provide facilities for multi-programming
whereby the CPU can handle a number of quite separate programmes
simultaneously, and multi-access whereby use can be made of the
CPU from a number of different locations simultaneously. These
facilities are necessary since the power and expense of very large
computers is such that they must operate at optimum efficiency, and
this is best achieved by the computer itself. Thus the operating system
will arrange for switching between one programme and another
and between one user and another so as to ensure that all the facilities are being used as intensively as possible. Such sophisticated
systems are required in legal information retrieval systems where
the aim is to provide immediate access to a centralized store of legal
information from a terminal situated in the lawyer's own office.
Such a system would also enable work for which speed is not so
essential to be cumulated into a batch which could be run on the
computer at a time when the demand for immediate access is not
high, such as the middle of the night. This might be appropriate in a
legal environment for, say, the creation of statistics relating to the
work of different courts.

3 PERIPHERAL DEVICES

As noted above, peripheral devices are defined negatively with reference to the CPU. This leads to a certain amount of overlapping. Some secondary storage devices such as fixed fast drums provide such rapid access that it is somewhat arbitrary to regard them as distinct from the core storage of the CPU. At the other extreme, the system may provide references to information which is permanently stored on microfilm which can be read only on a special viewer. It is a matter of arbitrary choice whether such viewers are, or are not, regarded as part of the computer system.

There is a vast range of peripheral devices, and what follows does not in any sense purport to be an exhaustive list, nor does it purport to describe all the variations upon particular devices produced by particular manufacturers. All of those which are mentioned, however, do have some potential for application in systems devoted to law. For convenience these devices will be considered in four groups : input devices concerned with the preparation of data in a computer assimilable form, storage devices to hold data so prepared, output devices to present data which has passed through the system to the ultimate user, and transmission devices to convey data from one location to another.

Input devices

In legal information retrieval systems at present, one of the most serious bottlenecks is caused by the unavailability of most legal materials in a computer assimilable form. This is partly because the devices for preparing information, at present held in conventional forms like books and documents, are so primitive. For many years little attention was paid to these problems since the CPUs themselves could handle so little information that linguistic applications, especially those like law requiring reiterative access to large amounts of archival material, were virtually impossible, and quite impracticable. Now that CPUs and secondary storage devices have so dramatically improved in capacity and performance, data preparation has become a serious problem.

The original technique was to employ human beings to transcribe the material to be entered into the computer system by re-keyboarding it. A keypunch was normally used. This is a machine with a keyboard rather like an ordinary typewriter. The operator simply copies the original document so far as is possible within the limits imposed by the range of characters available on the keyboard, but instead of producing typescripts produces instead either a series of cards or a continuous paper tape into which holes have been punched. The pattern of the holes represents the characters which have been copied, and after passing through a special reading head these are capable of activating the computer in the appropriate way. It will be appreciated that such copying is very boring, and the chances of erroneous transcription are high.

Various techniques can be used to reduce the incidence of error. One of the most simple, in a punched card system, is for the card to print out along the top in ordinary characters the contents of the card, so permitting the operator to make a visual check. This alone will rarely be sufficient, and in many systems a technique of mechanical verification is employed using a device similar in appearance to the original keypunch. It is, however, fed not with blank cards but with the cards which have already been punched, and are being verified. The operator goes through the motions of copying from the original source. When there is a discrepancy between the character which appears on the original card and the key being depressed on the verifier some indication is given to the operator of the verifier, usually by resistance to depression. If the original is wrong it can then be corrected. It is possible that some errors will creep through where both operators have made identical mistakes, but experience shows this to be rare, and seldom seriously important where it does occur. This is, however, an expensive and slow process roughly doubling both cost and time of preparation. It also imposes considerable administrative problems when very large amounts of data have to be prepared extremely quickly and according to uniform specifications. This has stimulated a search for some way of diminishing the degree of human participation in the process.

One avenue has led to the development of optical character recognition (OCR) devices. These devices use optical scanners to read the original text and to convert it into computer assimilable form. The development and operation of such devices has, however, revealed serious difficulties. Among the more intransigent have been those engendered by the enormous range of different forms of the same character in terms of typeface, style and size, and by the great amount of visual but non-verbal information conveyed on the printed page, in the form of such things as paragraphing, indenting and footnoting. Such considerations cause no difficulty for the human brain but present almost insuperable obstacles to the mechanical scanner. The initial reaction was to compromise, and to build devices which could scan either special magnetic characters or special styles of typescript. The former account for the caricatures of numbers to be found on the modern cheque. The latter are more acceptable in appearance, but for legal purposes still involve transcription from the original source into an ocr compatible form, with all the risk of error which that entails. Recently, more sophisticated ocr readers have begun to appear which can read directly from original sources, but these are expensive and have to be specially set up either by programming or by hardware adjustment in order to cope with each particular combination of symbols encountered in the source. This makes their use suitable only for very large volumes of material. Such devices are extremely complicated, and consequently very expensive, with the result that it is not yet possible to know whether they will ultimately prove a more reliable and economical alternative to the older keyboarding techniques.

The result is that there is at present no completely error-free method of preparing archival material for the computer. Accordingly, more sophisticated devices for detecting errors have been developed. Such devices normally embody some form of visual display of the data in its originally transcribed state. It is usual to associate a keyboard with such a device which can then be used to correct any part of the text which appears to be wrong. Many such devices are primarily intended for use as part of printing systems in which the data is being prepared for ultimate publication. As a result they often have facilities for the rearrangement of the original text in a variety of formats.

Storage devices
It will be apparent from the preceding subsection that information may be prepared in a variety of different computer assimilable formats, and these therefore constitute storage media in some sense. Punched cards, paper tape and magnetic tape can all be produced directly by transcription devices. Of these, punched cards and paper tape are unsuitable for most legal purposes where information is to be stored for long periods, and used reiteratively. So in most systems it is necessary as a preliminary process to arrange for the transcription of data held in such forms on to magnetic tape, though there

are devices which enable the initial transcription to be made directly on to magnetic tape.

The advantages of magnetic tape over punched cards and paper tape as a storage device is that it is much more durable and reliable, information can be packed much more densely on it, and it can be read into the CPU much more quickly. Thus a 2,400 foot tape could contain over 7 million characters, and be able to read them into the CPU at a rate of about 40,000 per second, or one per 25 microseconds. The whole tape could perhaps be transferred in about two minutes. In most modern systems these speeds are too slow to permit the use of magnetic tape as the main secondary storage medium. This is partly because such speeds are so much slower than the speeds of internal operation of the CPU, and also because magnetic tape has to be read serially, and this means that access to any given character on the tape will take on average about one minute, or half the time for a complete pass of the tape.

Failure to provide random access, the inability to jump from one character to another without passing over all the intervening characters has dictated the use of two other forms of magnetic storage in most systems. These are drums and discs. The former array the data on the outside of a rapidly rotating drum, the latter on the surface of a revolving disc. Both achieve their capacity for random access by having multiple reading heads which read a large number of channels or tracks of information simultaneously. They differ mainly in that discs can provide denser storage for more data, but transfer rates and access times are inferior. Discs also tend to be more readily interchangeable than drums. The sort of drum which has been used in the past might have a capacity of more than a million characters, a transfer rate of a million characters per second, or one per microsecond, and an access time for a given character of a few milliseconds. Discs are generally arranged in packs, all of the constituents of which can be read simultaneously. A typical pack might have a capacity of 140 million characters, a transfer rate of about 200,000 characters per second, or 1 per 5 micro-seconds, and an access time for a given character of about 75 milli-seconds. Other secondary storage media include variations on these devices such as the data cell and the magnetic card, but these do not seem likely to be used extensively in legal applications in the future.

The only other storage medium which need be mentioned here is microfilm. This is completely different from those described hitherto in that it can be produced directly from the original source material, and by the same token can be read directly by a human being without the necessity for any prior mechanical processing. It too constitutes an economic, compact and durable medium for storing information. Its great disadvantage is that it can not be processed directly by the computer, though there are devices which will convert some forms of microfilm automatically into computer assimilable form and vice versa; indeed such devices are often an integral part of the more sophisticated optical character-recognition systems mentioned earlier.

For legal applications it seems most likely that a combination of discs and drums will be used to store information which is to be searched or manipulated, while microfilm can be used for storage outside the computer system, ready for display to the user.

Output devices

The computer can always produce information in the same media in which it is put in, that is on punched cards, paper tapes or any of the magnetic forms, but while this may be useful where the output is to be used for input at the next stage of the operation, it is not appropriate for systems in which the output is intended to be used directly by human beings. For such purposes the information must be presented in conventional alphabetic form. The most common method of securing such an output is by the use of a line printer. These devices print a line at a time on continuous stationery which passes a print set contained on a rotating barrel or moving chain which is electrically timed to strike as the correct character is in the appropriate position. Such printers usually have a repertoire of up to 64 characters and can produce from 300 to 2,000 lines of up to 160 characters per minute. Such devices are clearly most suitable where large quantities of information are required very quickly.

In many legal applications, however, the user will wish to engage in a continuous dialogue with the computer, and will consequently require much smaller amounts of information much more slowly. He will also need to be able to intersperse his own responses. It is clearly advantageous for both processes to be conducted through one device. Two forms of terminal are available for this purpose. In both the user has a keyboard from which he can despatch responses directly to the computer. On a teletype terminal the answers come back through the same keyboard, and are printed on the same roll of paper as the responses of the user, and thus a complete record of the transaction is produced. On a video terminal the keyboard is associated with a screen, rather like a television screen, on which the information is displayed. Here the user can communicate with the computer either by depressing keys in the normal way or by using them to operate a cursor on the screen to indicate responses. These terminals may also have devices associated with them from which a printed, or hard copy, version of what appears on the screen may be produced.

Finally it should be noted in this connection that computer output can be used to activate conventional printing processes. This is an important feature of many legal applications in the field of legislation. Here the computer is used to produce not only the final draft of a statute, but also a detailed set of typesetting codes which can drive a high-quality printer to produce the conventionally printed pages which will then be bound up to constitute the statute book in its final form.

Transmission devices
One of the major economic trends in computing has been the dramatic reduction in the cost of using increasingly large computer systems. This has stimulated the growth of time-sharing multi-programming and conversational systems which for convenient use in turn necessitate the operation of terminals remote from the location of the CPU. This has stimulated the development of transmission devices. At first these operated over ordinary telegraphic lines, but the relatively low speeds of about 50 to 100 bits per second which were available are unsuitable for fast modern machines. The GPO has accordingly responded by the provision of a range of faster services more suitable for the demands of modern computing systems with conversational facilities. These require very large bandwidths, but already speeds of up to 48,000 bits per second are available in the United Kingdom for transmission between major cities. Where such facilities are available the only further device required is a modem, which links the terminal or computer to the data transmission link, automatically checking the accuracy of the information transmitted to an error rate of less than 1 in 10 million characters.

The remaining limitation on the use of such devices is the complexity of the operating software which is necessary to enable the CPU to cope with the demands imposed by such systems, and it is significant that many of the major manufacturers are seeking to meet this either by building a buffer unit into the CPU or by the provision of an entirely separate slave computer system which is used as a buffering device. Even so, the programming for such systems is formidably complex and there is scope here for considerable improvement.

4 PROGRAMMING

As previously pointed out the most fundamental, and in most modern large-scale systems so far the most complicated, programmes constitute the operating systems which allow computer systems to handle simultaneously many different jobs and many different peripheral devices. Such programmes may number their individual instructions in millions, and occupy permanently large portions of the CPU, and even secondary stores. The reason for this is that a very large part of the burden originally carried by individual users is now carried by the system. As the operating system has grown more complex, so programming by the user has become more simple. In conversational systems, the user often need do no more than signify his requirements in a very slightly modified and constrained form of his natural language, with perhaps the addition of a few simple symbols which can be quickly derived from a book. It is in this way that many legal systems will be presented to lawyers. They will probably be required to do no more than operate a video terminal according to a set of very simple instructions.

Such simplicity on the surface obviously conceals a programming substructure of some complexity. At the lowest level there is a machine code, or language, which is numerical and orientated to a particular mark of computer. This activates the computer directly. All higher programming languages must be translated into machine code before they can become effective. There is a wide spectrum of such languages ranging from basic languages which are mainly numerical and machine-dependent to general purpose languages which are mainly written in a form of natural language and are, in theory, machine-independent. For each such recognized language a further set of programmes known as an assembler or compiler must be provided to perform the task of translating the instructions written in the programming language into machine code. As the level of the programming language rises the programmes themselves become easier to write and to understand, but the efficiency of the use of the computer falls. This used to constitute a major disadvantage, and as a result most of the early programmes used in legal applications were written in basic languages or in machine code. But with the enormous increase in power and capacity of modern computers this is no longer such a serious drawback, and programmes are now commonly written in higher languages. It has the incidental advantage of utilizing the scarce skills of experienced programmers in a more efficient way by reducing duplication. This is further assisted by the use of standard sets of programmes, or library routines, which perform operations common to large numbers of users, and which have in the past been developed and made available by computer manufacturers as part of their service to their customers. Much the same effects are achieved by independent companies which specialize in writing and selling such packages.

Two conflicting tendencies in programming have emerged : on the one hand the tendency to develop higher and higher and more and more general languages until ideally all programmers will use the same language whatever application they are concerned with, and whatever machine they are using. This situation seems relatively unlikely to occur, though it would be facilitated by a greater degree of compatibility between the designs of computers made by different, or occasionally even the same, manufacturers. The continuing contraction of the computer manufacturing business may bring this closer. On the other hand one tendency is to orientate high-level languages to specific applications, in effect cutting out a separate user application programming function altogether. In such a legal environment the programming language would in effect be the ordinary language of lawyers, and all the programming expertise would be expended in writing the compiler. There are some signs of such a tendency in some legal information retrieval applications where an unmodified form of natural language is used by the lawyer, but as yet such systems have not been widely adopted, or rigorously tested. It is felt that the variety, volatility and ambiguity of natural language will impose insuperable obstacles to the complete realization of such an approach, though progress will almost certainly be made in this direction also.

5 FUTURE POSSIBILITIES

The computer has developed so far and so fast in the last twenty-five years that it is extremely hazardous to make any forecasts for the future at all. But on the other hand no projects being planned now can afford to ignore future possibilities, since the one thing that is certain is that when they come to fruition things will not be as they are now. Perhaps the best that can be done is to extrapolate from the trends shown in the recent past, taking into account research which is known to be under way.

The most dramatic feature of the recent past has been the increase in the speeds and capacity of cpus, both having increased by a factor in excess of 100 during the past decade, together with a much less than commensurate rise in either capital or operating costs. It is this which has helped to stimulate the current orientation towards multiple use of very large machines. Research currently directed towards cpu geometry and operation, based on large-scale integration (lsi) of components and parallel processing, and the development of new immediate access stores based on thin film and laser technology can be expected at least to maintain current rates of advance. Systems with four thousand times the power of the most powerful machine of the early 1960s are already under construction, and it is envisaged that instructions will be capable of being carried out at rates of up to 10^8, or 100 million, per second. Storage density of up to 645 million bits per square inch is being claimed for some laser-based memories, and elsewhere access times of less than one thousand-millionth of a second, 10^{-9} or one nano-second, have been achieved. Work is also proceeding on entirely different concepts such as chemical rather than electronic memories which may succeed before the end of the century and which, if they do, could bring to the computer the compactness, efficiency and economy of the human brain.

A further line of development in this area which has already got under way is a switch towards much smaller cpus. The same miniaturization which has reduced the cost and raised the efficiency of large machines, has had the effect of bringing powerful computers, at least by the standards of the recent past, within the range of the large individual user. If such machines are provided with large secondary storage capacity then in the case of jobs where there is relatively little computing compared with the amounts of data involved, the whole job can be carried out on the user's premises. The advantages include complete control by the user and dispensation with complicated operating systems and costly data transmission facilities. This could eventually become important in legal applications, but only if the costs of the computers are reduced still further to bring them within the range of the traditionally rather small and under-capitalized legal firm, and only if legal information becomes widely available in a computer assimilable form. As yet these developments are hardly under way but they should not be totally ignored.

Less spectacular progress has been made in the past with peripheral devices, and the future seems likely to follow the same pattern. The development of OCR for data capture has been very slow and seems likely to continue to be so, though it may well become increasingly effective for legal materials which present relatively few special problems. Voice input is also expected to develop slowly, and input from light pens seems unlikely to have any radical implications for legal applications. Advances may however be expected in secondary input devices such as magnetic tapes, discs and drums. It seems that techniques for denser packing and faster rates of transfer are well advanced. One research project envisages tapes with storage densities of up to $1\frac{1}{2}$ million bits per square inch, a tape reading speed of 1,000 inches per second, and a transfer rate of up to 6 million bits per second. More modest improvements are expected in magnetic drums, but a new form of disc is being developed which will have a capacity of up to 200 million bits, a transfer rate of around a million bits per second, and an access time of about 30 micro-seconds.

Output devices are likely to show a dramatic improvement with the further development of chemical as opposed to impact printers. These are under active development, and are reported as already having achieved, under laboratory conditions, speeds of up to 26,000 lines per minute. This is, however, unlikely to be of significance for most legal work where speeds, of that magnitude at least, are not critical. Data transmission is, however, likely to be of extreme importance, and the GPO is likely to provide a vastly improved service for the 1970s, with much greater capacity and speed and with automatic switching. As view telephones are introduced the cost and width of coverage of data transmission facilities should become susceptible of even greater improvement.

Software developments are most difficult of all to predict. It seems quite likely that some of the work currently done by programming in large-scale operating systems will increasingly be taken over by hardware. Prospects for universal high level languages do not appear especially good at present, but it is very likely that special legally orientated higher languages, or at least standard packages and macro-instructions, will become available.

2

Computers and the law of evidence

It is a matter of common knowledge that the use of computerized record-keeping has become widespread, and that it is increasing rapidly. It is therefore necessary to ensure that such records will be available as evidence in the event of litigation occurring in relation to any of the activities with which the records are concerned. A computerized system can only be justified if it is either more efficient or more economic than a conventional system, or both. It is likely to secure its increased efficiency by automating the transfer of records from one document to another, on the basis that mechanical transcription is less likely to introduce errors than human transcription. It is likely to secure its increased economy by aggregating large quantities of records into single files, so as to permit the largest amount of iterative processing. Both reasons are prone to reduce the contact between the human beings responsible for the records and the records themselves. This poses three main problems for the law of evidence. First, it may be argued that a computerized record is not as a matter of form a suitable vehicle of proof. This is because such records must have an ultimate human source which could be tapped instead, and because their form indicates the interposition of an automated process which might be unreliable. Secondly, it might be argued that if the record is to be used as evidence of the truth of its contents, that it violates the hearsay rule. Finally, it might be argued that there is no appropriate procedure for securing in court the production of records made by computers. These points will be considered in turn.

1 FORM OF COMPUTERIZED RECORDS
The first objection rests upon what is known as the best evidence rule.

This rule, which was once regarded as the most important single rule of the whole of the law of evidence, has now decayed, especially in England, to little more than a token argument of last resort for a party objecting to the admissibility of a piece of evidence. Although in origin quite separate, it has had some influence upon the development of the rule that the original of a private document must normally be tendered in evidence, and not a copy. Since most computerized records are held in magnetic form, and are as such illegible by the human eye, it is common to offer, instead of the magnetic version, a legible version which has been printed out by a line printer. The question arises of whether such a print-out will be admissible in evidence.

So far no British case has been reported in which this question has been discussed. It is therefore necessary to consider analogies. There is no doubt that in the case of a photograph the negative is the original, and that the prints are secondary evidence, and equally that reproductions of an ordinary document made by mechanical copying machines are also secondary.[1] On the other hand it was held in *Glyn* v. *Western Feature Film Co.*[2] that a synopsis of a film made by one who had seen it was preferable to the projection of the film in Court. It is possible that the Court was influenced by the context of copyright in which the question arose, and the necessity of developing a rule which could also be applied to a mimed play, evidence of which could only be given by one who had seen it. More modern analogies are provided by sound recordings on magnetic tape, and film of traces on a radar screen. It might be thought that a tape recording differs from a computerized record held on magnetic tape not only in respect of the difference between the information represented by the magnetic impulses, namely sounds in the one case and words in the other, but also in the more crucial respect that the sound tape can be reproduced directly for the jury by playing the tape over in Court, whereas the computerized record has to be passed through a printer, and perhaps even undergo a conversion programme, before it can be presented to the jury. In fact in the leading case on the admissibility of tape recorded evidence, *R.* v. *Maqsud Ali*,[3] this point could not be taken since the original conversation there was conducted in an obscure Punjabi

[1] *Nodin* v. *Murray* (1812), 3 Camp. 228.
[2] (1916), 85 L.J. Ch. 261 at 263.
[3] [1966] 1 Q.B. 688.

B

dialect which would not have been comprehensible to the jury. The question related to a number of different transcriptions of the contents of the tape into English via Urdu as an intermediate language into which the original had first been translated. It was held that the transcripts were admissible as the best evidence available, and were no more objectionable than photographic prints taken from unretouched negatives. It was also thought relevant that objects observed through telescopes, but not visible to the naked eye, could be deposed to in evidence. The broad rationale of the decision was that 'it does appear to this Court wrong to deny to the law of evidence advantages to be gained by new techniques and new devices.'[4] This was qualified only by the requirement that the accuracy of the recording could be proved, and the voices properly identified. These conditions appear to give the Court some latitude in admitting such evidence. Such a view gains support from the subsequent decision in *R. v. Stevenson*[5] where tape recordings were rejected on the basis that it had not been sufficiently well established that the tapes claimed to be original had not been tampered with, and that by analogy with the rule for photographs the originals should be retained in strict custody before the copies could be admitted. The prosecution need only show a *prima facie* case on these matters to secure the admissibility of the original tapes and transcripts made from them.[6] It seems that it is not necessary to identify the events recorded by the testimony of a human being who was present at the time, and a purely automatic system of recording will suffice. This was the situation in *The Statue of Liberty*[7] where an analogy was drawn with the admissibility of cards stamped by a machine to record times of arrival at, and departure from, work. The President of the Probate, Divorce and Admiralty Division summarized the situation so far as argument about form is concerned by saying simply that 'the law is bound these days to take cognisance of the fact that mechanical means replace human effort.'

2   HEARSAY

The most obvious objection that can be made to the reception in evidence of a computerized record is that to do so infringes the

---

[4] At p. 701.
[5] (1971), 55 Cr. App. R. 171.
[6] R. v. Robson [1972] 2 All E.R. 699.
[7] [1968] 2 All E.R. 195.

hearsay rule. Under this rule witnesses may only testify to the truth of matters of which they have personal knowledge. In the case of the computer print-out the reason for relying upon it is usually just because there is no human witness who can testify to the truth of the matters contained in it. The record will typically have been completed by an unidentifiable clerk who even if he could be identified will have no recollection of the transaction recorded, been entered into the computer system by a similarly unidentifiable operator who will know nothing of the details of individual entries, been processed in some way by the machine and will then have been printed out quite automatically. Even before the advent of the computer such a concatenation of events was so commonly the case in relation to commercial dealings that from very early times it has been necessary to develop exceptions to the rigours of the rule to cope with such situations.

In some respects these have developed differently in Great Britain and the United States. There was a general common law exception for declarations made by deceased persons in the course of duty in both systems, though in the United States a further distinct common law exception was developed for the shopbooks of parties. Subsequently there has been statutory intervention in both systems, in the United States in favour of Business Entries, and in England in a series of more general Evidence Acts, in 1938, 1965 and 1968. These will be considered in turn.

Declarations by deceased persons in the course of duty
This exception to the hearsay rule lies at the root of the new exceptions established in the United States, but has been largely superseded by the more radical statutes passed in the United Kingdom. It has been wholly supplanted in civil cases affected by the Civil Evidence Act 1968 which is not only broader in extent but which also specifically provides for the abolition of the common law exceptions.[8] In criminal cases it lingers on precariously since the Criminal Evidence Act 1965 is not quite so sweeping as its civil counterpart and leaves some scope for the operation of the common law exception, which is in this statute expressly retained.[9] It is further threatened by Part II of the draft Criminal Evidence Bill appended to the Eleventh Report of the Criminal Law Revision Committee 'Evidence (General)'

[8] Sect. 1(1).
[9] Sect. 2(1).

Cmnd. 4991, which proposes to replace the Criminal Evidence Act 1965 by very similar provisions on hearsay to those contained in Part I of the Civil Evidence Act 1968. Under the exception the declarant must be dead. This immediately creates a difficulty since in many of the computer record cases there may be difficulty in establishing the identity of the original recorder, or if this can be done, then in tracing his subsequent movements so as to establish that he is indeed dead. A further problem here is that the declarant must both have been under a duty to record the precise details recorded, and the record must relate to acts performed by the declarant. This latter requirement might well cause difficulty with many computerized records since the entry to the system is very likely to have been made by a clerk in a central office on the basis of information supplied by other employees. Such entries would not be admissible under the common law exception.[10] However, the exception would apply where the system provided for direct entry through remote terminals, say of moneys received or disbursements made.[11] The other principal conditions for the admissibility of records under this exception, namely that the act must have been performed, that the record should have been made roughly contemporaneously with the acts to which it relates, and the absence of any motive to misrepresent, should cause less difficulty. The question of contemporaneity might in some circumstances be difficult, but in view of the requirement that the record must relate to the acts of the declarant this is not so crucial here as elsewhere.

It may also be mentioned here that a further common law exception relating to the admissibility of declarations of deceased persons contrary to their interest might be invoked in vindication of computer records. This exception is also of restricted application in the United Kingdom in view of the two modern Evidence Acts, and because of the necessity of proving the death of the declarant. It is, however, freer in that the statement need not relate to the acts of the declarant, and that there need be no duty to record them, so to this extent it is more eligible in relation to the admissibility of computerized records. It is, however, subject to the different condition that the declaration should have been contrary to the interest of the declarant, known by him to be so, and relate to a matter within his personal knowledge. In this case, but not in that of a

[10] Brain v. Preece (1843), 11 M. & W. 773.
[11] Price v. Torrington (1703), 1 Salk. 285.

declaration in the course of duty, the entry can be relied upon to
establish collateral matters contained in it, which might in the case
of computerized records sometimes be of value. In some criminal
cases, where for example the record was not that of a business thus
excluding the operation of the Criminal Evidence Act 1965, and
where the act recorded was not that of the declarant thus excluding
the course of duty exception, but instead involved say an acknow-
ledgement of debt by a customer, a computerized record might be
proved under this exception. But such cases are likely to be rare.

Shopbooks
This American common law exception was originally based upon
English statutes of the seventeenth century, and justified on grounds
of necessity and trustworthiness.[12] In general, the requirements are
that the maker of the entry should be unavailable, that the entry
should have been made in the regular course of business, at or near
the time the transaction recorded occurred, and provided that there
was no motive to misrepresent the transaction. The person making
the entry should normally have made it on the basis of personal
knowledge, though this requirement is satisfied where he makes it on
the basis of the report of one who himself had personal knowledge.

In most states of the United States this common law exception
has been superseded by a Business Records statute. One of the jurisdictions in which the common law exception survives is Mississippi,
and it has there been applied to computerized records.[13] In this case
the record purported to show the balance which was outstanding on
a particular account. The procedure was that receipts were accepted
at branch offices, a record was forwarded to the central computer
where it was entered into the computer system, and the relevant
central files were updated. The accounting manager testified to this
procedure, and although the original records of receipts were held
at the branch offices they were not adduced in evidence, nor were
microfilmed copies of the branch records which were also held at the
computer centre adduced, and nor were any of the clerks who
accepted receipts called upon to testify. The state Supreme Court
upheld the decision of the trial judge that the central computerized
records were admissible in evidence under this exception on the basis
that three conditions were satisfied. First, that the electronic com-

[12] Wigmore, *Treatise on Evidence* (3rd ed. 1940), vol. V, para. 1518.
[13] *King* v. *Mississippi ex rel. Murdock Acceptance Corp.* 222 So. 393 (1969).

puting equipment was recognized as standard equipment; secondly, that the entries were made in the regular course of business at or reasonably near the time of the happening of the event recorded; and thirdly, that the foundation testimony satisfied the court that the sources of information, method and time of preparation were such as to underwrite its trustworthiness and justify its admission.

This decision reflects the liberal attitude taken to this exception in Mississippi where Wigmore's view that 'Courts must here cease to be pedantic and endeavour to be practical'[14] has long been judicially endorsed.[15] In particular, so far as the unavailability of the maker of the record is concerned, the Court has taken the view that this requirement may be dispensed with wherever the inconvenience of complying outweighs the utility of doing so. The first of the special requirements set out in the opinion is perhaps a little oddly expressed since it is hard to believe that the Court would wish to reject automatically a record produced by a machine that worked perfectly well, but happened to be unique, or to accept a record just because the machine was standard if it was using a set of experimental programmes for the first time, though the third condition might be used to deal with the latter situation. It can also be argued that the second condition was not met in the *King* case since the sheets which were printed out carried cumulative totals, and were not themselves made at or near the time of the original entries, though the basic data from which they were compiled was so entered. A Court might, however, take the view that such a delay was reasonable in the case of a computer system where the information was being held in an electronic and not human memory before reproduction, and thus not liable to decay and mis-recollection. It is in fact hard to understand why any more than the third of the conditions laid down by the Court should be regarded as mandatory, leaving the considerations dealt with by the first two to go to weight, or as factors affecting the decision arrived at in relation to the third factor. Such an approach would be in accordance with the liberal view expressed that 'the Court should apply these rules [admission of hearsay records at common law] consistent with the realities of current business methods.'[16]

---

[14] Wigmore, *Treatise on Evidence*, vol. V, para. 1530.
[15] *Grenada Cotton Compress Co.* v. *Atkinson*, 47 So. 644 at 646 (1908).
[16] At p. 397.

Business records

This section is intended to cover the various legislative formulae propounded in the United States to overcome some of the difficulties occasioned by the common law rule, and especially that flowing from the requirement of personal knowledge in the case of a composite entry. A model Act for 'Proof of Business Transactions' was propounded in New York in 1927, and subsequently adopted by a few states. This was followed by a Uniform Act on Business Records approved by the Conference of Commissioners on Uniform State Laws in 1936. This was adopted by the Federal Government and by most of the states. Subsequently, however, the American Law Institute's Model Code published in 1942 contained a further set of provisions relating to this exception, and it features also in the 1969 Preliminary Draft of Proposed Rules of Evidence for the United States District Courts and Magistrates. A feature of the latter draft, which is the only one of these to have been prepared in the computer age, is that it includes in its list of documents caught by the provisions 'a ... memorandum, report, record, or data compilation, in any form. . . .'[17]

The most commonly adopted form so far is, however, one based upon the Uniform Business Records Act. This attempts no definition of a record, extensive or restrictive, but instead leaves it to the interpretation of the Court. It requires that the custodian, or other qualified witness, testify to its identity and mode of preparation. Like the common law rule as interpreted in Mississippi, it also requires that the record should have been made in the regular course of business at or near the time of the act, condition or event, and that the Court should be satisfied that the sources of information, method and time of preparation were such as to justify admission.

The interpretation of the Nebraska version of this Act, as it applies to computerized records, was tested in *Transport Indemnity Co.* v. *Seib*.[18] Here too the state Supreme Court upheld the admissibility of the computerized records. The question related to the records of an insurance company which operated a form of policy in which the premium was calculated retrospectively according to a formula taking into account an advance premium and claims experience. These calculations were performed by the computer which also printed out all records of losses reported to the company and claims

---

[17] Rule 8.03, illustration 6. A similar form of words appears in illustration 7.
[18] 132 N.W. 871 (1965).

met by it. These records were proved by the company's director of accounting at such great length[19] as to entitle one to consider whether the statute had really achieved very much in the way of simplification. The Court took the view that the purpose of the statute, and of others like it in different states, was to fortify the old shopbook rule, and since it 'was intended to bring the realities of business and professional practice into the courtroom ... [it] should not be interpreted narrowly to destroy its obvious usefulness.'[20]

Thus here the breadth of the interpretation permitted the computerized record to be adduced even though it recorded only cumulative totals, and even though the original records were retained. Any objection on the latter basis being overridden on the somewhat surprising ground that the originals were probably also inadmissible on a strict application of the hearsay rule. *Prima facie,* such original records would appear to be more eligible than the computerized records for admission under the relevant legislation, and it is difficult to understand why such further records taken from the same source at one remove are not governed by the same objection. In this case the plaintiff was no doubt assisted by the fact that the records in question were originally submitted by the defendant, and their accuracy had never been disputed by him. The question of contemporaneity was also solved in a broad and liberal manner by taking the relevant time to be that of the creation of the original tape from which the records adduced in evidence were printed, rather than the time of printing itself which was indeed much later.

In Florida, which is one of the states which has enacted the Uniform Business Records Act,[21] an amendment has been inserted for the express purpose of dealing with computerized records. It now states that record includes 'a record kept by means of electronic data processing'. This is an interesting amendment since, as noted above, the Courts have interpreted the original form of words as applying to computerized records, and one of the strengths of the Uniform Act might be taken to be its reluctance to define a record. By providing a partial definition the Florida statute immediately creates doubt in relation to records which do not fall within the scope of the amendment, but are sufficiently novel not to have been in the minds

[19] His testimony, mostly by way of foundation for the admission of the computerized records, occupies 141 pages of the official Court record.
[20] At p. 875.
[21] F. S. A. Tit. 7, Ch. 92.36.

of the framers of the Uniform Act. Thus a record kept in an optical form in the context of laser storage technology might not fall within the strict definition but should in principle be admissible on exactly the same terms as a record held in any other computer assimilable format.

Evidence Act 1938

As a result of the Civil Evidence Act 1968 the 1938 Act now affects the reception of hearsay evidence only by Magistrates' Courts. It is an elaborate measure broadly making first-hand documentary hearsay admissible where the maker was for some reason or another unobtainable. In determining its impact upon the reception of computerized hearsay records it is necessary first to consider the definition of a document contained in it, and then any of the prescribed conditions which might be relevant. Documents are defined as including 'books, maps, plans, drawings and photographs'.[22] This is further elucidated by the definition of a statement as including 'any representation of fact, whether made in words or otherwise'. It is clear that the former of these, while not positively favourable to the reception of computerized records, is equally clearly not prohibitive since the definition is inclusive and must obviously extend to papers of the sort that a computer would print out. It is also possible that magnetic tapes and discs might be included though this is less likely since gramophone records which were, of course, well known in 1938 are not explicitly included, and seem closely analogous. The definition of a statement is, however, quite apt to include representation either on tape or disc.

The Act covers both the case where the maker of the statement had personal knowledge of the matters dealt with by it, and where he was merely acting in pursuance of a duty to record information supplied by one who did have such personal knowledge. In the latter case the record is required to be 'continuous'. There are difficulties in applying either level to computerized records. It is made a condition of admissibility that the maker should either have made the record with his own hand, or signed, initialled or otherwise recognized it, as one for which he was responsible. This is unlikely to be capable of being met in the case of computerized records. The record might, however, occasionally indicate the identity of its maker, or alternatively an extraneous writing acknowledging the

[22] Sect. 6(1).

authenticity of the record might satisfy this requirement. A further requirement is that the document should not have been made by one interested in the proceedings. It must, however, have been made either by someone with personal knowledge or by someone under a duty to record information supplied by someone with personal knowledge. These requirements limit the circumstances in which the computerized record would be useful. They would, for example, have led to the exclusion of the computerized records in both *King* v. *Mississippi ex rel. Murdock Acceptance Corp.*[23] and *Transport Indemnity Co.* v. *Seib*[24] since in both the record was made and tendered by a party to the proceedings. It is also a condition in the case where the maker has no personal knowledge that the record should be continuous, and the view has been expressed that this would exclude 'many business records, particularly under modern systems of record keeping'.[25]

Criminal Evidence Act 1965

This Act, which applies generally in criminal cases, broadly creates an exception to the hearsay rule for documents forming part of a record relating to any trade or business. A document is defined to include any device by means of which information is recorded or stored. This was, in view of the widespread use of computerized records at the time of the Act's passage, clearly intended to cover computers. It is perhaps a little unfortunate that the *document* is so defined since it makes it sound as if the computer itself is a sort of document. In fact, the print-out will normally be on paper and not in need of any special definition, but the wording here is clearly apt to include discs, tapes and punched cards. The definition of statement follows that in the Civil Evidence Act 1938. Other provisions of the Act are also favourably inclined towards the reception of computerized records. Thus the only requirement is that the original supplier of the information should have had personal knowledge of it, and it does not matter through how many hands it may have passed on its journey into the machine. It is also a reason for not calling as a witness the original supplier that, having regard to all the circumstances, he is unlikely to have any recollection of the matters dealt

[23] 222 So. 393 (1969).
[24] 132 N.W. 871 (1965).
[25] Law Reform Committee 13th Report, *Hearsay Evidence in Civil Proceedings*, Cmnd 2964 (1966), para. 16(a).

with. This will be most commonly the case in routine computer applications. Finally, many of the provisions which crippled the application of the 1938 Act to computerized records are either, like questions of interest, made into matters going to weight, or, like the requirement of the continuity of the record, abandoned altogether.

Despite the slight clumsiness in the approach to the definition of a document, this statute is simple, straightforward and sufficient to provide a satisfactory framework for the reception of computerized records in evidence in the area to which it relates.

Civil Evidence Act 1968

Part I of this statute is more sweepingly permissive in the reception of both documentary and oral hearsay than any previous enactment in the United Kingdom. It largely follows the recommendations of the Law Reform Committee.[26] It provides for the admissibility of first-hand hearsay in most cases where direct oral evidence would be admissible, and for more remote documentary hearsay where the statement forms part of a record compiled by a person acting under a duty. It also provides specifically for the admissibility of statements contained in documents produced by computers. Now that the requisite rules have been drafted this statute governs civil proceedings in the High Court and County Court except for bankruptcy proceedings where the strict rules of evidence do not apply, but it has not yet been implemented for proceedings in Magistrates' Courts.[27]

The provisions specifically relating to the admissibility of statements produced by computers will be examined first. Subsection 5(1) provides that a statement contained in a document produced by a computer shall be admissible in evidence provided that direct oral evidence would have been admissible, that the relevant rules of Court have been complied with, and further conditions set out in subsection 5(2) have been met. The requirement that the evidence shall consist of a statement contained in a document is not unduly restrictive since the definition of statement is the same as that in the

---

[26] *Ibid.*
[27] Civil Evidence Act 1968 (Co. 2) Order 1969 S.I. 1104/1969; Civil Evidence Act 1968 (Co. 3) Order 1970 S.I. 18/1970. The Criminal Law Revision Committee in its 11th Report Evidence (General) Cmnd. 4991 (1972) has recommended the importation of substantially identical provisions into criminal law.

1938 and 1965 Acts, while the definition of a document is much more elaborate :

10(1) (c) 'document' includes in additon to a document in writing – any disc, tape, sound track or other device in which sounds or other data (not being visual images) are embodied so as to be capable (with or without the aid of some other equipment) of being reproduced therefrom; and

(d) any film, negative, tape or other device in which one or more visual images are embodied so as to be capable (as aforesaid) of being reproduced therefrom . . . .

The provision of such sources as alternatives to documents in writing indicates that the Act envisages the reception of the original records as held in the computer, and that evidence admitted under it is not to be restricted to the normal print-out.

The requirement that direct oral evidence should be admissible is not restrictive since it is not necessary that any individual should have been in a position to supply it. The requirement relates to legal rather than physical possibility, and is designed to preserve from exposure computerized records to which privilege attaches, for example. The relevant rules of Court deal largely with questions of the procedure for exchanging notices.[28] The main conditions for the admissibility of such evidence are set out in subsection 2 of section five, and in the amplifying and explanatory subsections 3 to 6. It must be said at the outset that these provisions are extremely elaborate. The first condition is

. . . that the document containing the statement was produced by the computer during a period over which the computer was used regularly to store or process information for the purposes of any activities, regularly carried on over that period, whether for profit or not, by any body, whether corporate or not, or by any individual.[29]

It will be noticed that the document must have been produced during a period of regular work by the computer. 'Regular' is not defined, but is apparently different from 'ordinary' and 'proper' since these terms are used later in the subsection. It is not obvious why the work need be regular. If the computer is operating properly on irregular work, why should evidence so produced not be admissible? In principle it would seem that the question of regularity

[28] R.S.C. O.38, rr. 21, 24–7.
[29] Sect. 5(2) (a).

should be dealt with as a matter going to weight rather than admissibility.

A similar objection can be raised against the second condition

... that over that period there was regularly supplied to the computer in the ordinary course of those activities information of the kind contained in the statement or of the kind from which the information so contained is derived. . . .[30]

Here the further element of 'the ordinary course of those activities' is introduced. It is again not obvious what function this qualification serves. Why should the activity not be out of the ordinary, providing that the record was not produced by some malfunction of either computer or programmes? The further objection may be raised here that it would appear to exclude a document if there were a break in the supply of information of the type contained in the document. The first condition envisages the regular storing of information. It is quite possible that a business might take a number of orders over a period of a few months and enter their records into the computer system, and then when its productivite capacity was fully engaged, add different kinds of information relating to the orders. Since this subsection requires the regular supply of the same kind of information during the whole period of regular storage and processing it would seem that documents reproducing the information contained in the initial orders would be inadmissible. This sort of problem becomes endemic when statutes become over-elaborate and attempt to specify in minute detail the activities which they seek to regulate.

The third condition is

... that throughout the material part of that period the computer was operating properly, or, if not, that any respect in which it was not operating properly or was out of operation during that part of that period was not such as to affect the production of the document or the accuracy of its contents. [31]

Here the new concept of proper operation is added to regular use and ordinary course. It is suggested that the whole turgid repetition could be abridged by making the sole condition of admissibility that the computer should have been operating properly at all material times.

[30] Sect. 5(2) (b).
[31] Sect. 5(2) (c).

A final condition is

> ... that the information contained in the statement reproduces or is derived from information supplied to the computer in the ordinary course of those activities.[32]

Once again this seems somewhat redundant in the light of common sense, and what has gone before. The subsection goes on to define a computer as including various combinations of computers all elaborately specified, together with a sweeping up clause. This seems open to objection since it envisages the successive operation of any number of computers, and by treating the computer for the purposes of subsection 5(2) might be thought to weaken the conditions there set out in their application to any one of the computers operating in combination. All subsections must also be read in the light of subsection 5(6) which defines a computer as 'any device for storing and processing information'. This is incredibly wide. A tape recorder or a filing cabinet would apparently be included. It is hard to believe that this was intended, and it is possible that difficulty will be caused by it since section four which deals with second-hand hearsay generally is expressly subordinated to section five, so that the conditions set out in section five take precedence over those set out in section four to the extent of any conflict between them. In some respects, such as proof of regular operation, the conditions set out in section five are the more onerous, but in others, such as its requirement of a duty and of personal knowledge, section four is the more onerous, so there will be a temptation to exploit any overlapping created by the wide definition in section five.

Subsection 5(4) provides that the document produced by the computer may be supported by a certificate signed by a responsible operator or manager identifying the document, describing the manner of its production, giving particulars of devices involved in its production, and dealing with any of the conditions set out in subsection 5(2). It is significant that while the conditions set out in subsection 5(2) relate to a particular period, there is no specific provision here that the signatory should have been occupying his position at the relevant time, and he need only certify to the best of his knowledge and belief. This seems to permit a newly appointed manager to certify freely as to the operation of the system in the past. This is subject only to a criminal sanction imposed on one who wilfully

[32] Sect. 5(2) (d).

makes a material statement which is known to be false or not believed to be true.[33] It may be right that such considerations should only go to weight, but it is unfortunate that attention is not directed to this possibility in any parts of the Act which deal with the weight to be attached to documents produced by a computer.[34]

Subsection 5(5) expressly provides for situations where the input as well as the output is handled through peripheral devices, and where a service bureau's computer is employed in connection with the ordinary activities of the body to whom the information was originally supplied.

Section six provides that a statement contained in a document admitted under any of the principal sections, including section five, can be proved by the production of a copy either of the whole or of a material part authenticated in a manner approved by the Court. Where the document embodies only non-visual images this may be a transcript, and in the case of one embodying only visual images it may be a reproduction of the image. If it embodies both then it may be transcript and still reproduction.[35] This is a useful provision since it allows the proof of old records which are no longer in regular use, and which, if the print-out were to be regarded as the original rather than merely a copy, would not be able to satisfy the provisions of subsection 5(2). With the aid of this provision it is only necessary that the original record should have satisfied the conditions laid down by subsection 5(2), and the print-out will be admissible as a copy notwithstanding that the production of the print-out is wholly irregular, and follows a complete break in the activities which originally led to the compilation of the record.

Subsection 6(2) is a somewhat cryptic provision which seems to give the Court discretion to exclude a document altogether if the circumstances in which the statement it contains came into being or to be made, or the form and content of the document, justify a reasonable inference that it should be excluded. It is not at all clear how this section will apply, and what sort of circumstances will be regarded as going to the question of admissibility under it, rather than to weight under the succeeding subsection, 6(3). This subsection directs the Court to have regard to all the circumstances from which any inference can reasonably be drawn as to its accuracy or other-

---

[33] Sect. 6(5).
[34] Sect. 6(3) (c).
[35] Sect. 10(2).

wise in estimating the weight to be attached to a statement admitted under section five. In particular, it directs attention to the contemporaneity of supply, or recording for supply, to the computer with the occurrence of the events recorded in the statement, and to whether any person concerned with the supply of information or operation of the system had any incentive to conceal or misrepresent the facts. It seems wholly beneficial to have these considerations going to weight rather than to admissibility.

The most striking feature of these provisions is the substitution of the requirement of the regular operation of the computer system for that of personal knowledge of the facts either in the initial supplier of the information, or anyone else. This constitutes a breach not only with the past but with the other main liberalizing provisions of the Act. It is true that subsection 2(1) does not explicitly require personal knowledge, but as it deals only with first-hand hearsay, and requires that direct oral evidence *by him* (scil. the maker of the statement) should be admissible this requirement is in fact implicit. Subsection 4(1) contains an explicit requirement of personal knowledge in the maker or originator of the information contained in the statement. In subsection 5(1), however, the sole requirement is that direct oral evidence of the facts stated in the document should be admissible. But as in this case there is no link to any particular witness this amounts to no safeguard at all. The result is that any statement about a person contained in a computer system may become admissible in evidence irrespective of the means of knowledge or diligence of its supplier. It is possible that this might be mitigated by reference to subsection 6(2), though since that subsection also applies to statements admissible under subsections 2(1) and 4(1), where as noted above this danger does not arise, it is possible that this was not intended by Parliament. Given the wide definition of a computer for the purposes of section five, and given the precedence of section five over section four, it may well mean that an important safeguard can be eroded in relation to any documents which can be said to be contained in 'any device for storing and processing information'.

Under the general scheme of the Act the procedure will be for the party seeking to tender the computerized record to serve a notice pursuant to Order 38 rule 21 of his intention to do so, in the form prescribed by rule 24 which requires a copy of the material part of the record to be annexed, and which must contain particulars of a person occupying a responsible managerial position in relation to the activities for the purposes of which the computer was used regularly, and of a person occupying such a position in relation to the operation of the computer. The notice should also state whether the computer was operating properly at the material time, and give all relevant details of times when it was not. The opposing party may then serve a counter-notice under rule 26 requiring any person named in the notice to attend for cross-examination. In general, failure to serve a notice under rule 21 or to comply with the requirements of a counter-notice under rule 26 will render the record inadmissible. This is, however, subject to a residual discretion in the Court to waive the requirements when it is just to do so.

3 DISCOVERY

It has been noted that where a party seeks to adduce in evidence a computerized record which is under his control he must, pursuant to Order 38, serve a notice on his opponent with a copy annexed. It may, however, be the case that his opponent is believed to have a relevant computerized record under his control. Order 24 provides that after the close of pleadings the parties shall, subject to contrary agreement between them, give discovery of documents which are, or have been, in their possession, custody or power relating to matters in question in the action. 'Document' is not among the terms defined for the purposes of the rules in Order 1 rule 4. It has, however, been said in relation to the rule providing for discovery of documents that

We desire to make the rule as large as we can with due regard to propriety; and therefore I desire to give as large an interpretation as I can to the words of the rule 'a document relating to any matter in question in the action'[36]

It would be in the spirit of these words to interpret the rule so as to permit its application to computerized records. It might be objected that where no print-out was currently in existence the document could not be said to be in the custody, possession or power of the opponent. If document is given a sufficiently wide meaning so as to include magnetic tapes or discs, this objection might be met. The question would then arise as to whether production in that form, which might well be unintelligible to the other party, would be sufficient.

[36] *Compagnie Financière du Pacifique* v. *Peruvian Guano Co.* (1882), 11 Q.B.D. 55 at 62, 3

It is suggested that a better approach might be to construe documents within the power of the defendant so as to include print-outs which could be compiled by his order from tapes or discs containing the information in which the other party is interested. Some support for this suggestion may be derived from the practice in relation to copies of existing documents. The general rule is that a party subject to an order for discovery is not entitled to refuse to allow the documents to be photographed, and the Court may so order under its general powers if it is of opinion that justice so requires.[37] The justification for this is that there is sometimes no better way of obtaining exact copies than by photography. In the case of computerized records there will often be no better way than by the supply of a print-out. In fact the practice in relation to conventional documents is that the possessor of the documents will himself supply copies at the reasonable request of the other party, and upon payment of the usual charges.[38] Further support is supplied by Order 29 rule 3(1) which provides that

Where it considers it necessary or expedient for the purpose of obtaining full information or evidence in any cause or matter, the Court may, on such terms, if any, as it thinks just, by order authorize or require... any observation to be made on [any property... as to which any question may arise therein] or any experiment to be tried on or with such property.

This seems wide enough to require the running of a programme to secure a print-out of a document held in the computer in an unintelligible form.

It is, however, true that to secure the discovery of computerized records by reference to these provisions is unnecessarily clumsy, and that it would be convenient if a further rule were added to cater expressly for the discovery of such records. Such a rule should first define the concept of a document for the purposes of discovery in sufficiently wide a manner as to include all possible forms of computerized records, and should then seek to secure the provision by the party having such records in his control, custody or possession, of a legible copy of them, or the material parts of them, upon such terms as the Court thinks just. These terms would probably be such as to allow sufficient time so as not to disrupt the possessor's regular flow of computing, and as to provide for sufficient payment for computer time so as not to expose him to undue expense.

[37] Lewis v. Earl of Londesborough [1893] 2 Q.B. 191 at 192.
[38] Supreme Court Practice 1970, vol. 1, p. 383.

3
Privacy and computerized data banks

The initial development of the modern law of privacy was stimulated by the technology of the late nineteenth century; thus in their
seminal article on the topic Warren and Brandeis wrote :

Recent inventions and business methods call attention to the next step
which must be taken for the protection of the person, and for securing what
Judge Cooley calls 'the right to be let alone'.[1]

They referred to the dangers of photography and of mass circulation
newspapers. But the perils they responded to have been intensified
by the development of modern forms of surveillance vastly more
insidious than the 'surreptitious flashlight' to which they so quaintly
refer, and by the more systematic dissemination of personal information by means of computerized data banks. It is wholly understandable that such technological advance has produced in its wake an
increasing demand for more effective control.

In this chapter the problems of maintaining personal privacy
induced by the advent of the computerized data bank will first be
assessed, and the most promising safeguards against abuse will then
be considered. In dealing with the problems I shall discuss in turn
each of the concepts included in the title of this chapter, namely,
privacy, computerization, data and banks.

1 PROBLEMS
Privacy
It is clear that in a world where the reproduction of the species is
not accomplished spontaneously, and where survival depends upon
the cooperation of others, there can be no complete exclusion of

[1] Warren and Brandeis, 'The Right to Privacy', 4 *Harvard L.R.*, 193 at 195 (1890).

others from one's life. And other people have eyes, ears and tongues; they are curious, and they love to gossip. Indeed privacy hardly exists naturally in the most primitive communities, though it is still valued and often expressed in some ritualized form. But the facets of privacy most in issue today, such as a desire for seclusion, for anonymity and for the right to control the dissemination of information about oneself are very much the creation of, and a response to, urban civilization. In older, more rural communities the working life itself more often involved some seclusion, and so there a positive stimulus towards a more gregarious leisure life existed. In a modern industrial society the working life is more commonly crowded and full of contact with others, and the demand is for more seclusion. Indeed the contrast between the life of the housewife, which corresponds more to the older pattern, especially in the suburbs, and the life of her worker husband, is a familiar source of domestic tension. The argument is that the intensification of industrialization and the increasing pace of modern life have led to a greater demand for privacy when these very factors make it more difficult to satisfy it.

Modern industrialized society is characterized by mass production and mass consumption. They can only be sustained by the physical agglomeration of human beings in factories, and hence in towns and cities, and by the creation of pervasive marketing and selling techniques. To bring large numbers of human beings together and to coordinate their activities satisfactorily requires organization, and effective organization demands information to be successful. Without it the individual suffers. Until recently in New York it took up to fourteen days to assemble the information necessary for deciding whether or not to grant bail, but the decision had to be made in four days. To market the right product demands knowledge of the habits and preferences of the people, and to sell on the required scale seems to necessitate the provision of wide and rapid credit facilities.

The skeleton of the ogre is becoming apparent. The ordinary man must work cheek by jowl with his neighbour, he must divulge personal information so that his welfare may be provided for and his needs and wants satisfied. But his demand for privacy is still insistent. It has been persuasively argued that personal privacy is a necessary condition for the establishment of relationships of love, respect, trust and friendship. Unless we are left with a private area which we can choose to share with others these relationships cannot be established.[2]

[2] Fried, 'Privacy', 77 *Yale L.J.*, 475 (1968).

It is, of course, highly unlikely that any system will ever seek to intrude so far as to leave the individual with no secrets to share. But such relationships should not be seen in a digital framework as either existing or not existing. They should be looked at rather from an analogue viewpoint as being either more or less satisfying as the intrusion into personal privacy decreases or increases. The aim must be to maximize them so far as is consistent with the minimal external standards of life that are acceptable. It must be noted that these values are just as much threatened by a belief that an intrusion has been made as by actual intrusion. A man who is being overheard, but does not know that he is, will be more frank in his conversation than one who is not being overheard but who believes that he is. The privacy of the intruder is antithetical to the privacy of the person intruded upon. It is the fear of secret intrusion by unknown persons using undisclosed and perhaps inaccurate information which constitutes the greatest threat to the privacy of the individual. This fear must be dispelled, and a potent way of accomplishing this end is to secure greater publicity for what is going on, and to the extent that publicity is incompatible with the reason for using the information, then by securing greater public control over the use of the information and the creation of confidence in the impartiality and effectiveness of such control. It is here important to emphasize the necessity of avoiding exaggerated and hysterical criticism. Such criticism is likely to promote secrecy and to destroy confidence, and thus to exacerbate the dangers it seeks to eradicate.

In broad terms the infringement of privacy in the relevant sense comes in two ways. First, in the collection of personal information, and secondly in its use. My privacy is infringed by a surreptitious search of my house, and even though nothing is discovered which I would not have been ready to divulge publicly. This sort of consideration accounts for the feeling of insecurity engendered by the development of a telephone system which can be dialed to read the meters in a house without ringing, or giving any other indication that it is gathering the information.[3] My privacy is also infringed when information which I may have given willingly for one purpose is used without my consent for some different purpose altogether. It is true that these two senses tend to shade into each other since it may be thought that an unauthorized intruder into my data file in the second example is little different from the unauthorized in-

[3] See *Computer Weekly*, 12 March 1970.

truder into my house in the first. It is nevertheless convenient to consider them separately. From the point of view of data banks the second is the more obvious danger, but the first must also be considered.

In most cases the data held in a computerized data bank of personal information has been voluntarily divulged by the subject. There are however two clear exceptions to this, and a range of more dubious ones which indeed throw doubt upon the general assertion. A clear exception is constituted by the case given above where the information is collected without even the knowledge of the subject. This may be because it is collected secretly, or because it is supplied by other people. Where it is collected secretly a further distinction may be made between situations in which the subject does not know that the information has been divulged at all, where a private document is copied for example, and situations in which the subject, while knowing that the information has been divulged, does not know that it has been retained, a secret recording of an ostensibly private conversation for example. A somewhat similar distinction may be made in relation to information obtained from other people. Sometimes it will be obtained from them without the subject's knowledge at all, by questioning neighbours for example, and sometimes the subject will know that information has been given about him, but not what it was, as in a reference from an employer.

A second clear exception is where the subject himself gives the information, but under legal compulsion. A clear example is information given to the Registrar General for the census, or to law courts by a subpoenaed witness. In most such cases such compulsion carries with it some guarantee of protection from prejudicial use.

The more dubious exceptions are inherent in the difficult notion of voluntary disclosure. It can even be argued that disclosure under legal compulsion is voluntary since the subject can always refuse to divulge the information and take his punishment.[4] But this is surely too wide a view of voluntary disclosure. There are nevertheless infinite gradations of the voluntary. The Inland Revenue compels the disclosure of details of a man's income, but it may be argued that it does not compel him to have one. If instead he chooses to apply for Social Security payments he will have to disclose another set of personal details. Can either be said to have been disclosed voluntarily? A little further along the scale are the details required

[4] See e.g. Austin, 'Lectures on Jurisprudence', Lecture XXIII.

by an employer of an applicant for a job. In some cases, for example those requiring a high degree of responsibility, virtually the whole of the applicant's life may have to be revealed, in others virtually nothing. Here there may seem to be more choice. No one is compelled to apply for any particular job. But the labour market is not perfect, it is distorted by the patterns of available vacancies, the range of salaries paid, the skills of the applicant and the range of his needs. He may indeed be under very great pressure to apply for a particular job. Similar considerations apply to other requests for the 'voluntary' supply of information, to credit agencies, to insurance companies and to medical authorities.

The degree of voluntariness varies infinitely from situation to situation, and from person to person. It is perhaps true that the only truly voluntary disclosure is within the special relationships of love, respect, trust and friendship. Outside them a balance must be struck so as to ensure that the gains accruing to the individual from the transaction truly compensate for the invasion of his privacy involved. This is best achieved by close control over the type of information collected and the uses to which it is put. The balance is, however, a delicate one. It should not be assumed as an axiom for example that information gathered for one purpose should never be used for another. The privacy of the individual may indeed be better preserved by such an automatic data transfer. For example, where highly embarrassing personal information is required for a number of separate purposes, the subject may well prefer to give it once and then to forget about it, rather than to repeat it over and over again for each purpose. In such a case however there could be no objection to securing the consent of the subject, though this might itself present further problems.

Computerization

There is no doubt that the development of computers as data processing devices has accentuated concern over the problem of the preservation of personal privacy. It is worth considering how far this is justified. It has already been remarked that in older, more rural communities personal privacy was more restricted than it is in today's urban society. It may plausibly be argued that modern technology leads in many ways to the easier preservation of privacy. Consider the analogy of the telephone system. Under the older system with small manual switchboards operated by the village postmistress personal privacy for telephone conversations hardly existed at all. Modern automatic systems serving vast areas are much more secure. An individual call arouses no curiosity since there is no obvious indication of where it comes from or where it is going, and the numbers are so vast and so widespread that casual eavesdropping is likely to be unrewarding.

It can be argued that the computer has a similar effect in relation to personal records. By increasing the volume that can be stored in one place the need for local storage is diminished, and by the same token the number of points at which security is at risk. The transfer of records from words on paper to magnetic impulses on tapes at least introduces one further stage between obtaining access to the record and access to the information it contains. The use of more expensive systems discourages casual use, and encourages the greatest selectivity and accuracy in the data stored. The substitution of mechanical for human keepers eliminates curiosity and gossiping, for machines are not the one and do not engage in the other.

Why then is computerization made the focus for attack? To some extent it is an emotional reaction. Human beings are jealous creatures. They value their individuality as human beings, and resent the idea that their special human skills can be replaced. This is the Luddite mentality, graphically expressed in the moving saga of John Henry's competition with the steam hammer. The advent of the computer has moved this jealousy along the scale from the manual labourer to the manager, from the blue to the white collared worker, from the inarticulate and uninfluential to the articulate and influential. Such resentment is compounded by ignorance, an ignorance fostered by the exaggerated claims sometimes made about computers by those who live by selling them, but to a much greater extent a simple result of the pace of mid-twentieth-century technological advance. The modern computer is as far from the comprehension of the average manager as the watch from that of the nineteenth-century savage.

Such fears and resentment can be reduced only by convincing those affected that computers are simply tools to be used just like mechanical looms and steam hammers, and like them will enrich and improve the quality of their lives. The real lesson to be learned from the Luddites is that this can only be accomplished by the provision of a humane social system within and by means of which necessary adjustments can be made. It is probably the case that changes of the order of those inherent in the full capacity of modern computing can only be successfully and humanely accomplished by using that computer capacity. But even if such emotional, though by no means irrational, arguments are discounted, there are still effective counter-arguments to be raised. It is argued that the benefit of the computerization of personal data lies chiefly in a reduction of the cost of retrieving it. It is a simple application of the economies of scale to reduce marginal costs. The bigger and better cross-referenced the store, the greater the saving and the stronger the argument.

So far as security is concerned several questions can be raised. If there is only one centralized store its security may indeed be greater than that of any local store, but the rewards to be gained by breaking its security are correspondingly greater, and the real comparison should be between the cost of breaking the security of the central store and the cost of breaking the security of *all* the local stores. Indeed in a modern multi-user system with remote local access the situation embodies the worst security features of both centralized and local systems, since its true nature is to expose the whole of the information to the insecurity of the weakest local access point. In addition, risks are created at every point along the communication linkage.

There is some argument among the commentators as to whether it is easier to break the security of a computer or a manual system.[5] There can be little argument that the potential returns are greater in the former case. It has been suggested that the real difference between holding data in computerized and conventional form is that whereas in conventional systems it is cheap to retain data and expensive to remove it, in computer systems the converse is true, it is expensive to retain it but cheap to remove it.[6] This is a consequence of the relatively lower marginal cost of finding information in the computer system. But it is less true now than it was when Professor Miller wrote it, and it becomes less and less true as time goes on. While it is difficult to compute its extent accurately, all commentators agree that the unit cost of storing and manipulating information in computers is decreasing, and at an increasing rate. For the future it would be prudent to rely on different safeguards.

[5] Compare, on the relative success of the security of computer and conventional systems at M.I.T., Meldman, 'Centralised Information Systems and the Legal Right to Privacy', 52 *Marquette L.R.*, 335 at 353, and Miller, 'Personal Privacy in the Computer Age', 67 *Michigan L.R.*, 1091 at 1111.

[6] Miller, *op. cit.*, at 1139.

One fear is that information held in a computer system is more likely to be inaccurate than information held in a conventional system. Everyone is familiar with the stories of incorrect bank statements and gas bills. The GPO has tested this view by having the same data stored and handled by computers and by conventional means. It was found that the computer system made only one-tenth of the errors, and perhaps even more important, when it did make errors they became immediately visible to the operators of the system.[7] A further factor tending to promote accuracy within the computer system is the facility it provides for cross-referencing between different records which will tend to reveal inconsistencies and enhance the possibility of correction. Another advantage of the computerized system here is that the intrusion of errors in the data through mechanical malfunction is much smaller than through inaccurate transfer by copying in a conventional system. The most powerful guarantee against error, though, is the interest of the compiler and user of the records in having an accurate set of records. However malign his purposes may be imagined to be, they are liable to be frustrated if he makes his decisions upon the basis of inaccurate information.

There is a counter-balancing consideration, however. It is connected with emotional attitudes to computers. There is commonly enormous respect for their accuracy and infallibility. This may seem odd having regard to the gas bill jokes. But these are perhaps best seen as rather uneasy attempts to cut the computer down to size, and are indeed a symptom of an overly respectful attitude, the exceptions which prove the rule. It may be questioned why, if computer systems are more accurate than conventional ones, this attitude should be deplored. The reason is that it is not enough to compare the relative accuracy of the two types of system. Instead it is necessary to compare the relative gaps between the true and believed accuracy of the two sorts of system. This is the converse of the usual credibility gap. It is worse to have a very efficient system which is believed to be completely infallible, than it is to have a relatively inefficient system which is known to be inefficient, at least so far as the detection and correction of errors is concerned. Even when it is accepted that computerized systems may contain errors in the data their very size militates against discovery of error, and to some extent increases the cost of correction. The very size of the stores

[7] Hansard, H. L., vol. 306, col. 166, 3 December 1969, speech of Lord Gardiner L.C.

militates against comprehensive accuracy checks, though as indicated earlier cross-referencing can help to some extent. This is one of the areas where the pressure for safeguards is most insistent because the privacy of the individual is most threatened.

The question of accuracy is exacerbated by a tendency to confuse accuracy of fact with its completeness and evaluation. Thus a record of an arrest may be kept and printed out on demand to an authorized enquirer. The first question is whether the record is factually accurate, whether that subject was arrested on the occasion in question. But it is only the first question. It is highly misleading if there is no accompanying note of the dismissal of the charge, and the success of a consequential claim for false imprisonment and malicious prosecution. For this sort of reason the usual witness oath asks for the whole truth. Completeness depends upon the purpose for which the information is required. The entry 'married' may be complete for the purpose of a survey to determine the proportion of the population who have married, but may very well be seriously incomplete if used for Inland Revenue or Social Security purposes where it may well be necessary to know in addition whether the parties are still living together. This consideration gives some support to the thesis that records should be used only for the purpose for which they are compiled. But it is by no means clear that this would be universally desirable. Suppose a sexual psychopath with a record of homicidal attacks on small children is at large and can be positively identified by his medical record, surely the police should be allowed access to it. Or suppose an applicant for a post as a security guard in a bank has enormous debts, and a long record of criminal convictions, surely the employer should know. The real thrust of the attack should be aimed at the criteria for the cross-use of records, and their suitability for each purpose, rather than a blanket attack on the practice under any conditions.

There is a general danger to be avoided here. Because the increased use of computers has concentrated attention on the dangers to personal privacy represented by the use of records containing personal information, one reaction is to oppose the use of computers for these purposes. This might eliminate the problem, but the cure would be worse than the disease. Quite apart from the beneficial services which would be lost, attention would be diverted from the real evils. Computers can cause harm only when used to do it by human beings. The machine itself is innocent, and over-concentration on the part played by it diverts attention from the human purposes it is being used to effect. If, as seems to be the case, some files do contain records of arrests but no information on subsequent disposal, perhaps because this is difficult to obtain, the fault is not with the computer system but with those who are prepared to rely upon such incomplete data for any practical purpose. This is also true of the evaluation of the information in the file. Sometimes, as in the case of credit ratings, the information is itself in the form of evaluation. Such information is particularly prone to be misleading since the establishment of consistent and objective standards is especially difficult. The difficulties are multiplied if different evaluative systems are to be merged. In the relatively straightforward field of credit ratings the United States Association of Credit Bureaus took four years to harmonize the rating system between its different members. Evaluation is, however, sometimes implicit in the uses made of the information in the files rather than explicit in the information itself. Here the danger is of placing too much reliance upon unreliable sources which may have been used to compile the files. Much of the information on political associations especially relating to periods long before the information was actually gathered is a source of suspicion, and the use to which such information is put should be very closely examined.

Data
It is obviously the case that not all data banks threaten personal privacy. All depends upon the type of information in the bank, and the form in which that information is held. No amount of information about the nature and behaviour of celestial bodies threatens anyone's personal privacy, at least if the accuracy of astrology is discounted. It is personal information about human beings which gives rise to concern. Here a distinction is often drawn between banks of personal information used solely for statistical purposes, and banks of information used for the purposes of personal intelligence. This is a very relevant distinction if it can be maintained. The much debated proposal for the establishment of a National Data Bank in the United States hinged on this point.[8] The proponents of the scheme stressed the statistical nature of the in-

[8] 'The Computer and Invasion of Privacy'. Hearings before a Subcommittee of the Committee on Government Operations. US House of Representatives, 89th Congress 2d, 26–8 July 1966.

formation which would be used and published. In particular it was stated that police records would not be included, and that the information would not be used in any way involving the identification of individuals. These are broadly similar to the assurances customarily given in relation to census data, which is conceded to have a good record for confidentiality in the United States, and in most other countries. Any such guarantees need careful scrutiny, however, as illustrated in the United States Supreme Court case of *St Regis Paper Co.* v. *US*[9] where the assurances expressly related to the census returns, and were held not to cover the copies which were returned to the subjects.

Even in the case of statistical information purposes critics can point to the danger involved in the personal identification of the subject at the point of entry into the system. It is necessary, even for statistical purposes, to retain identified personal records if it is intended to use them for some continuing purposes, such as say the compilation of statistics on population movements or the incidence of re-marriage of divorced persons which might be highly desirable for help in arriving at decisions in the field of economic or social policy.[10] Such records are useless unless they can be identified and up-dated. It is argued that the retention of such identifiable personal files constitutes a standing temptation to the commercial exploiter and the probing bureaucrat, and a perennial source of danger of accidental leakage. Even the statistical information deliberately released presents some dangers. Fears have been expressed that comparison with other records may enable individuals to be identified.

A more serious risk is of an invasion of personal privacy as a direct result of the publication of the statistical information even though no individual details can be identified. Thus in the field of census returns there is a market among selling organizations for special blocks of data. If the block as a whole shows the correct characteristics the privacy of all the individuals comprised in it is liable to be infringed by, for example, aggressive direct selling techniques. It is immaterial to the individual concerned that he has been identified not solely by reference to his own return, but to those of his neighbours also. It might be supposed that most statistical pur-

---

[9] 368 U.S. 208 (1961).
[10] When, in an attempt to eliminate such identification in the British Census 1971, the questions referred to the past history, objections were then raised on that score also.

poses could be achieved on the basis of sample figures rather than by a complete collection, thus reducing both the intrusion into privacy caused by the collection of the information itself, and the risk to privacy if it should be disclosed. Unfortunately, if the sample were not compulsory it would be invalidated by the element of self-selection, and if it were compulsory it might well be regarded as unfairly discriminatory between those who were and those who were not required to participate. Nevertheless, this is clearly a possibility to be considered for some purposes, and has indeed been used for additional information in the census.

Fears are rightly greatest in relation to information which is avowedly dedicated to the creation of a record relating to the affairs of an identified individual for use in relation to him personally. Typical collections of this type are police records, vehicle identification, income tax returns in the public sphere, and credit ratings, bank statements and insurance files in the private. Concern is mainly centred on the possibility of cross-referencing between different files, on the inaccuracy and selectivity of information contained in them, and their use in an unauthorized manner. It may be feared that bank statements will be checked against tax returns; that old convictions for trivial offences will be raked up to deny employment; or that vehicle identification records might be used to compile a record of a person's journeys. These are very real fears, and must be assuaged if the individual is to feel private, but a sense of perspective is essential. The existing conventional systems are themselves quite insecure in these respects, and most of the information mentioned above is available at a price at present. Then there are very few authentic examples of the misuse of personal information of this type, and much of the case rests upon fears about what might happen in the future.[10a] It is as well to reflect that in so far as these fears depend upon malignity in human beings, the ends might be accomplished in other and even more unpleasant ways, whatever restrictions are placed upon the collection of information now. It would be ironic if the imposition of severe controls on the collection of personal information should lead to the burgeoning of organized crime and political subversion to such an extent that the democratic system itself should be overthrown, for that system is still the best guarantee of personal freedom and liberty that has yet been demonstrated.

[10a] See Report of Younger Committee on Privacy Cmd. 5612 para. 575, 6 (1972).

Banks

The metaphor of the data bank is now widespread, and perhaps deserves more attention than it has hitherto received. How strong is the analogy between a bank with money in it, and a bank with data in it, and what conclusions can be drawn from it? The strongest similarity, and perhaps the explanation for the usage, is that the store is built up by an accretion from a number of different sources. As money goes into an individual account, so data goes into an individual file. This carries a number of implications. First, the larger the accretion of accurate data the greater the utility of the data bank. Just as counterfeit money is useless to the money banker, so false information is unwelcome to the data banker. Secondly, if data is to be accumulated like money, it too must be fungible. It must be possible to add one piece of data to another in the same way as one pound or one dollar can be added to another. This means that systems of harmonization and classification must be established to make data coming from various sources compatible. In its proposals for the establishment of a National Data Center the United States Bureau of the Budget indicated twenty-one different collecting agencies for data which could usefully be combined together. The closest analogy to the National Center is perhaps the Central Bank. It is interesting to note the passionate and successful opposition in the United States to that institution also, and for very similar reasons. But the development and defects of the purely private system that grew in its place also carry their cautionary message. A further parallel between the two types of bank is that, at least so far as in private hands, they tend to be profitable to their promoters, and more significantly yield their profits in the same way, namely by hiring out the use of their deposits. Since the deposits have this value, it behoves those in charge of them to restrict access to authorized users, and to ensure this by the application of stringent security systems.

So much for similarities. There are important differences also. The most obvious is that a man deposits his money in a bank quite voluntarily, and for his own personal convenience. It is no direct concern to him how many others do so, and his convenience in no way directly depends upon this. A number of important minor differences flow from this. The depositor will expect to receive an exact account of his balance, and of any additions to or subtractions from it. He will expect to be able to withdraw the whole or any part of his deposit. None of these things necessarily applies to a data bank. As remarked earlier, deposits are rarely fully voluntary, and equally rarely is there any equivalent to the facility for receipt of a statement or withdrawal. A further difference is that many data banks are controlled by the government and do not exist for the purpose of making a profit by hiring out their contents, though there is perhaps an analogy to be drawn in regard to the social benefits expected to be achieved by their use.

From the security point of view there is the important difference that the value of the data in a data bank does not depend upon its appropriation if by that is understood the removal of the data from the bank. The benefit can be taken and the data left exactly as it was before. This means that security arrangements must be made much more stringent, not because the value of the data is greater than the value of money, nor because the likelihood of attempts to extract the contents is likely to be greater, but largely because the detection of an unauthorized intrusion is so much more difficult. A final difference is that money banks have a longer history than computerized data banks and have had time to establish a code of ethics in their employees and practices which have gained the confidence of the public.

No one would argue today that the accumulation of money in banks is a bad thing because it makes it easier for unscrupulous governments to impoverish the population, or easier for unscrupulous criminals to rob it. We know that they fulfil a useful purpose provided that they are properly controlled and operated, and provided that adequate security is established. This is surely the moral of the terminology of the data *bank*.

2 SAFEGUARDS

As already remarked, privacy is a delicate concept endangered as much by apprehension of infringement as by proved infringement. It is therefore not necessary to be able to show that infringements have taken place in order to recommend appropriate safeguards. The usual division of safeguards into categories such as administrative, technical and legal is not adopted here. Instead safeguards are divided into two classes by reference to their main function : those which are preventive and those which are remedial. It is proposed that both types should have legal force where necessary, and both operate so as to ensure that technical and administrative systems are adequate. Preventive safeguards come into operation immediately and are designed to ensure that the system does not break down at all; remedial safeguards come into effect after a breakdown has occurred and are designed to compensate the victim, punish the offender and prevent repetition of the breach.

At the very beginning of this chapter it was noticed that a modern law of privacy was first proposed to meet the challenge of current technology. It has been argued that the pace of change has been so rapid and increased so much that the common law technique of waiting for an offence to occur and to be litigated before providing a remedy is altogether too slow and cumbersome a process.[11] This is clearly right, but one should not necessarily and immediately move to the opposite end of the spectrum and propose detailed legislation instead. Case law may exhibit the vice of sloth, but it has the compensating virtue of flexibility. The danger is that legislation may be too precipitate a technique and establish rules which are either not sufficiently precise and can be evaded, or too precise and rapidly become obsolete. The dangers were illustrated by the case of *St. Regis Paper Co.* v. *U.S.*[12] where the legislative guarantees of privacy were held either to be too vague to be applicable, or too precise to cover copies of the returns since the text referred only to the returns themselves. In that case the situation was immediately remedied by further legislation,[13] but had the original guarantee appeared in a case rather than a statute it is inconceivable that it would not have been extended by analogy to cover copies.

To counter these difficulties it is suggested that a method be employed so as to combine the strengths of the speed of statute and the flexibility of case law. For many preventive safeguards it is suggested that this might be achieved by the creation of a licensing agency with powers to make rules binding upon those operating data banks. The agency might be a public body like that envisaged in England by the National Council for Civil Liberties,[14] or a private body established by the computer industry itself, as proposed elsewhere.[15] In either event it will be necessary that the agency has

---

[11] Miller, 'Symposium on Computers, Data Banks and Individual Privacy', 53 *Minnesota L.R.*, 211 at 240.
[12] 368 US 208 (1961).
[13] 13 U.S.C. 9(a) (3) (1964).
[14] See its draft Personal Information Bill, Younger Committee, appendix F.
[15] Grenier, 'Computers and Privacy: A Proposal for Self-Regulation', 1970, *Duke L.J.*, 495.

C

legal powers of compulsion. Similar standards should be applied in both the public and private sphere, since the public must have confidence in both. It is indeed probably the case that the threat to privacy is greater in the public sphere just because of the greater power of government, which creates a fear, however unjustifiable, that it may be used. And as has been stressed the threat lies more in the fear of infringement than in its reality.[16] It is true that government data banks are already controlled by parliamentary methods, and by special offices like that of the Ombudsman. Such safeguards are valuable, and should be retained, but their existence is no substitute for the wider range of safeguards to be proposed here.

Preventive

It is here proposed to pay more attention to the nature of the various safeguards than to the precise machinery for enforcement. As indicated above it is suggested in general terms that rules be established by a controlling agency with powers to make them legally binding, and with powers to modify and adapt whenever experience or advances in technology indicate that it is desirable. These safeguards are divided, somewhat arbitrarily, into three sections dealing with data, systems and personnel. Most have been suggested already in different places and at different times, though not arranged in quite this form.[17]

DATA : The most important safeguard is that public justification should be given for all data which it is proposed to collect. Each collecting agency should be required to specify in detail precisely what it intends to do, and how the data it proposes to collect will assist it to do it. Any such application should be submitted to a searching scrutiny, since it is so easy for means to become ends, and for data to be collected for the sake of collecting data, or for the sake of justifying the investment in the system for collection. It is not enough to provide for the publication of questions, and for them to be allowed if unchallenged, as is often the case at present. Each question should be automatically challenged, and the burden of

[16] See Younger Committee Survey. Report, ch. 6 and appendix E.
[17] See esp. Westin, *Privacy and Freedom*, ch. 14; Miller, 'Personal Privacy in the Computer Age', 67 *Mich. L.R.*, 1091 at 1207; Warner and Stone, *Data Bank Society*, chs 10 and 11; Peters and Ware in Proceedings of Spring Joint Computer Conference 1967; Lister, 'Civil Liberties and the New Information Technologies', paper delivered to American Civil Liberties Union, New York, 1970.

proving it necessary should lie on the potential collector. Any such enquiry should also probe the possibility of the data collected being made available to other agencies, and the possibility of this agency seeking to augment its data from other agencies.

It is appreciated that whatever the rules about the exchange of data, it would be unrealistic to suppose that all situations in which it might be desirable could be foreseen and specified in advance. It might therefore be necessary to provide a means of overriding the regulations. But the general conditions under which this should be possible should be as stringent as possible, perhaps only where this is the only way of saving life, and the rules should provide for the decision being taken at the very highest level of responsibility. Rules should also specify permitted methods of collecting particular types of data including such questions as the selection and authentication of human beings involved in the process.

At this stage also the quality of the information to be collected should be checked against the purposes for which it is proposed to use it. Some information may be of such low quality that it should be collected and used for only the most idiosyncratic purposes. Thus it may perhaps be thought permissible to allow the collection of hearsay about political attitudes, but only so long as the sole purpose of using it is to enable the personal security services to guard prominent public figures from physical attack. It would be absolutely essential that the purposes of obtaining such data should be stringently limited, and any such limitations rigidly enforced. It would probably be desirable for all data to be classified on the basis of its sensitivity and its potential value so as to establish the most stringent precautions in relation to the most vulnerable data, such as records of political attitudes or medical records. The most sensitive types should probably be physically separated from other information and protected by special systems from casual access. A further precaution, incredibly enough not always taken at present, is that programme testing and demonstration work should always use special dummy data and not that actually in the current working files.

It has already been suggested that there may be positive advantages in providing facilities for the cross-referencing of data in different files. Repeated personal intrusion may be avoided, unusual situations provided for and accuracy enhanced. Nevertheless the dangers are serious, and evident. It has already been suggested that advance application for cross-referencing facilities should normally be made. But implicit in this suggestion is another and perhaps equally important one. It is that data should generally be stored by reference to some unit other than the individual identity of the subject, whether this be by name, number or some other unique characteristic. It is generally better that individual files relate to particular subject matters, and the personal data relating to any given person should be dispersed among them. This not only makes sense from the point of view of efficiency, since cross-referencing will be a relatively unusual activity, but it helps to still the greatest fear of all, which is the compilation of a personal dossier containing everything that is known about a particular individual.

Such diffusion of information is one of the most potent guarantees of individual privacy at present. Newsday magazine in the United States once conducted an experiment by selecting an individual and securing his premission to gather as much information about him as they could. Without using any illegal methods, or by patronizing services which offer to supply confidential information for a fee, they were able to compile a dossier which astounded and horrified the subject. In the state of present systems such an enterprise is expensive, but in a computer system the cost will be reduced, and safeguards must therefore be created to restore the balance. In a different way the control is still an economic one. By keeping the data dispersed in a number of files, each with its own independent security, the cost of obtaining complete information about any individual is hopefully rendered uneconomically high.

An obvious safeguard which is easily underestimated is that of providing physical security for the data. But this is, after all, the main safeguard offered by money banks, and their contents are in some demand by the unscrupulous also. In addition to adequate physical security, personal data can be encoded. Indeed it must be coded to be held in a computerized data bank at all. Additional enciphering is envisaged here. This too should probably vary in complexity according to the sensitivity of the information held. For the most sensitive data it would be possible to split the file and hold each different part in a different place with an independent coding system, thus artificially introducing further dispersal of information, with the difference here that none of the information would be meaningful at all without the other parts. Such measures would clearly be extremely expensive, and a balance will need to be struck in each case.

One of the most serious problems lies in ensuring the accuracy and completeness of the data in the files, accuracy here extending to form and contents whether factual or evaluative. As mentioned earlier, some errors will be revealed by the comparison of records from different files, and for this reason, and provided security can be maintained, regular cross-checking might be advisable. But some things will appear in only one file, and others will appear incorrectly in several. This raises the further problem that such is the normal accuracy of the data and operation of the system, that it might be very difficult to persuade the agency that all the computers contained the same wrong information. There must then be more than simple cross-checking systems.

A rather extreme suggestion from a number of quarters is that the subject should be informed whenever information about him is being held in a data bank, and that he should be entitled to require a print-out of his record. This is thought to be the equivalent of a writ of *habeas corpus*. There are obvious difficulties in any such suggestion, especially if this is to be regarded as being unqualified and of universal application.[18] It would be absurd to allow a patient whose medical record states that knowledge of his condition would probably kill him to be entitled to see his record, or for the police to open up their *modus operandi* files to criminals interested to find out which features to avoid in their next crime. Similarly some information is given only on condition that it is kept from the notice of those to whom it refers, references from employers or teachers for example. So there must clearly be some restrictions upon any such right.

It is further suggested that the analogy of *habeas corpus* is hardly helpful so far as procedure is concerned. It is possible to require such formal and cumbersome processes as full Court appearances where the conditions are of such rare occurrence as those leading to a *habeas corpus* application. After all we only have one body, and it is very rarely falsely imprisoned. There are innumerable pieces of information about one held in a multitude of locations, and claims could easily be made frivolously. It may be argued that the proceedings in Court only come on in the event of a refusal to

[18] See Younger Report, paras 613–18. Cf. US Fair Credit Reporting Act 1970, U.S.C. 15 §1681.

produce, and that they could easily be avoided by producing the information upon demand. But the rules for holding and withholding data are likely to be a great deal more complex than those relating to wrongful imprisonment, and disputes will be, to such an extent, more common.

Cost is also a serious consideration here. The reproduction of all records would be a very serious expense, and questions would arise as to who should bear it.[19] It will be all the greater, if, as already suggested, personal information is kept on a large number of different files, when the task of coordination and organization necessary to assemble a complete record will be daunting. It would further be necessary to devise some procedure by which the individual could challenge the data held in his file. Clearly he could not be given *carte blanche* to change it whenever he wished, and to whatever extent, without giving some proof that the existing version were inaccurate. It is even possible that such an intended safeguard would have a positively harmful effect. To make it work the system would have to provide for the assembly of a complete dossier with some ease, but this would create dangers of information being divulged to unauthorized persons by either impersonation or intimidation of the person entitled. Thus an employer might make the production of the complete print-out a condition for employment. These points are not raised with the intention of rejecting the idea entirely, but merely seek to reveal some of the questions to which attention is necessary, and to suggest that it is highly unlikely that any simple blanket safeguard will ever be appropriate for all situations.

A more modest proposal is that a subject should have the right to be informed that an enquiry has been addressed to the system in relation to a record relating to him. The precise details of any such proposal would require careful elaboration since it could be adopted in a number of different ways. It might be envisaged that the enquiry should in such a case be held up pending the consent of the subject; or it might be envisaged that the enquirer should if challenged by the subject be required to reveal, either to the subject or some impartial arbitrator, his reason for requiring the information; or it might be combined with the previous proposal

---

[19] The Younger Committee points out that the postal cost of sending one letter to each person on the files of the largest UK Credit Bureau would exceed its current turnover (para. 615).

and such a challenge made a necessary and sufficient condition for ordering a print-out of the record to be supplied to the subject; or it might be envisaged simply as a way of warning the subject of those who had made an enquiry so that he could take the matter up with them if he chose to do so.

Yet another proposal, this time designed more with regard to the quality of the information, is that there should be strict rules enjoining the removal from the records of stale information, perhaps incorporating an automatic cut-off point. This idea gains some support from the decision in *Melvin* v. *Reid*[20] that to make public very old criminal charges is an invasion of privacy even though they are accurate and a matter of public record. But here too it is apparent that no universal rule of thumb is possible, and that special rules would have to be developed for each different sort of information and use.

None of these points are raised with the intention that such suggestions should be abandoned completely, but solely in order to indicate the need for careful consideration before they are implemented, and for adopting a measure of flexibility in the application of any suggested safeguard. It is, however, clear that some form of audit, not necessarily by the subject himself, is desirable, in the hope of eliminating some of the errors which cannot be detected by an automated comparison of different records. In any event it will be necessary to establish some machinery to decide upon the correct version in the event of an inconsistency being shown, and the further tasks indicated above might be assumed by such a body.

A final suggestion here is that it might prove desirable to create some sort of advisory committee, perhaps containing representatives of users and subjects, which could channel suggestions to the agency responsible for establishing the conditions under which licences would be granted. The precise structure needs to be worked out in detail, but experience suggests that such a body is sometimes a more sensitive barometer for the measurement of public pressure than institutions of a more formal character such as Parliament or the office of the Ombudsman. It is not suggested that these other avenues should be closed, simply that they should be augmented.

SYSTEMS : Here again a number of safeguards are available, and their precise degree of deployment should probably vary with the sensitivity of particular situations. It should be possible for a licens-

[20] 112 Cal. App. 285, 297 Pac. Rep. 91 (1931).

ing authority to determine which of the safeguards should be made a condition for the granting of any particular licence. For the purposes of this discussion it is assumed that the computer system incorporates a multi-user capacity with remote terminals, partly because this seems the most likely line of development in relation to data banks, and partly because it poses the greatest security problems.

The most obvious safeguard for any system is the provision of physical security for all parts of the equipment, central processor, peripheral devices, communication lines and remote terminals. Simple precautions like the supply of lockable machines are remarkably, though not completely, effective. Already in most systems remote terminals can only enter the system by quotation of some identification code which has to be accepted by the computer. Such codes should be kept secure, and varied at irregular intervals. Operators too should have personal codes which could operate in the same sort of way. Such codes can be employed to impose an automatic definition of the range of material permitted to that operator at that terminal at that time for that particular ask. In some cases it might be best to make the codes interactive rather than fixed. The computer could print out a random number say, and the user be required to manipulate it in some variable way such as adding a digit representing the time of day. This might minimize the danger of codes being physically lost.

A further possibility is to make the interaction unique to the operator, and in the future this may take the form of having the computer check finger or voice prints. In the case of specially sensitive information it might be desirable to establish rules to provide for the authority of a superior before information is divulged, and this too could be made to depend upon a form of coding. Systems already exist in which the superior's own terminal is automatically interrupted for approval when the special information is demanded. This constitutes a further safeguard against unauthorized requests. It is sometimes useful to require some statement of the need for the information as part of the routine request code. This is of assistance in connection with the suggestion to be made later that all usage of the system should be recorded. This will, in addition, assist with the auditing processes discussed earlier. In a well established system a measure of automatic auditing can be accomplished by the comparison of patterns of actual activity with the established pattern of activity. Such a comparison would reveal sudden changes in the amount or type of activity of given units of the system. Such deviation could be brought automatically to the notice of superiors or security workers in the ways described earlier. Similar monitoring could also be applied to output though it must always be remembered that such safeguards themselves pose privacy risks.

The operating system will require periodic checking against a master copy of the original version, since many other safeguards might be overridden by unauthorized alteration. Such operating systems should themselves be prepared in secure conditions, and preferably by personnel having no knowledge of or conection with the personnel to be engaged in actual operation, so far as this is technically feasible. All other programmes should be subjected to similar checks, and it might even prove to be desirable in extreme cases to write software in such a way as to allow progressive minor alteration as part of the security precautions, and thus imposing a temporal limit to some forms of breach. This may seem excessive, but there is some evidence that no system is completely immune to the talented and dedicated programmer.[21] Another possible counter-measure here is to employ staff whose job is solely to try to break the security of the system, and thus to furnish continuous testing of it. Strict security should be maintained for all programmes and operating manuals. There should also, so far as possible, be segregation of users from programmers, and programmers from the data file. To minimize the danger of alteration of programmes and data it will almost certainly be desirable to impose very strict limitations upon the ability of remote terminals to alter, add to or delete any information existing in the files. For this reason it is envisaged that most of the remote terminals will normally be of a read only character.

The operating system should further contain stringent precautions against any data being left in the central store after being used, so as to minimize the danger of its being picked up by an unauthorized terminal, even by accident. Terminals too should be designed so as to minimize the danger of their being photographed or overlooked while in use, and so as to eliminate absolutely every trace of the information they have displayed after use. It is probably impossible

[21] Hansard, H. L. vol. 306, col. 121 per Earl of Halsbury who asserted that in no United States Government system had the security survived for more than six months.

to devise precautions to eliminate all risks of eavesdropping, but some additional steps should probably be taken in this direction. All devices might, for example, be provided with shields to guard against electronic survey from outside. Communications lines and switching centres should also be rendered as invulnerable as possible to 'wire tapping' in any form. The scrambling of all data transmitted over communications lines might also constitute a further safeguard here.

It may be felt that all these precautions will cost a great deal in terms of reduced speed of operation on account of coding processes, loss of storage space to provide for elaborate recording and comparison techniques, and generally in money to pay the salaries of specialized security staff, and for otherwise unnecessarily sophisticated equipment. One estimate puts the loss of storage at 20 per cent,[22] and another quotes a figure of an extra ·007 seconds an operation to allow for encoding and decoding.[23] It must, however, be remembered that not all these precautions need be taken in all situations, but in every case a balance should be struck depending upon the special factors involved.

PERSONNEL : As remarked earlier one of the reasons preventing similar fears about the activities of money bankers is that public confidence has been created in the bankers themselves. This is also true of most other persons in whom it is customary to repose confidences, such as accountants, doctors and lawyers. In all of these cases a professional ethic incorporating obligations of keeping information confidential has been created, and is expected to be generally respected and enforced. The best guarantee of confidence in the data processing area would be the establishment of a similar code of ethics, perhaps by the institution of some sort of professional status for those working in the field. It may be objected that such a status would be inappropriate for the programmers, operators and maintenance staff even if generally appropriate for the higher managerial staff. But such objections may be met by reference to comparable areas. We rightly expect the nurse and lawyer's clerk to be as discreet as their principal. Once the ethic has been established it tends to pervade the institution and to infect all those in contact with it.

The first essential step towards inculcating such an ethic is to establish control over the membership of the profession. This in-

[22] Behrens, 'Computers and Society', 91 *Science News*, 532 (1967).
[23] Hoffman, paper *CGTM* 76, Stanford University.

volves control over both entry and dismissal, and is an obvious precaution in the case of those handling delicate personal information. Those who are to be entrusted with it must be, and be seen to be, of such a calibre that the public can feel confidence in them. They should be accorded the status and financial recompense to signify their worthiness of that confidence, and to reduce the material temptation to abuse it. It should be made a condition for entry that the candidate has been educated in the means of securing privacy for the data he will handle, and to this end he should take regular instruction during his training. Entrants should also be made aware that even after being admitted they are liable to forfeit their status if they should be guilty of any breach of confidentiality, by carelessness as much as by deliberate dereliction. All this entails the creation of an organization which can set the standards, select potential entrants, educate and examine them, admit them, control them, and, if necessary, deprive them of their status. This is no more, and no less, than the function of any of the well established professional bodies.

It may also be necessary to recruit special security and enforcement personnel within the various agencies operating data banks. It may be objected that this might undermine the morale of the staff, and that it is incompatible with the professional status suggested above. This is indeed a serious danger, and to some extent the suggestions are alternative. But if it is made clear that the primary task of such a force would be to guard against threats from outside the agency it might be more acceptable. Provided that the operation is conducted with a due sensitivity to the feelings of the personnel there should be no overwhelming objection on this score, and where the most sensitive information is being handled it may well be absolutely essential. Similar security forces operate in banks and secret government establishments without leading to particularly dire results.[24]

To summarize this section of the chapter. The major precautionary measures which give the best promise of preserving personal privacy, and confidence that it is being preserved, are strict control over the methods of obtaining data, the purposes for which it may be used and assessment of its usefulness for achieving those purposes; the provision of systems which are physically and operationally as

[24] For a similar view in relations to Local Authority applications see 'Computer Privacy', Notes of Guidance for Local Authorities, a Report of the Computer Panel of LAMSAC (1972).

secure as possible; and the creation of a professional ethic among the workers in the field. Only if all these fail need recourse be had to the remedial safeguards described in the following section.

Remedial

This section deals with the remedies available when an individual's privacy has been violated. It is perhaps a little odd to regard such remedies as safeguards since they only apply after the damage has been done in most cases. But such remedies usually have some deterrent force in preventing the occurrence of similar breaches in the future, and exceptionally some are available against a merely threatened intrusion.

Some confusion has been caused by the assertion as a vindication of such safeguards of a 'right' to privacy. It has been suggested that to legislate to create such a right is inconsistent with the general common law scheme of development which advances by smaller and more precisely defined steps.[25] Jurisprudential terminology in this field is in some confusion, but it is perhaps permissible to extend the analogy of property in this respect. Our enjoyment and use of our property is a privilege in the strict sense, but a right in a more general sense. Nevertheless this privilege or right is protected by very specific duties imposed upon others not to interfere, in relatively well defined ways, with our property. Here too we wish to enjoy our seclusion and anonymity, and it is possible to specify in relatively precise terms the sorts of remedies that can be used to furnish such protection. As in the case of property these remedies need not all be of one sort, tortious, contractual, equitable or criminal, but may be expected to extend into many different areas.

It is the elaboration of specific remedies and their concatenation which is important. Accession to vague affirmations of the general doctrine such as article 12 of the Universal Declaration of Human Rights, or article 17 of the United Nations Convention on Civil and Political Rights, or article 8 of the European Convention for the Protection of Human Rights and Fundamental Freedoms, while helpful is not conclusive since such articles are necessarily in general terms, and while they might indeed be used to invalidate systems which provide no remedies at all, do not prescribe any in particular.[26]

The account of possible remedies which follows, most of which are

---

[25] Hansard, H. C. vol. 794, col. 914 by Mr Angus Maude MP.
[26] See Younger Report, esp. chs 2 and 23.

of a legal character, is based mainly on the British system, but has some reference to other systems, and especially to that of the United States in relation to the tort of invasion of privacy.[27] One reason for not concentrating exclusively upon that possible remedy is that where the essence of the complaint is the invasion of personal privacy, it is somewhat quixotic to compel the subject to institute public procedings complete with all the trappings of calling witnesses, undergoing cross-examination and proving the degree of damage, in order to secure redress.

The remedies will be discussed in relation to four possible defendants : against the employees of a centre where violation has occurred who were responsible for the violation, against the centre itself, against an individual violator not an employee of the centre, and against the user of the information. It is appreciated that this is not a completely exhaustive catalogue of possible defendants, but it is felt to be sufficient to illustrate the range of the remedies available. Some remedies might be used in a number of these situations, and these will be discussed only where they seem most appropriate. Once again it must be stressed that the aim is to illustrate a possible range, not to suggest that all safeguards should be applied in all situations.

AGAINST EMPLOYEE : Since this part of the chapter is arranged by reference to those responsible for the violation, it will be appreciated that it does not follow that the subject of the information is necessarily the party in whom the remedy inheres. A typical example of this sort of situation would be one where an employee of a centre were suborned to supply personal information from the files to an interested third party. Such an employee might be exposed to pressure from four possible sources : from the state, from his employer, from his professional body, and from the subject. Pressure from the state would be exerted through the criminal law. Thus it is already a criminal offence in England for government employees to divulge confidential information,[28] and there are special provisions dealing with such matters as Census information,[29] taxation information,[30] and some medical records.[31] There is, however, no

---

[27] See Younger Report, appendix I (Great Britain) and appendix J (other states).
[28] Official Secrets Act 1911, sect. 2. The section covers a wider range of situations than that indicated in the text, and is currently under review.
[29] Census Act 1920, sect. 8(2) and Census Regulations S.1. 1970/481.
[30] Taxes Management Act 1970, sect. 6 and 1st Sch.
[31] N.H.S. (Venereal Diseases) Regulations 1968.

general criminal offence though it has been suggested[32] that the very
wide definitions in the Theft Act 1968 might make such conduct
theft, but this seems very dubious.

Pressure from the employer would no doubt take the simple form
of dismissal from employment, since such conduct would clearly be
in breach of a term of the contract of employment, implied if not
express. Such a sanction would be reinforced if a further consequence were that the employee should also forfeit his membership
of his professional body, as this would prevent his being able to secure
similar employment elsewhere where he would have the opportunity
of repeating his conduct. The subject might have any one of a number of causes of action in tort, but discussion of these will be post-
poned. The only difference made to the eligibility of the tort action
in virtue of the violator's being an employee of the centre is that
this might render the centre liable vicariously for the tort of their
employee. It is no defence to such a claim that the employee was
acting in breach of specific instructions from his employer,[33] or that
he was committing a crime,[34] or a tort[35] whether or not that tort was
committed for the benefit of his employer,[36] provided always that
the conduct in question took place in the 'course of the employment'.

AGAINST CENTRE : The situation envisaged here, of which that dealt
with above is an example, is one where a centre undertakes to keep
personal information confidential, and in some way or another it
fails to do so. Criminal remedies are less obviously appropriate here
since most centres will be corporate entities, and there are well
known reservations about the utility of applying to them the full
rigour of the criminal law.[37] The possibility should not, however,
be entirely dismissed. A more effective means of exerting pressure
might however be through the licensing system suggested earlier.
A licence could be revoked, or suspended, or continued only upon
certain conditions. In the case of revocation or suspension any desirable changes could be made conditions for renewal. Since these
remedies would strike in a substantial way at the profit-earning
capacity of the centre they might well constitute a most effective
safeguard. They have the additional element of flexibility, and could

[32] Jacob and Jacob, 'Confidential Communications', 119 *New Law J.*, 133 (1969).
[33] *Limpus* v. *London General Omnibus Co.* (1862), 1 H. & C. 526.
[34] *Dyer* v. *Munday* [1895] 1 Q.B. 742.
[35] *Mersey Docks Trustees* v. *Gibbs* (1866), L.R. 1 H.L. 93.
[36] *Lloyd* v. *Grace Smith & Co.* [1912] A.C. 716.
[37] See e.g. Williams, 'Criminal Law: The General Part', para. 283.

be used to divert resources into those areas where they could, in the light of experience, be most safely employed.

The main source of pressure here, however, is likely to be the aggrieved subject of the information. His most obvious cause of action in the case of a private centre with whom he was dealing would be in contract. It is highly advisable for any such person to insist upon the inclusion of an express term guaranteeing confidentiality into the contract.[38] The main advantage of the remedy in contract is that the duty can be specified in precise terms appropriate to the particular subject matter of the contract. It is also possible in some cases to prevent the breach by obtaining an injunction, or even by repudiation for anticipatory breach. Even after breach repudiation may often be a more effective remedy than damages, as many agencies will have budgeted in reliance upon the continuation of existing contractual arrangements. Unfortunately it is not always the case, even with private agencies, that the subject of the information is in a contractual relationship with the centre. In such cases the first recourse will be to the law of tort. As remarked in the previous section, if an employee has committed a tort the chances are that the employer will be vicariously liable, and will, of course, make a more tempting choice of defendant. But if no employee can be shown to have committed a tort, the question of the original tortious liability of the centre will arise.

Where, as suggested earlier, there are statutory regulations dealing with safeguards and the violation occurs as a result of breach of one of them the subject might have a cause of action for breach of statutory duty, since it is clear that the safeguard would have been directed towards protecting the plaintiff against just this sort of damage.[39] Even if there are no statutory regulations, breach of the conditions under which a licence is granted might be very helpful in establishing a cause of action in negligence. This could relate to any of the matters dealt with in the previous section, namely data handling, system of operation or selection and control of personnel. Some authority for such a claim is afforded by a New Zealand case in which a doctor was held to have been negligent in disclosing private personal information about a female patient to her husband.[40]

[38] See Lickson, 'Protection of the Privacy of Data Communications by Contract', 23 *Business Lawyer*, 971 (1968).
[39] *Gorris* v. *Scott* (1874), L.R. 9 Exch, 125.
[40] *Furniss* v. *Fitchett* [1958] N.Z.L.R. 396.

If it is not possible to establish a case of negligence there is no clearly applicable tort of strict liability in English law. Perhaps the most promising analogy is provided by the tort established by the case of *Rylands* v. *Fletcher*[41] which gives a remedy against one who for his own purposes gathers and keeps on his land something not naturally there and which is liable to cause mischief if it escapes. It would require only a slight extension of the notion of the thing stored there which has already been applied to electricity,[42] and of the concept of an escape, which has unfortunately been construed in a rather less generous way.[43]

A further possibility which has been mooted is the treatment of the centre as a trustee of the information gathered, and hence susceptible to an action for breach of trust by the subject of the information.[44] There is however little basis in English law, at least, for any such development. The great advantage of a remedy in equity however is the availability of the injunction to restrain abuse. This has suggested the more promising line of applying the equity to restrain breach of confidence. This, however, is a relatively obscure branch of English law, and has so far been applied mainly against the users of information obtained in breach of confidence, and will accordingly be discussed later.

AGAINST AN INTRUDER : While it is perhaps most likely that security will be broken, if at all, by someone with inside knowledge it does not follow that such a person will necessarily be employed by the centre at the time of violation. It is also possible that the security might be broken from the outside, by wire-tapping for example. In either case the remedies in contract and through professional action described in the first section above will be unavailable. However, there is at least one important additional form of action available against intrusion from outside. This is the action in tort for trespass. It was the great traditional bulwark of personal privacy in England in the eighteenth century especially. Its essence is to provide a remedy for any intrusion on to the land of the plaintiff. In relation to most data banks this will mean that the remedy will be available to the centre rather than to the subject of the information.

The subject himself, however, would have the remedy in respect

---

[41] (1868), L.R. 3 H.L. 330.
[42] *National Telephone Co.* v. *Baker* [1893] 2 Ch. 186.
[43] *Read* v. *Lyons & Co. Ltd.* [1947] A.C. 156.
[44] Miller, 'Personal Privacy in the Computer Age', 67 *Mich. L.R.*, 1091 at 1226.

of some forms of data collection, such as a secreted microphone.[45]
The principal defect of this remedy is that it depends upon a physical
intrusion on to the plaintiff's land, and there is thus no remedy in
trespass in respect of the more insidious techniques of surveillance
from outside.[46] In England the rule is the same though assisted by
the early realization that even when outside the plaintiff's land the
intruder is unlikely to be on his own, and thus someone has an
action in trespass.[47] This may, however, be of no avail to the
subject if the owner of the land trespassed upon is uncooperative.
And where the information is collected from a public utility like a
communication network neither the subject nor the utility has an
action.[48] Nor is there generally any remedy in trespass, or nuisance,
for surveillance from the intruder's own property even though it is
done for commercial gain through the publication of the information so obtained.[49] Nevertheless trespass does deal with some of the
more obvious forms of intrusion and is a useful weapon in the
armoury of remedies.

In addition to any civil remedies at the hands of the occupier
of the land intruded upon, it is possible to bring some pressure to
bear through the criminal law and local bye-laws, but without
some more drastic addition to the range of criminal remedies, as
has been proposed principally to deal with industrial espionage in
all its forms, this can not be regarded as a major safeguard.

AGAINST USER : Of course in many, if not most, cases the user and
the intruder will be the same person. So far as the kernel of the
complaint is the use of the information the remedial safeguards
are considered here. The roots of the modern law of both England
and the United States in this area are to be found in a few English
mid-nineteenth-century cases,[50] but the subsequent development has
been very different.

In the United States a new tort of infringement of privacy has
emerged, recognized in all but a tiny handful of states and having
given rise to over 350 reported decisions since 1905. In England
there has been no comparable burgeoning of authority, and the thin

[45] As in *Sheen* v. *Clegg*, *Daily Telegraph*, 22 June 1961.
[46] *Goldman* v. *US* 316 US 129 (1942).
[47] *Hickman* v. *Maisey* [1900] 1 Q.B. 752, where the intrusion took place from a public
highway the ownership of which was vested in the plaintiff.
[48] *Paine & Co.* v. *St. Neots Gas Co.* [1939] 3 All E.R. 812 at 823 per Luxmoore L.J.
[49] *Victoria Park Racing Co.* v. *Taylor* (1937), 58 C.L.R. 479.
[50] Principally *Prince Albert* v. *Strange* (1849), 1 H. & T. 1.

trickle of cases has taken a different line in the direction of breach of confidence. This is partly due to the fact that the tort in the United States has a number of different facets,[51] some of which give rise to remedies in defamation in England. Of those facets the most appropriate in connection with data banks is that where private personal information is made public. This differs from defamation in that traditionally justification is a defence there whereas truth is no defence to a privacy action, and there is also an important difference between publication which is essential to defamation and making public which is a requirement in breach of privacy. The latter requires a much wider range of exposure than the former.

In the United States the tort of invasion of privacy has been used to give a remedy where unpaid debts were made publicly known,[52] or where old criminal charges were raked up in a film.[53] Unfortunately it has some drawbacks as a safeguard. As conceived by Warren and Brandeis it was especially aimed against press intrusion, and as such has to be balanced against the public interest in knowing what is going on in the society so as to make the democratic processes work.[54] This consideration brings it into conflict with the very powerful commercial and parliamentary strength of the press lobby.

It is in most cases dependent upon the establishment of the privacy of the information in the first place, although as demonstrated earlier much information buried in various locations in the public domain becomes sensitive when it is dug up, assembled and exposed to the glare of modern publicity. It further depends upon the information being made public in a way which will by no means always be true of information extracted illicitly from a data bank which may indeed be kept very secret by the user. This drawback is further accentuated, if, as suggested by Warren and Brandeis, defences similar to those of qualified privilege in defamation are made available. Then there is the difficulty in determining whether or not the subject may not himself have given implied consent to publicity by doing something in public, or arousing public interest in his activities. Then again the information to which publicity is given must be something which an ordinary person would find

[51] Prosser, in his important article 'Privacy', 48 *Calif. L.R.* 383, (1960) distinguishes four.
[52] *Brents* v. *Morgan* (1927), 299 S.W. 967.
[53] *Melvin* v. *Reid* (1931), 112 Cal. App. 285.
[54] US Freedom of Information Act 1967 is an indication of the pressures exerted in this direction.

offensive.[55] Finally, there is a difficulty in defining at all adequately the interest of the plaintiff which is being infringed, and consequently in establishing satisfactory criteria for the assessment of damages. For these and similar reasons some of the most perceptive commentators in the United States have expressed considerable reservations about the potentialities of this particular tort.[56]

As stated earlier the common starting point for developments in both the United States and England was the old case of *Prince Albert* v. *Strange*[57] where the Prince sought an injunction against, *inter alia,* the publication of a catalogue compiled by the defendant which described some private etchings of members of the Royal family made by the Prince exclusively for his private use. It was decided that quite apart from any question of property in the etchings themselves, an injunction would lie to restrain a breach of confidence. The confidence seems to have been treated as synonymous with the privacy of information about another, especially when it had been obtained surreptitiously. This ruling was later applied to restrain the wider publication of photographs commissioned by the plaintiff.[58]

But in such cases the law is obscured by the presence of the further feature of a contract between the parties, raising the possibility of breach of an implied term. This factor is also present in the vast majority of cases dealing with commercial secrets. In *Triplex Safety Glass* v. *Scorah*[59] a term imposing a limited obligation of confidence was even implied when a wider express term designed to achieve the same result was struck down as an unreasonable restraint of trade. Even in *Argyll* v. *Argyll,*[60] where one of the parties to a marriage was restrained from publishing marital confidences, the contract of marriage was one of the factors influencing the Court. It should be stressed that the importance of the contract lies in its endowing the information with a confidential character since it is clear that a third party can be restrained from making use of such information, and not only a party to the contract.[61] The scarcity

---

[55] Cp. *Melvin* v. *Reid* (*supra* n. 53) with *Sidis* v. *F.R. Publishing Corp.* 113 F. 2d 806 (1940). Some indication that English Law would adopt a similar view is furnished by *Sports Agency* v. '*Our Dogs' Publishing Co.* [1916] 2 K.B. 880.
[56] See e.g. Kalven, 'Privacy in Tort Law – Were Warren and Brandeis Wrong?', 31 *Law and Contemporary Problems* 326 (1966).
[57] (1849), 1 H. & T. 1.
[58] *Pollard* v. *Photographic Co.* (1889), 40 Ch. D. 345.
[59] [1938] Ch. 211.
[60] [1967] 1 Ch. 302.
[61] See e.g. *Ashburton* v. *Pape* [1913] 2 Ch. 469.

of recent cases in which such a contractual element is absent undoubtedly obscures and diminishes the value of this doctrine for the present purpose where there might well be no contractual element in the situation at all. The remedy is further limited by its unavailability in respect of matters of public record,[62] or in respect of 'iniquitous information',[63] or to restrain its use in evidence in a Court of law.[64] It is unclear precisely how the remedies it supplies would be applied in the data bank situation, though it does seem clear that the only possible plaintiff is the party to whom the information is confidential.[65]

Apart from these somewhat dubious remedies in tort and equity there is also some possibility of bringing the influence of the state to bear through the criminal law. In particular, it might be thought that criminal libel might afford a remedy since there, by contrast to civil defamation, truth is no defence, indeed the adage is 'the greater the truth, the greater the libel'. This remedy is, however, little used nowadays, and would in any case be very often hampered by the availability of qualified privilege as a defence. A further possibility to prevent some unauthorized uses of information might be by way of the crime of blackmail. This applies where the user is seeking gain by making demands without believing them reasonable accompanied by menaces without believing them to be proper.[66] It is apparent that these remedies are unduly limited.

In general also it will be apparent that the remedial safeguards are unduly limited at present. They would be vastly improved by the introduction of the precautionary safeguards suggested earlier, more especially if some of them are given statutory force. Outside the fields now adequately provided for by contract and trespass there is a great need for the rapid emergence of new torts and crimes, and new remedies specially designed to meet threats to the privacy of the individual. There is some ground for hope that by focusing attention on the weaknesses of the present situation the computer may prove to be the catalyst necessary to bring such a development about.

[62] *Saltman Engineering Co.* v. *Campbell Engineering Co.* [1963] 3 All E.R. 413 (decided in 1948).
[63] *Gartside* v. *Outram* (1856), 26 L.J. Ch. 113, recently approved in *Initial Services Ltd.* v. *Putterill* [1968] 1 Q.B. 396.
[64] *Butler* v. *Board of Trade* [1971] Ch. 680
[65] *Fraser* v. *Evans* [1969] 1 Q.B. 345.
[66] Theft Act 1968, sect. 21.

4

Computers and legislation

This chapter will attempt to explain and describe the application of computerized techniques to legislation. This should be understood in a broad sense to include subordinate legislation, rules and regulations as well as statutes, and reference to the latter should normally be taken to include the former. The practical application of computerized techniques is more advanced here than in most other legal areas. This is explained partly by the nature of the material and partly by the nature of the process. This is best explored by comparison with case law, and the first section briefly compares these two sources of law. The remaining sections deal with the application of computerized techniques at different stages of the legislative process, namely preparation, drafting, passage and printing.

1 LEGISLATION AND CASE LAW

To a lawyer faced with a legal problem, legislation presents two not unrelated difficulties. The first is to find the relevant legislative material, and the second is to understand and apply it correctly when it has been found. Both can be attributed to the form of legislation, and this in its turn can be explained by its function. The primary function of legislation is to establish authoritative rules for the future. It is true that this normally entails also repealing or overruling some of the rules of the past, but this is incidental. Case law on the other hand is primarily concerned to dispose of a dispute between two parties. In so doing new law is often created. Few would now deny that cases make law, but no one would deny that statutes do, though such a view was once held. The contrast is between legislation which preeminently establishes new rules for the future, and adjudication which necessarily resolves disputes which have occurred in the past. Both may sometimes do other things also, but they do not typically or necessarily do them. From this difference in function flow important differences of form. Thus judgements in cases contain long descriptive passages outlining the dispute before the Court, and even longer expository passages setting out the law as it applies to that dispute. The operative part of the decision is well established in form, concise in expression and un-ambiguous in effect. It it rare even for the most ingenious and assi-duous counsel to raise compelling doubts over the interpretation of some such phrase as 'judgement for the plaintiff', provided that the issues have been precisely defined, as they usually are.

Legislation contains no comparable descriptive passages, nor, now that preambles have passed out of fashion, does it normally contain an exposition of the precedent state of the law. It is wholly operative. The task for the lawyer is a different one for each of these types of law. In relation to case law he must construe from the exposition of law rehearsed in the judgement the changes, if any, which have been made by it. To this end a vast apparatus has been developed to enable him to distinguish between *ratio decidendi* and *obiter dictum,* and an elaborate hierarchical distribution of authority be-tween different Courts has also been established. There is no authori-tative text of the *ratio decidendi* of a case to be found anywhere in the judgement of a Court, and especially not in the predominantly appellate Courts where multiple concurring opinions are permitted.

Legislation raises different problems. The problem is not one of how authoritative any particular part is, because every word is authoritative, and equally authoritative; though somewhat similar questions may arise in relation to legislatures which have a limited or subordinate jurisdiction. The problem here is much more one of meaning and interpretation, because unlike orders in cases, the operative words of a statute are almost never specific. In comparing all cases and almost all statutes this is necesarily true. The order in a case decides a dispute; it lays down no rule. To suppose that it does is to confuse the concepts of *ratio decidendi* and *res judicata*. Legislation nearly always establishes rules, and it is a characteristic of most legal rules that they apply to more than one set of particu-lars, and in that sense are necessarily not specific. For practical reasons also legislation is more general in tone, and tends to apply to a wider range of instances. The process of legislation has its impact here. Statutes are generally expected to last for a long time.

They can not all be continually brought back for amendment and expansion as the Jacobins discovered in France.[1] Legislative time is just too short. By contrast it is by no means unusual for case law to be made the subject of gradual elaboration and crystallization by subsequent cases over very long periods of time.

It may thus be accepted that legislation, on account of its function and the process by which it is enacted, has acquired a form which makes it difficult to understand, and because of that also difficult to find. This difficulty of finding legislation is exacerbated by its sheer bulk. The 90th Congress in the United States alone enacted 640 public Acts running to 2,300 pages of text in the Statutes at Large, excluding private statutes, proclamations, joint resolutions and constitutional amendments. But this is just the tip of the legislative iceberg. In the first year of that Congress 18,517 measures were introduced of which only 453 were eventually enacted, yet track had to be kept of all the rest. If, as in the United States, interpretation of legislation may be assisted by reference to the official Congressional Record, then for that first year of one Congress, it would be necessary to consult twenty-seven volumes extending to 37,507 pages. The volume of rules, regulations and orders made under this legislation by departments and agencies is still greater, and defies estimation, even though some indication of its magnitude may be gathered by considering that the Federal Register for 1968 runs to 20,072 triple column pages.

In the case of the United States it is also necessary to consider the legislative activity of the component states. Their output is not so intensive as that of the Federal Government, but it is by no means insignificant. In the years 1966 to 1967 the fifty states together with Puerto Rico and the United States Virgin Islands considered 136,006 measures in regular sessions, and a further 5,553 in extra sessions, of which 44,441 eventually became law. There is no reliable way of calculating the volume of legislative discussion relating to these measures, nor the number of rules, regulations, orders and ordinances made under them by the states. Nor is a reliable estimate possible for the output of lesser authorities such as cities, towns, municipalities and counties though it has been calculated that there are over eight thousand such subordinate rule-making authorities in the United States alone.

[1] See Law of August 16–24, 1790 tit. II art. 10 for their unsuccessful attempt to devise a continuous revision system.

In Great Britain the legislative load is smaller. In 1968 for example, only twenty-seven statutes received the Royal Assent, but they still occupied 2,532 pages of the Public General Statutes. The factor by which bills exceed acts is also smaller than in the United States, but even so during 1969, Parliament had before it 240 bills, though this figure includes separately some bills which lapsed in one session and were reintroduced in the next. As in the United States the volume of rules and regulations exceeds that of legislation, and the six volumes of statutory instruments for 1968 amount to 5,660 pages. Here again there is no reliable way of estimating the output of legislation by inferior bodies such as county, borough, district and parish councils.

It will be appreciated that this enormous bulk of material makes the task of finding any particular measure difficult, especially since, as already noted, indexes and summaries are inappropriate tools with which to dig. The task is made completely impossible if the legislation is not available in printed form. Already in most countries the mass of material has made the Government printer the largest publisher in the state, and in many the process is on the point of breaking down. So far, high priority items, such as drafts of bills, for the relevant assemblies, are generally unaffected. But the strain of producing these on time piles up further difficulties lower down the list. The result is that almost all government printing establishments are running far behind schedule, and slipping further back all the time. The worst effects are often most apparent in small states where the printing is contracted out. In these places it is as much as can be done to get the actual legislation printed. Subordinate legislation is often not printed, and if available at all appears in a variety of less formal and often quite unsuitable formats.

It is against such a background of mounting frustration and failure that attention has been increasingly turning to computer orientated assistance. This is often in the form of a system providing the full range of services required to put legislation through every stage of the legislative process, from the initial gathering of information to the final printing of the statute, which then itself becomes part of the material available for searching. The remainder of this chapter considers these steps of the process in turn.

2 PREPARATION

The preparation of materials by legislators with a view to the passage of legislation embraces a diverse assortment of processes, of varying degrees of formality. Initially it is often highly informal. Someone has an idea, and in reflecting about it brings into the forefront of his mind with great speed and a minimum of effort an enormous array of relevant information. But this is too informal and too unreliable to serve as more than a starting point. The information assembled in this way must be written down, checked for accuracy and amplified. It is then that the difficulties emerge, and artificial aids have to be used. The precise nature of these difficulties and of the techniques by which they can be overcome will vary with the nature of the legislation in question, and the purpose for which the information is needed. The range of materials required in connection with, say a constitutional amendment, a new criminal statute, an appropriation act or a traffic regulation will vary enormously. So will the needs of different bodies; a committee considering the policy of a proposal, the draftsman or drafting committee, other affected legislative committees, individual legislators during discussion in the chamber, and executive personnel will all require different information concerning the legislation. Perhaps the most acute information problems arise in connection with codifying enactments, but as this impinges more than is convenient in this chapter upon the different problems of case law, consolidating legislation will be considered here instead. It was indeed the problem of collecting all the relevant legislative material for the production of the Hospital Law Manual which first convinced Professor Horty, the doyen of computer applications in law, of the necessity of finding some more satisfactory way of assembling this sort of legal information. In states where the law already exists in the form of an enacted code the problem is less acute, but still exists for legislative materials other than statutes. And conversely, as already noted, the initial preparation of a code strains conventional resources more than any other activity.

Faced with this task of collecting all the legislation in a particular area with a view to consolidation, the lawyer's first reflex is to look for some existing collection from which to start. This procedure is, however, impossible when the area is a new one, and unsatisfactory when it is an old one which has been substantially impinged upon by new developments. At best this technique is no better than the printed sources it relies upon, and the schemes of classification and indexing devised for them. It is hardly surprising that this technique yields poor results, and that lawyers like Horty when faced with such tasks have been driven to look elsewhere for assistance.

The computer became an eligible possibility towards the end of the 1950s when for the first time it began to be feasible to use it for linguistic as well as mathematical applications. It had the virtues of speed, accuracy, and most important of all, complete indefatigability. Its most outstanding drawback was its complete novelty in the field of law. This meant that no one knew how to harness its capabilities, which, in a conservative profession was itself a disadvantage. The conservatism of lawyers is largely the obverse of their salient virtues like their reliability. Their slowness to change is at least in part a reluctance to adopt any new technique or practice until they are sure that it will work. The scene was thus set in the early 1960s for the experimental testing of computer applications in the field of the retrieval of legislative materials.

For further development in this area to succeed, it was necessary that a number of important issues be resolved correctly. The most important of all was to decide upon the nature of the information upon which the computer was to be put to work. One attractive approach was to draw up a list of key concepts relevant to the particular field under investigation, and then to characterize each document by reference to these concepts in a computer assimilable form. The computer would then be able to find upon command all the materials relating to a given concept, or combination of concepts. Such an approach would utilize the first principle of computer application which is that the machine should be set to those tasks which it can perform more efficiently than a human being, while the human being, and especially the human brain, should be set to those which it can perform better than the computer. Here the characterization of the meaning of a document in terms of key concepts is preeminently a task for the human brain, while the sorting of those documents once they have been so characterized is clearly a task for a machine. An advantage of this approach is that by using familiar key concepts it makes it easy for the lawyer to use the system with a minimum of training and a maximum of self-confidence. An advantage of using the computer to sort the information is that it permits a much more specific search to be made than would be possible by using conventional methods.

Conventional techniques will permit a combination of about five facets with ease. Thus the first might be represented by the selection of a volume dealing with a particular broad area of law relating to the problem, say a book on criminal law. The index might then be used to select two main topics, say arrest and mistake, and perhaps one subheading under each main heading, say arrest by a police officer and mistake of fact. Then, by comparison of entries under these two subheadings, references to those passages dealing with the criminal implications of arrest by a police officer labouring under a mistake of fact would be identified. The computer does not depend up memory or putting fingers between pages in the same way as the human being. It can combine as many facets as required without any difficulty at all.

Such a computer system is, however, subject to two types of limitation upon its efficiency. First, it is limited by the efficiency of the indexing system which has been selected so far as its depth and general adaptation to the particular class of request is concerned. Secondly, it is limited by the degree of consistency with which the selected scheme has been applied. Unless the computer scheme is substantially superior in one or other of these respects, it may be better to computerize the existing indexes. But this would only be advantageous as compared with traditional methods either if more precision were required, that is that the searcher wished to combine more facets than was convenient by manual methods, or because a computerized system offered some other advantages in terms of increased speed, lower chances of error, more remote access to materials, instantaneous display of the required information, or other incidental advantage. Against these, however, should be weighed the undoubtedly less attractive ambience for the lawyer of electronic machines than that of calf-bound volumes, and much more important the loss of an easy browsing facility.

Professor Horty, it is thought rightly, rejected the computerization of existing indexes. He saw that the problem was more fundamental than mere inconvenience. However much care was taken, the system would still be incapable of providing reference to all the information which might be needed, especially in the field of legislation. The reason for this was the relative poverty and inflexibility of the concepts used in conventional indexing. The terms are few because of the need to keep the bulk of the index down so as to make it convenient for manual use, and also to avoid a multiplicity of borderline judgements, or duplicated references. Clearly the more terms used the more borderlines there will be between them, and the more possible categories into which to insert any given reference. The terms are inflexible partly because of the necessity for the lawyers using the system to be familiar with them, and partly because of the nature of the publishing process. Once a printed book has been published, the index achieves a fixed form. The economics of publishing then demand that even where there is a new edition, or where the book is published in loose-leaf form, the new index should not be so radically different from the old as to entail the re-indexing of the whole of the original work.

When the lack of compatibility between different conventional indexes, and the relatively low degree of care and skill with which they are compiled are considered, the argument against their reproduction within a computerized system becomes very strong indeed. But these arguments go further than merely making a case against the automation of existing indexes. They also tell against the development of a computer orientated indexing system of any sort, not perhaps so much in theory but certainly in practice. The problem is that in practice the framers of a special computer orientated index are unlikely to be able to achieve the necessary improvements in detail and flexibility without at the same time further sacrificing the already defective standards of utility and consistency. Another practical argument is that such a system must involve the development of the indexing system before the scheme can be put into effect, even on an experimental basis. This means that the framers will be committed to the expenditure of large sums of money without the means of demonstrating whether or not they are on the right track. It will, of course, be even longer before any such scheme can be expected to show a financial return. It is also legitimate to reflect that it is unrealistic to expect the framers of any new system to improve the present system radically in a suitably short period of time, considering that the present system represents the culmination of years of progress by countless dedicated professionals, and is still quite unsatisfactory.

For these reasons, Professor Horty and others were attracted by a different approach, and one making a more fundamental breach from the techniques of the past. This was to bypass the problems of indexing and classification completely in the initial stages, and to work with the raw material constituted by the words of the original document. Such an approach allowed work to start almost immediately, and for continuous sustained testing as it progressed.

It further avoided all problems of harmonizing different existing indexing schemes. It may be objected that this approach breaks what has been described as the first principle of computer applications, namely that the computer should do what it can do better than the human brain, and that the human brain should do what it can do better than the computer. But the trouble with indexing was that even though the human brain was better than the computer, it was still not good enough.

It was therefore necessary to develop a set of processes which would achieve better results without breaking the principle. It may be true that a computer cannot at present be programmed so as to distil the meaning from a document. To suppose otherwise is to ignore the relative failure of machine translation despite the enormous expenditure of time and money devoted to it. The extraction of meaning from the arrangement of words and symbols is an extremely complicated process demanding the application of rules which we are neither accustomed nor perhaps able to articulate completely. Some thinkers, like Professor Chomsky, assert that such rules are innate rather than learned, which suggests that the difficulties of articulation may be even more severe than had hitherto been believed.[2] But while this may amount to an argument against some systems of mechanical indexing, it is not necessarily an argument for the complete abandonment of the goal of using computerized methods to find relevant legislative materials for the legislator. The question is whether any acceptable alternative exists to the preparation of indexes or lists of key concepts in order to find legislative materials.

The answer suggested by Professor Horty, in the field of legislation at least, was that the occurrence of words in the text of the relevant materials might be an acceptable substitute. This is a plausible view. It is not very surprising to argue that the meaning of a document is related to the words it contains. The human brain, whatever also it might bring to its task, must at least refer to those words as a starting point in determining the meaning of a document. Here, at least, is a task for which the computer is more apt than the human brain. The detection of the presence of a given word merely involves a set of simple mathematical calculations. These calculations can be performed so fast and so accurately that very large quantities of material can be scanned in minute periods of

[2] See e.g. Chomsky and Halle, *The Sound Pattern of English* (1968).

time. The complete text of the statutes in force in the United States can be scanned so fast that the answer appears instantaneous to the searcher. It will also during that instant have been double-checked. Imagine how long it would take a human being to conduct such a search and how unreliable the answer would be, not because human beings cannot read, but because they are by comparison slow readers, and they get tired, bored and distracted, especially if asked, as they are at present, to perform unrewarding and undemanding tasks.

Here there is a perfect application of the principle of allocating to the computer tasks it can perform more efficiently than a human being. The example also shows that computerized methods are in certain situations quicker and cheaper than any others. The development of modern technology is such that the speed of response and the cost of processing now present no problem to the application of computers in the legislative sphere, though they once did. It may be noted that these two factors are directly linked in an inverse way, since computer processing time is charged for by reference to the time it takes. The only serious financial obstacle to such applications lies in the cost of preparing the basic documents in a computer assimilable form, but as will be shown in a later section, even this problem is well on the way to being solved, at least for legislative materials.

The real problems are not practical and technical but theoretical and legal. They involve the selection of material to be stored in such a system, the form in which it is to be stored, and the efficiency of such a system in finding relevant information. These will therefore be considered in turn in the special context of legislative materials.

Selection of material

It has already been suggested that there are substantial advantages for computerized methods in using the raw text of the documents as the basic information. The question here is which texts are to be included. This must obviously depend upon the particular application under consideration. To revert to the example of a consolidating statute, it will obviously be necessary to have all the existing statutes of the jurisdiction on the relevant topic available. But this raises a problem. If the proposal for consolidation arises just because it is difficult to find all the law in the relevant area, how can those who are proposing to use the computer find all the information in the relevant area to set it to work? It looks like a vicious circle. It was this precise difficulty which first plagued Professor Horty and his team at the University of Pittsburgh in their efforts to collect together all legislation relating to public health. They were aware that however hard they tried to find all the relevant legislation in Pennsylvania there would still be obscure sections which were relevant tucked away in the crevices of statutes dealing for the most part with quite different subjects.

The resolution of this problem resembles that employed in relation to the identification of concepts, namely to postpone it at the preparation stage by resisting the temptation to isolate particular subject areas in advance, but instead to prepare a much larger body of material within which that which is sought is known to be located. The computer can then be employed to achieve any desired selection. Thus if one's primary interest is in the Pennsylvania health statutes, the best strategy is to prepare the most appropriate larger set which is known to contain the health statutes as a sub-set. In this case the most likely such set would be the whole of the Pennsylvania statutes.

At this point a second basic principle of computer application in law may be stated. It is that in designing an information retrieval system, the structure must be determined by the needs of the user. This principle carries two implications of unequal weight, namely that nothing should be provided that is not needed, and everything that is needed should be provided. The second of these is incomparably the more important. But needs are difficult to identify, especially when they are to arise in the future, and in a context which will be so significantly different from anyone's experience as to be virtually unimaginable. It is a little like conducting an opinion poll in Neanderthal times to see whether the radio should be developed. The difficulty is that the availability of a new facility creates its own demand, and nowhere more than in a highly competitive context. This means that the bias should be towards providing more rather than less than is required, though practical and economic considerations will impose outer limits. Thus in the field of legislation it will be necessary to anticipate as many of the needs of the legislature as possible, and to prepare the most appropriate set of documents which is known to include them.

Here it may be noted that the use of the text of the original documents as basic input has a further advantage. It presents, as will be demonstrated more fully later, no inherent obstacle to further expansion. This is not true of indexed systems. These tend to be orientated towards particular users and uses in their selection of index terms and concepts. Thus indexing systems in medicine and law differ significantly enough for books on interdisciplinary subjects like forensic medicine to be difficult for one or other of the two professions to use. A system using the original text experiences no such problem. Any new subjects may be introduced without difficulty, since there is no hindrance to the adaptation of any intellectual scheme of arrangement. Thus if a state were suddenly to consider making fundamental changes in its educational system, there would be no difficulty in making books and periodicals dealing with education available to the legislators through the computer system even though it had originally been envisaged that it would only deal with legal materials. Ultimately all written material everywhere in the world will be made available in computer assimilable form, and this particular problem of collection will cease to be troublesome. But that is still a long way off, and until then the question of selecting the most appropriate set of materials to process in order to satisfy the needs of the legislators and other users will remain.

Form of material
It might be thought that the decision to store raw text rather than keywords would exhaust this problem. This is far from the case. First, there are questions relating to the general way in which the information is to be structured. This will be largely determined by the way in which the retrieval side of the system is arranged. For some purposes it will probably be enough to finish up with references to the statutes in which the relevant information is contained. If this were the only demand it might be sufficient to divide up the data only by reference to the statutes in which it occurred. For other purposes, however, it might be desirable to know exactly where within a statute in terms of section, subsection or even smaller unit, a given piece of information was to be found. This would necessitate a different approach in which even smaller units would have to be indicated to the computer. Whatever the decision, the machine must be programmed to recognize the units chosen. Since a system coping with legislation must be linguistic, one of the basic units

clearly has to be the word, though even this is more complicated than it sounds. There are problems with numbers and dates, and with other logically discrete units which function like words, but are composed of arrangements of words, letters, symbols and figures such as titles of, and references to, statutes. These questions will be discussed at greater length in the next chapter.

Leaving them aside, a basic choice must still be made about the larger units by reference to which the words are to be located. This is a choice of whether to select physical units such as page and line, or logical units such as document and sentence. The former makes it easier to find the occurrence once it has been indicated, the latter is more effective as a device for detecting a relevant occurrence. The latter is therefore the more eligible since it is more important to identify the correct document than to give a reference which may be useless even though it can be found easily. In general, once a document has been correctly identified it can be found by conventional means, whereas if it has not been identified it cannot, *ex hypothesi*, be easily found by conventional means. So it is better to divide up legislation by reference to the logic of its construction.

The precise way in which this should be done must depend upon the form of the document in question. In the case of statutes, most working schemes use the statutory section as the document rather than the statute itself. This is understandable when one considers that under many forms of parliamentary procedure each section has to be voted on separately, and thus has to be capable of being understood independently, at least to some extent. The full meaning may indeed demand reference to other sections, or even to wholly extrinsic documents. If the section is to be regarded as the basic unit, it would be possible to design a system in which the only smaller unit would be the word. In fact, most systems also employ the sentence, or subsection, as further intermediate units.

If the only units were to be words and sections, the organization of the material would be particularly simple. It would merely be necessary to indicate the beginning of each section to the computer. This is probably best done by allocating a special character to be inserted in preparation for entry into the system. Such insertion should present no great difficulty, since separate sections are clearly separated from each other in the original.

In selecting the appropriate character for this function care must, of course, be taken to select one which will never appear, even by

D

accident, in the body of the text. For this reason a composite character is usually employed. This raises a minor dilemma since the longer it is, the less likely it is to get into the text by accident; but the shorter it is, the more efficient is the process of input. In an ideal system it would be as well to dedicate a special key for this function with a special mode of depression to guard against accidents. This would not seriously slow down the keyboarding process since fresh sections come relatively rarely, and always at a point when there is a psychological break in the flow of work. Once the character has been inserted, the computer will be able to recognize the beginning of each new document and will automatically allocate a running number to it. If a conversion table is then prepared between these numbers and the usual form of reference to the statute, it is possible for the computer to use these numbers for internal use while accepting from the user, and printing out for him, references in the usual form.

Identification of words presents a somewhat more difficult problem. It is not appropriate to signal the beginning or end of a word in the way just described since this would slow down the keyboarding process too much, and in making the text visually unfamiliar would impair many of the informal checking procedures which a typist customarily uses, and which contribute significantly to the accuracy of the final product. If special characters are not to be inserted, then reliance must be placed upon ordinary punctuation and spacing. This entails the formulation of special rules to deal with hyphenated words, and word-splitting between lines. It also involves the development of an efficient checking system to ensure that none of the conventional word terminators have been inserted accidentally into the middle of a word, since there can here be no question of special protection for these keys which are in constant use.

Decisions must also be made about the treatment of numbers. Are they to be treated as words? If so, the language immediately acquires an infinite number of words, and further decisions become necessary about the treatment of punctuation such as the comma which terminates ordinary alphabetic words but appears in the middle of large numbers. If they are not to be treated as words, valuable information may be lost to the system.

There is also the problem referred to earlier of the larger combinations of words, numbers, letters and symbols which together constitute single units. Statutes frequently refer to earlier statutes by titles in such a form when repealing or amending them. Or a statute might refer to the 'United Kingdom'. There is little obvious purpose served by treating such a reference in the same way as any other sequence of two words. In any event a decision must be made whether to do so or not. Similar decisions must be made in relation to all other proposed subdivisions or other units. It is suggested that the most useful practice is to mark all conceivably useful divisions and units so as to enhance the flexibility of the searching systems, allowing the precision to be sharpened or blunted as need dictates and response indicates.

So far consideration has been given only to the division of the raw text, and the indication to the computer of such division. But the thrust of insistence on the use of raw text is simply that it should not be subtracted from, not that it should not be added to. It is a minimum not a maximum. Perhaps most especially in considering legislative users of computers, it is necessary to bear in mind appropriate forms of addition to the text as it appears on the printed page. Professor Horty, for example, in his original work found it useful to add to the text of the section of each statute, a title, a scope note and an indication of the legislative history of the section.

There may be two reasons for adding to the text. The first is to improve the efficiency of the system for retrieval; the second is to provide further information for the user. Additions of the former type would not normally appear as part of the print-out of the results of a search, though they may have been essential to its success. Additions of the latter type must be printed out, since the justification for their inclusion is that they may be needed by the users. The additions inserted by Professor Horty as mentioned above were primarily of this type. It is easy to think of further references which might be added, to definitions of words contained in the section, to cases in which the section had been discussed, or to the parliamentary as opposed to the legislative history, for example. It is, however, necessary to bear in mind that such additions further encumber the input process, which is in any event the most recalcitrant problem for legislative applications at present. They should therefore be introduced only if really needed by the users, and if not readily accessible in some other way, or capable of being made available by independent input into the computer system.

Efficiency of system
Before considering the efficiency of such a system, it is first necessary to sketch out the basic principles upon which it proceeds. It has

already been pointed out that on account of the absence of pre-indexing and the minimizing of alteration of the original text, the computer is left with an undigested mass of words in its store. The problem is to devise a method of using that unwieldy mass to such effect as to achieve better reference to the documents represented by it, than can be achieved by using the best efforts of human indexers. The one avenue, as previously indicated, is to set out to identify a document by reference to the words which occur in it, and the way in which those words are combined. Here legislation has some advantages over case law as raw material upon which the computer is to work. If the statutory section is to be regarded as the basic document, then documents are short. This is one result of the austerity of legislation as compared with case law. It is also relatively economic and precise in its use of language. One word one meaning and one meaning one word is the motto for the draftsman. The result is that problems of synonyms and antonyms, and particulars and generalizations, are much less acute than they are in case law. Even the range of grammatical variation is smaller, the incidence of past tenses and adjectives being very low in most legislative materials. There are fewer problems with footnotes, citations and proper names.

All of these factors can be regarded as favouring the application of computer techniques to legislative material. They tend to operate to restrict the range of words which the user of the system must specify to indicate documents in which he is interested. When presented with a legislative retrieval problem, the searcher must first formulate a relatively precise characterization of the subject area, and in a conventional system as previously described this will usually be general at first so as to permit the selection of a book from the shelves, and will then become more precise so as to select a term or terms to look up in the index.

The steps are similar in the computer system except that after the mental characterization of the subject area, the user arrives not at the words likely to have been used by the publisher and indexer to characterize the meaning of a relevant document, but instead the words which are likely to appear in the text of such a document. Since the user will normally be familiar with legislation in the relevant area this should not prove to be too difficult. Even if he is not, the use of the terms which he would use to search a conventional index will probably suffice to give him a lead, since it has been discovered that a surprisingly high percentage of index entries simply reflect the occurrence of the word in question in the original text. In indexes to the New York and Maryland statutes, for example, more than 86 per cent of the entries were found to be of this type.[3] But in a computer system the user's task is not completed with the selection of appropriate terms. There is a special expertise in combining them in such a way that only documents in which the user is really interested are retrieved.

This technique has to be learned, and two of the longest established systems employing this approach in the United States have elaborate training and follow-up programmes. Aspen Systems Corporation, which is the contemporary manifestation of the University of Pittsburgh project, provides courses for users, and elaborate manuals to guide the framing of searches, and has plans for introducing more advanced courses. Project LITE, an acronym of Legal Information Through Electronics, is a system working under the aegis of the United States Air Force, providing access to a wide range of materials of interest to government departments and agencies by these techniques. It too provides courses and manuals, and in addition conducts follow-up studies to ensure that the correct information was supplied.[4] Both organizations also offer facilities for assisting users in the formulation of searches.

The reason for such intense concern is that a computerized information retrieval system involves a voyage between the Scylla of false drops and the Charybdis of over recall. This jargon may be translated as defining two ways in which unwanted information is retrieved by a computer system. A false drop typically occurs when, although the occurrence of a precise word was specified, it happened to occur in irrelevant documents, perhaps because it had more than one meaning. Suppose the searcher was interested in some aspect of the political structure, and asked for documents containing the word 'election'. Documents dealing with the equitable doctrine of election would be false drops.

Over recall occurs when the word whose occurrence is specified is not sufficiently precise to define the searcher's real interest. Suppose the previous searcher to have been concerned only with

---

[3] Fels and Jacobs, 'Linguistic Statistics of Legal Indexing', 24 *University of Pittsburgh L.R.*, 771 (1963).
[4] But see McCarthy, 'LITE – A Progress Report', 64 *Law Library J.*, 193 (1971), on an interesting recent change of emphasis in this respect.

elections of representative peers. Directly relevant documents would be swamped by a deluge of others on other types of election. Searchers must also be constantly aware of the problem posed by grammatical variations of the same word and by synonyms and other equivalents, though as mentioned above the problem is even more severe in connection with case law, and will be discussed in the next chapter.

The selection of the best search terms is only the first step in formulating a successful computer search, however, and the technique of combining them together must now be briefly considered. Most systems allow at least the use of operators to indicate conjunction, disjunction and negation, corresponding to Boolean 'and', 'or' and 'but not'. The use of such operators may be illustrated by reference to the example of the user interested in documents relating to the election of representative peers. He might specify the retrieval of documents containing the word 'election' *or* 'elections' *and* 'peer' *or* 'peers' *but not* if 'equity' or 'equitable' also occurs. A further refinement added by many systems to help the searcher is the ability to specify the degree of contiguity within which the words are to appear, as defined by the units into which the document is subdivided within the system. Thus in the example the conjunction of 'election' and 'peer' might be accepted if both occurred in the same document, but could be more precisely defined by retrieval being limited to those documents in which the words occurred within five of each other. Such contiguity can also be made directional so that only documents in which the word 'peer' followed within five words of 'election' would be retrieved. In this way the computer can distinguish between 'man bites dog' and 'dog bites man'. Such a facility also permits the system to detect documents in which a particular phrase occurs, since each individual word can be specified, and required to occur one immediately after the other.

The same techniques can be applied to each sub-unit into which the document has been subdivided, and this makes apparent the sense of employing a logical rather than a physical scheme of subdivision. It is much more meaningful to ask for documents in which given words appear in a particular sentence, say, than to ask for references to pages on which they occur in a given line. To revert to the example of the researcher interested in the election of representative peers, if the sentence is the unit, he is safe in asking for all documents in which the word 'representative' is immediately followed by the word 'peer' in the same sentence. If the same technique is used in relation to information stored by reference to page, line and word, retrieval may be distorted in two ways. First, cases where 'representative' occurs as the last word in one line, and 'peer' as the first word in the next line will not be recovered, even though they both occur in the same sentence. Secondly, and conversely, documents in which 'representative' is followed on the same line by the word 'peer' will be recovered even though they occur in different sentences, and are separated by a full stop.

The question then arises of whether this theoretical full text method will work effectively in practice. This is very hard to measure accurately and precisely. In the original experiment at the University of Pittsburgh, tests were made by comparing the performance of lawyers using their ordinary methods with that of others using this new computerized technique. Those using the traditional methods were given problems and asked to prepare lists of legislative documents which they thought that they would need to read to decide whether or not they really were relevant to the problem they had been given. Those using the computer techniques were given the same problems, and the computer printed out lists of references as a response to the terms prepared by the lawyers. These lists were then given to those who had prepared the original problems for them to assess the relevance of the materials indicated by both techniques. They used a threefold classification according to which 'A' signified that the lawyer would indeed need to read the section, 'B' that he might have to read it in the light of additional facts which might be present but which had not been stated in the problem, and 'C' that the document was clearly irrelevant. When twenty-four such experiments had been carried out, it was found that the conventional methods yielded 429 'A' statutory sections, 10 'B' and 69 'C', while the computerized techniques yielded 837 'A' sections, 50 'B' and 547 'C'. In all, 871 'A' sections were retrieved and 54 'B'. The precise number of 'C' sections seems not to have been established, but the results can be evaluated without this information.

A convenient way of expressing the results of such information retrieval experiments is in terms of precision and recall. These will be discussed in more detail in a later chapter in relation to case law experiments, but may be shortly defined here. Precision expresses the relation between the number of relevant documents retrieved and the total number of documents retrieved. Recall expresses the relation between the number of relevant documents retrieved and the total number of relevant documents in the collection. For the purposes of calculation it has to be assumed that there were no other relevant documents in the collection than those retrieved by one or other of the two methods, and judged relevant by the evaluators. The figures may be calculated first on the basis that both 'A' and 'B' documents were relevant. Conventional methods then show 86 per cent precision and 47 per cent recall; computerized methods 62 per cent precision and 96 per cent recall. These differences are only to be expected. The computer finds more relevant documents, but at the expense of throwing up more irrelevant documents. Conventional techniques are on the other hand more conservative, they retrieve little that is irrelevant, but are by no means comprehensive.

Part of the apparent difference in precision is explained by the browsing facility in conventional methods which allows the human brain to operate on the initial output so as to reject parts which are obviously irrelevant. This can occur quite unconsciously. According to the techniques used in this experiment the computer was allowed no such advantage, and the output is completely without the benefit of any form of post-editing. If 'B' documents are not regarded as relevant, both figures fall for both techniques. Conventional methods then show 84 per cent precision and 46 per cent recall; computerized methods 58 per cent precision and 95 per cent recall. Some caution must however be exercised in the interpretation of these results. It will be obvious from the fact that there were on average 36 'A' and 2 'B' sections judged relevant to each problem, that the problems were drafted very widely.

Such problems reflected the sort of work undertaken at Pittsburgh in the preparation of the Health Law Manual, and are probably relevant to the sort of preparation necessary for consolidating legislation. They might not be so valid for other types of legal work, and further research would be desirable. The width of the problems also affects the validity of the results in another way in that it makes the determination of the relevancy of any given statutory section to the problem so much more a matter of opinion.[5] That this is the

[5] Cp. the experience of the joint ABA and IBM experiment in case law as reported by Eldridge, 'An Appraisal of a Case-Law Retrieval Project', Computers and the Law Conference Proceedings, Kingston, Ontario, 1968.

key feature in this type of evaluation of a retrieval system is indicated by the depression of both precision and recall figures for both computerized and conventional techniques upon the changed assumption of the relevancy of a 'B' rating.

It is surprising that the results of no further or more rigorous experiments have been published. In their absence any attempt at evaluation must rely upon the opinions of the users of the established systems which employ these techniques. The view has been privately expressed by some users of the LITE system that the volume of relevant material retrieved through the system which would not have been found in any other way, justified the relatively high proportion of irrelevant material which was returned. It was also said that experience in using the system was effective in reducing the volume of irrelevant material returned. One way of reducing the amount of this is, of course, post-editing. The main objection to this is that it interposes a human being between the user and the material, which is precisely what the full text method is designed to eliminate. This general sense of satisfaction with the system seems also to hold good for the experience of Aspen Systems whose boast it is that no legislative body once having taken their service, has ever cancelled it. It seems that lawyers rapidly acquire and value the feeling of security that knowledge of comprehensive coverage brings. The expansion of computerized systems among state legislatures has been particularly rapid.[6]

By 1970 Aspen was providing retrieval services for twenty states in America, and in addition serving a number of government agencies, large private corporations and some larger cities. Data Retrieval Corporation of America, a later entrant to the field, provided facilities for a further six states at that time. Yet another private firm, Autocomp Inc., which concentrates more on smaller legislative bodies, has assisted with work in further states of the United States and participated in devising the system developed for the province of Manitoba in Canada. In England a particularly advanced system has been developed by Dr Niblett at the Culham laboratory where a segment of the British statutes dealing with atomic energy has been prepared in such a way that a browsing facility has been included to reduce the amount of irelevant material

[6] See Elkins, 'A Survey of the Use of Electronic Data Processing by State Legislatures', Institute of Government, University of Georgia, 1971.

D*

retrieved.[7] In addition, British statutes in the field of public health law have been made accessible in conjunction with the early work conducted at the University of Pittsburgh. It is probably safe to assume in the face of this successful expansion that most other governments in advanced countries either have considered or are considering the introduction of a computer based retrieval system for legislative purposes. This use is rendered more attractive if it can be linked to other uses of their existing machines, or if there are other legislative uses to which a computer solely dedicated to the legislature can be put. Two such possibilities will now be considered.

3 DRAFTING

It has already been remarked that to draft legislation is a highly skilled and extremely demanding human task. The legislative draftsman is torn between the instructions of the sponsors and the necessity of parliamentary passage, restricted by the inherent limitations of language and the capricious construction often put upon it by the Courts, and confined within and by his awareness of the boundaries of his personal foresight. No one who has ever attempted to draft any legal document, much less a statute, can have any illusions about the degree of difficulty which it presents. It is clearly beyond the power of any computer to perform it in its entirety from start to finish. The question is simply whether it can help at all, and, if so, how.

Drafting legislation is traditionally a task for specialized lawyers. Their precise mode of operation varies from one legislature to another, and even from one draftsman to another. Most probably start by drafting private documents before moving on to legislation. There are also analogies between the rules of construction which are applied by the Courts to the two types of document. The result, whether cause or effect is immaterial, is that there are great similarities of style between them. It is also the case that in this area advances in the private field have generally preceded advances in the public. It is therefore worth considering first the development of computer aids for the drafting of private instruments, and then the extent to which they could be applied to the drafting of legislation.

The only computer aid in substantial use at present in this connection is a computer assisted automatic typewriter. This is used for

[7] Niblett and Price, 'The Status Project', UK Atomic Energy Authority Research Group Report CLM–R101.

drafting documents which have a substantial amount of material in common, but which have to be adapted to the special needs of a particular client. It is most useful when there is more individual variation than would normally be found in a credit-sale agreement or insurance policy, for example, where all that is necessary is the insertion of the names of the parties on a standard form, though as will emerge later, standard forms are themselves not without significance in relation to some different drafting problems in the legislative field. Nor is there much scope for the use of the computer assisted typewriter in the preparation of a unique and specific document.

There is still a great range of transactions falling between these two extremes where the amount of variation is greater than just the names of the parties, but not in practice unlimited owing to similarities of interest among large numbers of clients, and to the desirability of using well established, and so safe, means of advancing them. Wills, conveyances, deeds of trust and articles of corporate association are among the documents of this sort which come immediately to mind. It is convenient to take a will as an example. There are some very common situations which most testators wish to provide for, and there are relatively few ways of doing so. The standard practice in this situation is still to refer to a precedent, taken either directly from a published precedent book or from a private set compiled over the years by the individual lawyer, or most commonly a combination of the two. The advantage of this is that it saves the duplication of effort involved in thinking through each of these situations afresh every time it arises, and it also permits a body of knowledge to be built up and strengthened over a period of time. The technique is in a sense self-justifying. At the same time it does not inhibit the moulding of the particular will to fit any needs peculiar to the particular testator.

It is now becoming increasingly common to use a computer-assisted automatic typewriter in this situation. There are a number of possible variations of the technique, in part dependent upon the precise configuration of the equipment employed. In essence, however, the technique depends upon the prior production of a set of standard clauses for input to the system by the use of the automatic typewriter. Where a variation in these clauses is likely to occur very often, for example the use of masculine and feminine pronouns, or of plural and singular forms, it may be best to prepare separate standard clauses incorporating each set of variations. Where the variation is likely to be unique, as with proper names, it is better to leave a space on the tape to be filled manually at a later stage. These standard clauses can then be given code numbers for speedy access. Once they are available on tape the production of a final version of a will for signature can be accomplished much more quickly.

During the interview with the client the lawyer can jot down the code numbers he will need. If there are no special requirements outside the scope of the standard clauses this list of code numbers can then be given to the typist with all necessary information about the names of the parties and beneficiaries, and descriptions of the property comprising the estate. The tape can then be used to drive the typewriter at a much faster speed than a typist could attain, and without any chance of error, stopping only at the appropriate places for the manual insertion of the names and descriptions. The document which emerges will, subject only to checking the manual insertions, be ready for signature. Even in the more complicated cases where some of the clauses have to be specially drafted, the process will be substantially improved. There will still inevitably be a number of standard clauses, and the preparation of these by the machine will provide a context in which the effect of alternative drafts of the new clauses can be more readily appreciated. It will also be clear that by the addition of such new clauses to the standard repertoire, the usefulness of the system can be constantly increased.[8]

It is apparent that public statutes rarely present problems of this precise type. They are necessarily general in their application. But there are some similarities, sometimes more pronounced the lower one moves down the legislative ladder. Local authority regulations, for example, may well contain standard inspection and penalty clauses. It is best if these are cast in a common form so as to prevent arguments from being raised upon the basis of minor differences in terminology. No one familiar with the volume and ingenuity of the learning devoted to the distinction between 'wilful' and 'malicious', 'permit' and 'allow' or 'custody' and 'possession' can be ignorant of the dangers inherent in such casual variation. So one

[8] See generally Allen, 'Law-Office Typing with the IBM MT/ST', 16 *Practical Lawyer* 13 (1970), and in connection with wills Boucher, 'Drafting Wills with the Aid of Fill-In Forms and an Automatic Typewriter', *Modern Uses of Logic in Law*, September 1964, p. 45.

way in which the computer could be used by the legislative draftsman would be to facilitate the use of such recurrent phrases by the
automatic inclusion of a single common form.

At present the use of such standard clauses seems undesirably
haphazard. The compilation of a list of such standard clauses would
in itself be a most useful exercise. Its availability and regular use
would sharpen drafting, and perhaps even infuse some sense into the
canon of construction whereby different meanings have to be imputed
to different forms of words in order to carry an imputed intention to
achieve a different effect on the part of the legislators by the use
of a different form of words. Adherence to the common form would
then involve less effort than departure from it. It is postulated that
this would tend both to reduce the incidence of deviation and increase its rationality.

This would, however, accomplish little since so much legislative
drafting is not in common form, for the reasons advanced earlier.
It has been remarked that the most extreme case of common form
drafting is achieved when a standard form is adopted. Such a form
permits no variation for individual cases beyond the details relating
to the parties. It is absolutely essential therefore that the draft is the
best possible for the purpose for which it is devised. Here there is a
parallel with legislation. Both standard forms and legislation affect
large numbers of individual transactions. Both are inconvenient and
expensive to change, once they have been settled. This wide effect
and long life demand the highest quality in the original draft. It
is significant that here too the first initiative in the use of unconventional means to achieve such excellence came in the private area.
As long ago as the late 1930s the drafting of insurance documents
was being tested by the application of symbolic logic.[9] It is being
increasingly suggested that similar techniques should be applied to
the drafting of legislation.[10]

A distinction must be made between two types of ambiguity
which may occur in legislation, semantic ambiguity and syntactic

[9] Berkeley, 'Boolean Algebra and Applications to Insurance', 26 Record of
American Institute of Actuaries, 373 (1937), 27, *ibid.*, 167 (1938).
[10] See esp. Allen, 'Toward a More Systematic Drafting of the Internal Revenue
Code: Expenses, Losses and Bad Debts', 25 *Univ. of Chicago L.R.*, 1 (1957), 'Beyond
Document Retrieval Toward Information Retrieval', 47 *Minnesota L.R.*, 713
(1963), 'Symbolic Logic: A Razor-Edged Tool for Drafting and Interpreting Legal
Documents', 66 *Yale L.J.*, 833 (1957), and Fitzgerald 'Law and Logic', 39 *Notre
Dame Lawyer*, 570 (1964).

ambiguity. Semantic ambiguity is a consequence of the relative imprecision of language, and is indeed necessary if legislation is to have the range and flexibility necessitated by the impracticality of continuous, or even frequent or rapid, change. It simply connotes that words have a central core of meaning surrounded by a penumbra of uncertainty. For example, a typed letter is clearly within the central core of meaning of the word 'document', but a label on a bottle, a banner with writing on it, a signed painting, an autographed cricket bat, a punched card without writing on it, a gramophone record or a roll of computer tape fall within the penumbra. Syntactic ambiguity occurs when the structure of a whole sentence is considered and yields more than one possible interpretation of the relationship between its constituent parts. It is especially prevalent when conjunctions like 'and' and 'or' appear, or where negatives appear in complicated constructions containing qualifications and exceptions. A moment's reflection will bring examples to mind, especially to a lawyer's, since such constructions are so frequently a focus of litigation. To take the simplest example possible, amendment VIII of the Constitution of the United States prohibits the infliction of 'cruel and unusual punishments'. It is clear that a punishment may be cruel without being unusual, and unusual without being cruel. It is therefore logically possible to construe the amendment as prohibiting punishments which are both cruel and unusual, or those which are either cruel or unusual. Much more complicated examples appear in the literature. It is indeed infinitely more difficult to find sections which are not susceptible of this analysis, than to find those which are.

The only justification for this sort of ambiguity in drafting is that the result may be more elegant than the circumlocutions demanded by greater logical precision, and is certainly likely to be shorter. Consider the appearance of the statute book if 'if and only if' were to be substituted for 'if' wherever it was meant. But since such ambiguities do undeniably lead to practical difficulty in Court and out, and given that few people read the statutes at all, and those few more for practical guidance than aesthetic satisfaction, such an excuse is quite unacceptable. It is necessary to consider therefore how such syntactic ambiguity can best be avoided, and whether there is any role which computers can usefully play.

One possible technique is to translate the proposed draft of a statute into the notation of a system of formal logic, say Boolean algebra, to programme the computer with the axioms of the system, and then to allow it to test the draft for ambiguities and contradictions. This is a relatively simple logical job for the computer, fitting in well with the principles employed in its own construction, and can be performed very quickly and cheaply once the draft and axioms have been prepared, and the computer programmed. What the machine cannot do is to prepare the original draft, or to amend it once a logical error has been detected. There would still be a substantial saving of skilled time and effort if the draft could be prepared by unskilled personnel. Unfortunately this is not possible. Crucial and extremely difficult questions of interpretation, just those which the Courts wrestle with under the present system, will arise at this stage. Thus the services of trained lawyers will be required to prepare the original drafts for the computer. In fact this process of preparation would itself be the stage at which the syntactic ambiguities were faced and resolved. Once it had been completed, the testing by the machine would be likely to reveal only trivial errors. This does not seriously affect the utility of the technique. It is quite likely that this sort of logical scrutiny will only be accomplished under the pressure of some such goad as preparing the draft of a statute in a form susceptible of computer testing. This may well be the justification for the introduction of such a system, especially when it is remembered that the actual computing will be very cheap, and can be accomplished on virtually any available machine, certainly on any machine capable of handling the retrieval problems arising at the preparation stage, discussed above.

An interesting elaboration of this technique has been developed by Professor Allen.[11] This involves the logical analysis of statutory text in the form of what he describes as normalized language. This language permits the representation of the contents of a statute, or indeed any other document, in the form of a diagram which illustrates the logical relationships between its constituent parts. Thus a prescription like 'a person who kills another human being with malice aforethought is guilty of murder' might be regarded as containing three elements:

if a person has killed another human being	S1
and if he had malice aforethought	S2
then he is guilty of murder	S3

[11] Allen, 'A Language Normalization Approach to Information Retrieval in Law', 9 *Jurimetrics Journal*, 41 (1968).

In Allen's notion this would represented diagrammatically ·

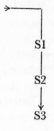

Figure 1

If it were the rule that recklessness was regarded as different from malice aforethought, but equally led to guilt, and if this is given the code s2a, then the diagram would be amended to read :

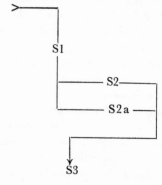

Figure 2

Here it will be seen that the path to s3 can be traced either through s2 or s2a, thus indicating that they are alternative conditions of liability. The diagram may also be modified so as to indicate the conditions for any of the categories used. Thus if intention, but not accident, counts as malice aforethought, this might be shown in a separate diagram the culmination of which is s2. In this way a completely interlocking network of categories can be established. Legislation is regarded as the prime input, but case law, commentaries or other types of legal source can easily be added. The diagrams can be displayed in looseleaf folders or held in computer store. Such a system, if successful, would eliminate by the use of the diagrams all vestiges of syntactic ambiguity.

If this were completely achieved it would constitute a major step towards the establishment of retrieval systems far more ambitious than those described earlier since the output would be the information itself and not merely references to the documents in which it might be found. Thus the input of 'a person has killed another human being with malice aforethought' would lead to the output 'guilty of murder'. This would be not only a retrieval system but a legal problem-solving system. The example gives an indication, however, of the weakness of such a system, a weakness to which Professor Allen draws attention. Everything depends upon the skill of the person who prepares the documents for input. A legal document can be 'normalized' in any number of different ways. Professor Allen, while admitting this, seeks to minimize its importance by stressing the flexibility of the system. Concepts can be freely broken down into their constituent parts, as indicated in the example for 'malice aforethought'. The system is, in the usual jargon, 'open-ended'. This implies both that concepts can be broken down, and that new concepts can be added. But this seems to overlook the possibility of the need for change in the converse direction. Concepts may not only be mistakenly omitted but also mistakenly inserted, and not only mistakenly stated at too general a level but also unnecessarily subdivided. It is not clear that these possibilities are satisfactorily provided for.

Even if they can be, too much responsibility is still reposed in the analyst. His judgement is constantly interposed between the input to the system and the user of it. This objection is also anticipated by Professor Allen, who suggests that it can be minimized by printing the original text alongside the representation of the 'normalized' version, and presumably by the provision of a separate index to the text so presented. It is unclear how this would apply in any computerized version of the system, nor would it entirely meet the objection. A user might well conceptualize a problem differently from the analyst, and not know of any relevant provisions which might give him a clue as to where the analyst's version was to be found. The major advantages of such a system all depend ultimately upon the quality of the analysis of the input. This problem raises just those difficulties which have defeated indexers and analysts for centuries. It is not obvious why they will all suddenly be solved. Until they are, satisfactory normalized sentences can not be created; and when they are, normalized sentences will be less necessary. The

problems are fundamentally similar to those which will be encountered in the discussion of the prediction of judicial decisions. Everything depends upon the concepts used to categorize individual situations. This is a matter for choice and judgement, not logic. Too
much attention to logical manipulation courts the danger of dis-
tracting attention from the nature of the entities being so manipulated.

The conclusion then must be that in the field of drafting the computer has a relatively modest role to play at present. It can assist
draftsmen in the use of common forms to meet recurrent situations;
it can provide a spur for the recognition of syntactic logical problems; and it can test final drafts for logical errors. These uses can
be accomplished relatively cheaply in the present state of technological development and by the use of established human skills. The
achievement of these goals should be regarded as the immediate aim.
It will furnish a firmer foundation for embarking upon the as yet
unsolved problems which can be seen lying further ahead. That
those problems seem at present also insoluble should neither dis-
courage, nor distract from, the solution of those that can now be
solved, and whose solution will itself constitute a significant step
forward.

4 PASSAGE AND PRINTING

The most extensive use of computers in the legislative process, at
least in the United States, is as an aid to legislatures in processing the
legislation coming before them for consideration, voting and ultimately for printing. All of these processes are, in the most advanced
systems, highly integrated, and they will be discussed together here.
The pattern in most legislatures in the United States is fundamentally similar, though there are of course minor difference in terminology and function in different places. Florida will be taken as an
example.[12] There, legislative proposals are first printed, and may
then be introduced in Senate and House, a daily calendar lists the
business of each body for the day and a daily journal notes the
action which has been taken, the legislative reference service issues
a daily summary of all proposals presented, the enacted laws are

[12] Study of the working of the state legislatures is enhanced by the excellent series
of studies produced by the Center for State Legislative Research and Service,
Eagleton Institute of Politics. See e.g. C. Lynwood Smith Jr., 'Strengthening the
Florida Legislature'; on the point in the text see especially ch. 7.

then printed as slip laws, and finally these are included in the volume of session laws.

This rather abbreviated summary gives some indication of the number of versions generated by a single legislative proposal, even though it omits the multifarious modifications which may be made at different stages, during the passage through the legislature for example. If the proposal has to be manually retyped at each of these stages an enormous amount of effort is duplicated, and opportunities for error are multiplied. Much of this can be avoided by the introduction of a computerized system, and an increasing number of legislatures,[13] including Florida which was among the earliest, have adapted such systems to deal with at least part of the work.

The description which follows is not an account of any particular system, but instead indicates a general pattern which may, of course, be adapted to meet local requirements. As already remarked, the economics of the system dictate the closest possible coordination of legislative processes and services. The computer both permits such coordination and finds its use justified by it. In particular, it is desirable to link the printing process with that used for the preparation of copy. For this reason one of the first tasks confronting the designer of any such system is to determine the range of typefaces required for the different publications envisaged, and to establish the appropriate codes and programmes to enable them to be produced by the photo-composition device which will produce the final copy. The coding for printing will probably be most economically inserted at the initial input stage, but there is no necessity for such symbols to be displayed at any stage where they are unnecessary. Thus they would normally be displayed when the printing instructions were being proof read, but not when the text itself was being proof read since their presence would tend to distract the reader.

Once these preliminary decisions have been made, the next task is to get the text of a proposal into the system. This is best done by the use of a terminal with a typewriter-like keyboard linked to the main computer system, probably by way of a smaller slave computer either built into the terminal or acting as a buffer between it and

---

[13] Elkins, *Survey of the Use of Electronic Data Processing by State Legislatures* (1971) shows that at that time thirteen states had computerized drafting systems in operation and five others had them in the course of development; eight had computerized printing systems in operation and nine others had them in the course of development; and only thirteen states were not using electronic data processing for some legislative processes.

the main machine. It is generally, and rightly, regarded as desirable that all proposals should be printed prior to their consideration by the appropriate legislative organ. This means that the printing codes will need to be inserted by the operator at the input stage. This is facilitated if a visual display device is associated with the keyboard. The operator will then have displayed before his eyes a representation of the data being fed into the system. As yet there are no video display devices which can cope with the variety of typefaces which will appear in the final printed version, so what the operator will see will be the text, in upper and lower case with margin justification, together with the codes for printing instructions.

Some features, like the maintenance of a running line number, will be generated completely automatically by the programming of the terminal. Others, like the margin justification, will be semi-automatic in the sense that the operator will simply have to adjust the spacing and to break the words, with the machine doing the rest, though by building in a hyphenation dictionary even this last task can be made largely automatic. Still other features such as the selection of upper or lower case, the typeface including type, style and font size, and indentation and paragraphing are more within the province of the operator. Once the operator is satisfied that the version displayed on the screen is accurate it can be released into the computer system.

It will be noted that in this system direct entry to the computer is envisaged. There is no necessity for the production of any intermediate version, whether typed or punched on to cards or paper tape. These could certainly be introduced if they were necessary for any reason, but in most cases it will probably be preferable for the operator to use the terminal and video display to establish the correct format, and for that to be entered into the system without any further intervening processes. This input will then be stored in the computer's memory for retrieval purposes, and will also be used to drive a photo-composition device which will produce a high-quality printed version of the proposal for distribution to the legislators, or any other interested parties, prior to legislative consideration.

The next stage may be to draw up a schedule of proposals for consideration by the legislature. For such purposes it might be convenient to install a terminal in the office of the clerk to the legislature. In compiling such a schedule, the operator would be able to draw upon the computer's memory to review the proposals awaiting consideration, in order to allocate them to the correct body for discussion. It may be noted that if there happen to be well defined rules for such allocation this process can be completely automated. Thus if proposals are scheduled in order of submission except where a proposal has been certified as extraordinary and as having priority over all except similarly certified proposals, it would be simplicity itself to programme the computer to produce a list in the desired order. The computer would also be able to instruct the photo-composition device to print from the list so compiled, and in this way the basis for a printed daily calendar would be laid. Other information such as summaries of the proposals prepared by the legislative reference service could also be keyed in in a similar way to enable the final version of the calendar to be compiled and printed. There are even schemes for the automatic preparation of such summaries themselves, but their success has not so far been so conspicuous as to justify their recommendation. Nevertheless, summaries compiled by human beings can be easily introduced into the system, and printed either as part of the bill, or in the calendar, or wherever else is appropriate in the light of the customs of a particular legislature.

The computer system can be employed in a number of further ways during the actual chamber discussion of a proposal. For these purposes it will be most convenient to have further terminals installed on the floor of the chamber. Another possible refinement is the provision at the desk of each legislator of a console consisting of keyboard, video display device, and voting unit. Then as each proposal comes forward for discussion the computer memory can produce the original version of the proposal in the form of a visual display. If an amendment is proposed, the operator of the control terminal can enter it into the system together with the names of its sponsors, and this information also can be displayed to the legislators, while at the same time a record is being prepared for printing in the daily record of the proceedings.

A further possibility is that the individual legislators may use their video displays as electronic scratch pads for trying out different forms of words, until they arrive at a version which they wish to suggest. By the use of the appropriate procedures it should then be possible for that version to be displayed directly on the video screens of the other legislators. Indeed several versions could be displayed at once for purposes of comparison. Once a version has been agreed and made the subject of a proposal, it would be possible for that version to be entered directly into the central system for registration and for printing the relevant publications. It may be mentioned that terminals and final printed versions can in these respects reproduce the usual methods of indicating amendments by scoring or under-lining. The great advantage of using a computer system to assist in this way is that it permits the consideration of a multitude of dif-ferent forms in the context of the rest of the proposal in a particularly effortless and convenient way. The elimination of paperwork is in this respect an inestimable boon. Discussion may also be expedited since the provision of a common display for all legislators of the point under discussion will serve to eliminate one common cause for delay and excuse for irrelevance.

It is a relatively easy matter to link the voting procedure into the system. If a vote is to be taken in which names are not recorded, the display panel can be used to display the result instantaneously. The voting itself will also be a simple matter of pressing the appro-priate button, and not a time-wasting business of counting hands, assessing noises or dawdling through a lobby. If names are to be recorded, the procedure will be the same so far as the legislators are concerned, namely a matter of pressing the appropriate button on the console, but the screen will show the names of the voters for, against, and not voting. These names can be sorted and displayed in whatever way is deemed most suitable, whether alphabetically by name of legislator, by name of legislative district, or in order of seniority. It is possible to have it displayed in one form on the screens at the legislators' desks, and in a different way in the official record, even though the basic material for both is derived from the same set of actions.

When a proposal has finally passed through all of its legislative stages, it usually requires signature by the titular head of the state. At the present time the document presented for signature is a cleaned up version with all traces of amendment and addition eliminated. There seems no special advantage in this, since if it is convenient for legislators to have this information so as to be able to see what they are doing, it is hardly less desirable for the head of the state to be able to see it also. But whatever the practice, the computer system can be designed so as to produce a final version of the proposal in the required form. And because the need for further proof-reading and checking is eliminated, this can be printed in a matter of days rather than months, as is regrettably often the case at present. This is an important advantage since legislation often comes into force as soon as it has been signed, and those affected by it should be able to obtain a copy of it immediately. Photo-composition techniques are now well enough advanced to produce copy of as high a quality and versatility as traditional letterpress methods. A further advantage of this technique is that the final version can be produced in any desired size by the application of simple photographic enlargement methods. This process can be repeated to produce volumes of session laws and even revised codes with similar savings of time, effort and expense.

This brings the process full circle for now there will be a new and completely up-dated body of law for the legislators to work with in the preparation of still further proposals in the never-ending legislative assembly line. It might perhaps be added that such systems need not wait until legislation has been passed before making it accessible for retrieval through the computer. It is simply a matter of systems design and programming, and the more advanced systems do in fact tend to make information available from the time that it has been entered into the computer, and before it has been put in the permanent store. Indeed some of the phases described above require that such access should be possible. Another point purely dependent upon systems design is that of security. It is clearly desirable to allow a terminal operator to change a word which has been mis-keyed without the necessity of first indelibly implanting the incorrect version in the computer's memory. On the other hand it is even less desirable to allow the janitor's young son to erase the complete legislative records of the state by accident while playing with the keyboard. Nor is it always wise to allow even authorized users of the system, like legislators, complete freedom to revise all the records. Such situations present few problems in practice. The initial preparation, as already described, incorporates a buffer stage, and entry into the main memory is not made until a version is believed to be satisfactory. Even then appropriate procedures can allow authorized amendment. Simple coding routines can provide against unauthorized use by either legislators or small boys. In practice, in legislative systems security seems to have presented no serious problems.

The advantages of such a system are largely those of improved accuracy, and a consequent increase in the speed of production. More ancillary services can also be provided more easily in such a system, and at a lower cost, since a single input can generate any number of different output versions. It has also been indicated how amendments might be dealt with more rapidly and more relevantly. The keystone of such a system is the marriage of computer handling of the data with the process of printing it. Since the cost of such printing is in any event comparable with that of conventional printing, the rest of the services can be financed by it. And where, as in the legislative process, there is a demand for a number of slightly different versions of the same basic material at different times and in relatively small numbers, the cost advantage of the computer printing process becomes substantial. The result is that such a system is both better and cheaper than the conventional alternatives. So far such systems have been mainly employed by legislators for bills and acts, but there is no reason at all why similar economies should not be made in the preparation and printing of subordinate legislation where, if anything, the need for greater speed and accuracy, and improvement in form, is still more apparent. It seems, however, that this is increasingly being appreciated and that an expansion of computer applications in this area is already under way.

5 CONCLUSION

So far most legislatures have progressed no further in their use of computers than a few of the applications described in section 4. But once a computer system has been installed, demand for its extension tends to grow, and since the initial demands upon it usually fall short of its capacity, it makes economic as well as political sense to satisfy them. This means that the drafting aids described in section 3 should be seriously considered, since they make only very modest demands upon computing power. The retrieval facilities described in section 2 make greater demands, but they also yield the highest returns, and may become increasingly viable economically as demand for such facilities by the private practitioner grows. It is most likely to to grow in an atmosphere in which such facilities are known to be available to government lawyers. For the time being, legislatures can be expected to lead the private profession in large-scale applications, if only because of the already significant concentration of computing power in the hands of government. The Federal Government in the United States alone has over five thousand computer systems in current use with a consumption of over 150,000 man-years of work, and at a cost of over 2 billion dollars.[14] Even in Great Britain the Central Government had 182 computers installed in 1969 with a further thirty-four ordered with a cumulative investment of the order of 40 million pounds.[15] When the resources of state governments in the United States and local governments in Great Britain are added to this, it is neither surprising nor unreasonable to find and expect legislative applications of computers to lead and continue to lead the field of legal applications of computers.

[14] Inventory of Automatic Data Processing Equipment in the United States Government. The figures in the text are a projection from those given for financial year 1968.
[15] 'Computers in Central Government Ten Years Ahead', Civil Service Department Management Studies 2 (1971).

5

Computers and case law: problems and techniques

This chapter will deal with the general subject of information retrieval as applied to case law. The special problems posed by case law are first examined, and then the efficiency of different techniques by which they might be overcome is considered. 'Case law' is used here in a wide sense, comparable to that ascribed to legislation in the previous chapter, and includes not only the decisions of Courts in the strict sense but also decisions of other tribunals. Retrieval problems arise wherever previous decisions have the power to influence future practice.

1 GENERAL PROBLEMS

No lawyer can doubt that case law presents retrieval problems; but many lawyers can and do doubt whether the use of computers will solve them. Some doubt the ability of computers to solve the problem as a matter of theory. They hold that the process of finding relevant authorities is so complex that it can only be solved, if at all, by the application of human reason. Others doubt the ability of computers to solve the problems as a matter of practice. They hold that the volume of material is so great that it is inherently beyond the power of any computer to handle it efficiently. Others doubt the economic viability of such attempts. This view is basically the same as the previous one. Some doubt even the advisability of attempting to solve the problem.

Desirability of applying computer techniques

The remaining sections of this part of this chapter will attempt to meet the first three of these objections, but the last, the doubts about the desirability of even attempting to use computers to solve the problems of case law must be faced here. The argument of the doubters is an attractive one. They agree with the advocates of computer methods that the present system is breaking down under a weight of authority too great for efficient searching by conventional means. But whereas their advocates conclude that more efficient and computerized searching techniques will solve the problem, these doubters suggest a much more radical solution. It is no less than the abandonment of the whole common law system of *stare decisis,* or at least its substantial modification so as to restrict to a trickle the range of materials which may be referred to in litigation. They argue that merely to improve the pre-trial searching techniques will do no more than shift the problem from the pre-trial to the trial stage, in much the same way as piecemeal improvements to the road system in towns shift the traffic jam a mile or two from the outskirts to the city centre where it is liable to cause infinitely more trouble. The suggestion is that a more efficient pre-trial search will reveal so much more relevant information as a result of searching a greater mass of data, that trials will take even longer and judgements will become still more constipated with discussion of authority. This in turn will generate an even larger data-base, and a vicious circle will have been established ending only with the total paralysis of litigation. It is argued that such improvements in information handling as have already taken place, such as the improved system of reporting in England since the middle of the nineteenth century, and the improvement in research tools like encyclopaedias and citators especially in the United States, have already had the effect of lengthening trials, and concomitantly in increasing the length of time taken in preparation and waiting for a trial to come on.

In England in the ten years from 1958 to 1967 the number of days spent in trying cases at assize increased by approximately 90 per cent while the number of cases increased by only 15 per cent,[1] but of course both figures are relevant. So, too, in the opinion of the Beeching Commission, waiting time had risen to an unacceptable level.[2] The situation is even worse in the United States.[3] There is, however, no evidence that this admittedly regrettable state of affairs has been occasioned by the increased citation of case law. Since

---

[1] Figures calculated on basis of Royal Commission on Assizes and Quarter Sessions (Cmnd. 4153) para. 145 and app. 5.
[2] e.g. paras 65, 412.
[3] See Mitchell, 'In Quest of Speedy Justice', 24 *Univ. of Florida L.R.,* 230 (1972).

many of these cases are unreported it is not possible to propound any confident explanation. However, some indication may be gleaned from reported cases. These are likely to embody more references to case law than unreported ones, and perhaps to that extent are over-favourable to the thesis that the delays are occasioned by increased citation. In fact citation of cases shows a decline rather than an increase over the relevant period.[4] The solution which tends to be advanced by the doubters is usually that the amount of case law reported or referred to should be restricted.[5] This may be done either by fiat, or by providing a code to supplement the existing case law, or by both. Experience is universally discouraging to such attempts. Where Tribonian and Portalis failed others can hardly hope to succeed. Nor have they. Thus the codification of the English law of Sale of Goods has hardly checked the proportion of references to pre-code cases.

Professor Diamond has compared the citation of authority in code cases with those in other areas of the law of contract in order to examine the apparent effects of codification.[6] His study reveals that in 1965 the citation of pre-code authorities in the code cases was only 3 or 4 per cent less than the citation of cases of the same vintage in cases in the uncodified areas, expressed as a *percentage* of total citation in the two areas. Such a reduction seems unlikely to have a startling effect on the length of time taken to hear cases. On the other hand the overall average *number* of authorities cited in the code cases is about four per case less than that in the uncodi-fied areas,[7] and this may make some slight difference, though how far it can be attributed to codification as opposed to the general nature of the topics codified is, of course, dubious. It must also be remembered that in the absence of any express prohibition the tendency is for case law to grow upon the back of codification, as Diamond's figures also reveal. The most that can be said then is that codification may administer a slight temporary check upon the cita-tion of case law, but its true justification must be sought elsewhere.

In fact the citation of case law is never likely to sink below a fairly high minimum level. The reasons for this are familiar, and

---

[4] Taking the All England Reports Volume 1 of 1958 and 1967 as a basis for comparison there is a decline from just over one case cited per case on average to exactly one case cited.
[5] e.g. *Law Reform Now* (1963).
[6] 'Codification of the Law of Contract', 31 *Mod. L.R.* 361 (1968).
[7] 12.9 as opposed to 17.3, i.e. about 25 per cent less.

need not be rehearsed here at great length. The main one is that the legal system can only make room for general legislation by diversifying questions of interpretation, application and supplementation among the Courts, and thus requires facilities for the citation of case law to achieve that consistency which efficiency and justice require.

No widespread computerized system has yet operated long enough in the field of case law to permit any accurate assessment of the level of citation it will induce. In the absence of such evidence, theoretical argument must suffice. Does it necessarily follow that as the range of materials available for citation increases so the amount of relevant material to be cited must increase proportionately? Only if one assumes that the criterion of relevance so as to compel citation is itself both absolute and constant. It is surely arguable that it is neither. It may even be the case that just because lawyers are aware of the inefficiency of their conventional research tools they are driven to cite cases of remote relevance, whereas if they could be sure that their methods were efficient they could be content with fewer. It is like shooting an animal in the dark, one shot through the heart would be enough if it could be seen clearly, but when it is indistinct a large number in less vulnerable but more obvious spots are advisable. It may be objected that while this argument may hold for the purposes of citation, it will not work for the pre-trial search phase, since it assumes that the lawyer will already have distilled the most relevant from the less relevant authorities. But such an argument makes assumptions about computer searching techniques which may not nowadays be justified. The techniques of computer assisted selection will be described later. It is possible for such selection to take place very quickly as part of the ordinary search leading to the choice of the cases which will actually be cited.

The argument that the range of citable data should preferably be reduced, and in any event not increased, depends upon assumptions about the nature of such material which may be questionable. If volume is to be reduced, what principle should be employed? If it is to be kept at its present level, is the present selective process the best that can be devised? At present any case reported by a barrister may be cited to an English Court. The great majority are reported in the regular law reports published by the Incorporated Council for Law Reporting, or by one of the commercial publishers. In Great Britain alone, however, *Where to Look for Your Law* 1962 lists

over a thousand series of which 30 are current. These include innumerable series of specialized reports in particular fields, sometimes
published as a self-contained series, like the Lloyds List Reports or
the Rating and Valuation Reports, and sometimes included as a
reports section in a periodical like the *Criminal Law Review* or *The
Conveyancer.* Then there are reports of special tribunals like the
Commissioners for Industrial Injuries Decisions. Legal papers like
the *New Law Journal* publish their own reports, and so do some
general newspapers like *The Times* and *The Guardian.* Unreported
cases may also be cited, and the Bar Library contains transcripts
of all unreported Court of Appeal decisions.

This proliferation is indeed a valuable safeguard for the profession
on account of the somewhat capricious methods of selecting cases
for reporting in any one particular place. Then there are large private
collections compiled by institutions like insurance companies or local
authorities who frequently litigate in special limited areas. The use
of these sources is particularly oppressive since they are, in practice,
accessible to only one of the sides in the dispute, and notwithstanding
the salutary rule that counsel is obliged to inform the Court of
authorities against as well as for his particular point of view, the
private litigant is still liable to be prejudiced. His counsel is unlikely
to be so familiar with these areas, he will have less time to consider
any unreported authorities referred to, and most important of all he
will have had no opportunity to check the selection of relevant
material or to compare it with that which has been rejected as
irrelevant. Even when access to unreported materials is allowed, as
with the National Insurance Commissioners Decisions, its use is often
difficult on account of the absence, or low quality, of indexing
made available.

In addition to such domestic materials counsel is free to cite
foreign materials as persuasive authorities where he expects them
to help his case. This expands the size of the potential data base
enormously. A similar situation obtains elsewhere, and in the United
States is exceptionally acute on account of the very high volume of
law reporting per head of the population, and the regular use of
authorities from neighbouring jurisdictions.

If this mass is to be cut down, a number of expedients could be
adopted. It would be possible to prohibit the reporting or citation
of unreported cases, foreign cases, old cases or cases decided by
lower Courts, or indeed any combination of these. The difficulty

would be to ensure that good authorities were not omitted. Holmes maintained that the cases of the current generation contained as much law as was necessary.[8] But this view is not supported by the pattern of English citation, since about half of the cases cited in one series of reports in 1969 date from more than fifteen years earlier. Nor does a scrutiny of cases cited in recent reported cases support the elimination of unreported, foreign or lower Court[9] cases, since they often are cited and sometimes decide the outcome. Thus in 1972 I All England Reports alone and omitting foreign appeals, references can be found to nine United Kingdom but non-English series, five different Australian series, and others from Canada, New Zealand and the United States. The same volume contains references to thirteen unreported cases, one of them Canadian, to cases reported only in *The Times,* to one case reported in the Yearbook for 1535, and to another appearing only in the 1903 version of a textbook. So if these sources had been eliminated the Courts would have been prevented from referring to what were presumably relevant materials. It is surely more sensible not to restrict the data-base in any such arbitrary way but to provide instead more satisfactory search techniques so that the lawyer can discover quickly just which cases among the mass are relevant to his needs. It is this that the computerization of the retrieval of case law seeks to achieve.

Volume of material

It is extremely difficult to estimate the precise volume of case law material in any common law country, bearing in mind the diversity of sources indicated above. Lord Gardiner has asserted that in England in 1963 there were well over 300,000 reported cases.[10] This figure at least provides a rather conservative lower limit. These cases will themselves vary enormously in length and language, as may be seen by selecting volumes at random at say one hundred year intervals for the last five hundred years. Each series has its own form and style so that the assessment of the total volume of even the reported cases is completely speculative. As is frequently the case, the computer is not only the best device for solving the problem; it is the only one for assessing its magnitude. And it has not yet been used.

It is, however, possible to glean the current rate of accretion of

8 'Path of the Law', 10 *H.L.R.*, 457 (1897).
9 As suggested by Sir Hartley Shawcross
10 Law Reform Now (1963) p. 10.

decided cases from the official statistics. Of course not all of these cases are reported, even though decided by Courts of record, but their number gives some idea of the available pool for reporting. The statistics show that 306,625 cases were decided in the higher Courts in England and Wales in 1971.[11] So far as the major reports are concerned *Where to Look for Your Law* 1962 lists 30 current series for England and Wales. It is very loosely estimated that this represents 5 million words of text. In the United States the position is much worse. Some figures for the period ending in 1958 are to be found in the statistical appendix to *Automatic Retrieval of Legal Literature: Why and How*. These show that taking the regional reporter system and the US Reports alone the annual accretion rate in 1958 was something in excess of 60 million words per year.[12] It is estimated that the comparable figure for 1971 is 69 million.[13] This ignores all state reports, reports of other tribunals, reports in specialized series, reports in newspapers, and unpublished private reports. All of which may be usable. This is a formidable rate of increase, but can perhaps be matched by the rate of increase in other fields. Thus United States medical periodicals increased from about ten in 1850 to fifty in 1900, and then to about 810 in 1950. Other scientific fields are experiencing comparable rates of increase. The principal difference from law, however, is that in law the rate of decay is so much lower. It has already been indicated that about fifty per cent of all cases currently cited were decided more than fifteen years ago. Indeed almost 20 per cent of the cited cases in that sample were over seventy years old.[14] The reason for the relatively slower decay of legal materials lies in the difference between the nature of scientific and legal information.

Scientific literature is for the most part descriptive of phenomena and processes, and is used to provide information about such phenomena and processes. As knowledge of the phenomena and processes advances so the information is modified and expended. Legal information is quite different. Case law is not valued for its description of phenomena but for the rules it prescribes. Prescriptive rules do

[11] Civil Judicial Statistics 1971 (Cmnd. 4982) pp. 20, 21. Criminal Statistics 1971 (Cmnd. 5020) p. 188.
[12] Statistical Appendix to Automatic Retrieval of Legal Literature: Why and How, Tables A5, A11, A12, A13, A14, A15, A16 and A17.
[13] Calculated on the same basis as the tables in the Appendix supra.
[14] Diamond's figures for cited cases for 1965 are comparable. See 31 *M.L.R.*, 366 (fig. 2).

not develop naturally like descriptive rules, but only by the operation of further prescriptive rules. If a new scientific discovery is made, then all other scientific rules are modified to accommodate it as a matter of course. If a new legal rule is prescribed, it is a matter for the application of sometimes rather obscure and complicated rules of the legal system itself to determine what effect it is to have on the existing corpus of legal rules. The essential point is that because legal information is prescriptive it is valued for its own sake, and not for the light it throws on some external phenomena. The medium really is the message.

It has already been shown that cases and statutes have different forms on account of differences of function.[15] These differences extend to the precision of the rules relating to modification. It is much easier to determine whether a statutory section has ceased to have effect than to decide the same of a case. Statutes when once repealed are dead, though new legislation may sometimes be enacted in identical terms. Cases, although they may be overruled by other cases, can now always be resuscitated, at least by the House of Lords, and without benefit of legislation.

It is also true that the overruling of cases is much more rare than the repealing of statutes. There is a much greater variety of techniques for the modification of cases, once again largely on account of the form of case law. It is true that cases are sometimes overruled not by another case, but by a statute. If this occurs then judicial resuscitation is impossible, though even such cases are more likely to be invoked in the course of analogical reasoning on collateral points than are repealed statutory sections. But ignoring this, the overruling of case law by statute is never so neatly executed as the repealing of a statutory section. The latter is nowadays usually accomplished by the compilation of a table of repeals and consequential amendments. The former has to be gathered from the enacting words of the statute. Thus the Civil Evidence Act 1968 includes a section specifying repeals and a schedule of consequential amendments. Where the Act affects a rule of case law, however, such as the rule in *Hollington* v. *Hewthorn Ltd.*[16] in Part II, the case is nowhere mentioned by name, and both fact and extent of abrogation must be deduced from the enacting words. The effect of this relative imprecision in overruling together with its rarity relative to explicit

[15] Above, p. 70.
[16] [1943] 1 K.B. 587.

E

statutory repeal on the rate of decay of case law and statute can be gathered from a comparison of references to case law and legislation on a basis of age.

If the indexes of cases and statutes noted in the 1969 volume of the All England Reports are considered it will be found that only 7 per cent of the references to statutes are to those passed before 1900 whereas 19 per cent of the references to cases are to cases decided before that date. Similarly, only 24 per cent of the references are to statutes passed before 1944 as opposed to 40 per cent for the cases. The complete table is :

	pre-1850	1851-99	1900-44	1944-53	1954-63	1964-69
Cases	11	88	120	48	89	181
Statutes	4	22	61	88[17]	87	107

Table 1

A further effect of the form of case law tending to expand its volume is the absence of a decisively authoritative text. As any report authenticated by a barrister may be quoted, so the number of citable versions of any particular case increases. Of course in the event of a conflict between different versions, the semi-official Law Report version will normally be preferred to the oral account of a barrister who claims to remember a contrary version. But often it is not so much a question of conflict as of completeness, and except in the case of written judgements comprehensiveness is more difficult to maintain. The further back one goes the more acute this problem becomes, and many older cases appear in up to about a dozen different versions, none of which can be arbitrarily rejected. A further factor of the same sort is that a case may be reported at each of its stages. In England this is rarely more than three, and may be less now that provision for leap-frogging has been introduced,[18] but in the United States the figure could be much higher. Even in England, however, the effect of both of these factors if a case is to be considered a basic document is to multiply Lord Gardiner's figure considerably.[19]

[17] This figure is abnormally high on account of the inclusion within the period of two important codifying statutes, Companies Act 1948 and Income Tax Act 1952. The new versions of these will no doubt alter the chronological pattern of reference significantly.

[18] Administration of Justice Act 1969. Pt. II.

[19] In the first section of the *English and Empire Digest* seventy-five references are provided for nineteen cases. About four per case.

Form of material

As explained, the number of reports of cases and the length of their valid life can to some extent be ascribed to their form. This section considers the direct effect of form upon the retrieval problem. It has been shown in the general comparison of case law and legislation that because of its function a case is much more diffuse in form than a statute. On the other hand, an individual statute tends to cover more ground than the average case. This makes direct comparison of relative length difficult. Statutes have in fact tended to become longer in recent years. The average length increased by a factor of four between 1810 and 1960. Reports of cases are also longer, though because of the protean forms of case law no directly comparable figures can be provided. However, if the reports of cases decided in the House of Lords are isolated, as a basis for comparison, the increase seems to be by a factor of three, though even here the comparison is weak on account of the very different pattern of jurisdiction in the House of Lords in the two years. A better comparison may be that between reports of cases and statutory sections since these are the units generally considered to be basic documents in most existing retrieval systems. If this measure is taken it is obvious that reports of cases are much longer. In 1972 the average length of a case reported in the All England reports was approximately 4,000 words, while thanks to the work of Dr Niblett it is possible to state with precision that the average length of a document, normally a section, in the Atomic Energy legislation is 310 words, and slightly under half that in the subordinate legislation made under it.[20]

There are also considerable differences of content and style. Statutes are drafted in concise prescriptive terms. This leads to a relatively high incidence of abstract nouns, and a relatively low incidence of proper nouns, adjectives and adverbs compared with documents in general. In addition, the vocabulary is relatively confined on account of the omission of colloquial expressions, the absence of narrative description, and the necessity for consistency at the expense of elegance. Though even at this level of generality it must be admitted that styles show great historical development. Thus the nineteenth-century habit of assembling long lists of relatively specific synonyms in statutory sections has long since been abandoned in favour of single more generic nouns. Statutes also include little internal cross-reference except in relation to repeals and consequential

[20] Niblett and Price, 'The Status Project', UK Atomic Energy Authority Research Group Report CLM-R101, fig. 1.

amendments. And as remarked earlier they never contain specific references to case names.

The statistics quoted throughout this section in relation to case law show a great deal of internal cross-reference both to other cases and to legislation. This clearly has an important effect on the comparative vocabulary of cases and legislation. The vocabulary of case law is not only greater than that of legislation at any particular moment of time, but increases at a vastly greater rate since new proper names are constantly added, being either the names of persons or things involved in the litigation in question, or in references to extraneous material. The rate of addition of new words to the vocabulary of legislation is much lower, probably lower than the rate of increase in English vocabulary generally.

A further consequence of the differences of form and function between case law and legislation, and especially of the discursive nature of case reports, is that the incidence of articles, prepositions, conjunctions and auxiliary verbs tends to be higher. Such words, often referred to as common words, are measured as a byproduct of some computer systems, and it has been found that the incidence tends to be about 10 per cent higher in case law than in legislation, in terms of the proportion of common words to the total number of words in the text. It should, however, be noted that the elimination of common words from computer storage does not necessarily achieve a comparable reduction in storage required, since common words usually comprise fewer characters than the average text word. In most systems, however, the effects of a common word list are measured in terms of reduction in words concorded. Thus in my own research I found that a common word list of about 150 words achieved an approximately 60 per cent reduction in the case law materials I was working with. Niblett states that a list of about 100 words reduced his legislative materials by more than 50 per cent.[21]

A further difference relates to frequency of repetition. It might be thought that since the vocabulary of statutes is more limited it would follow that for a given number of words of text the frequency of repetition would necessarily be higher. This depends, however, upon the unit within which repetition is considered, and it is helpful to distinguish between repetition within a document and repetition within collections of documents. If the statutory section is to be taken as the document, then since it tends to be short the incidence of

[21] *Op. cit.,* p. 11.

repetition is low. On the other hand, since statutes tend to contain a number of sections dealing with related aspects of the same general subject the incidence of repetition between different documents within the same statute is high. But conversely, as the order of statutes in most collections is random the incidence of most repetitions between different statutes is low except for such words as 'commencement', 'repeal' and 'enacted' which tend to be repeated in all statutes whatever their subject matter.

In reports of cases the incidence of repetition varies according to the format of the report, but in the most common type, that exhibited in the semi-official reports, the incidence of repetition within a document tends to be very high. Thus the report of a case decided in the House of Lords might easily contain nine different versions. The most laconic will be the list of index terms contained in the telegraphic abstract printed after the title, then there is the headnote, the argument of counsel on both sides and perhaps five judgements. The number can be even greater if there are several parties and if they employ more than one counsel each, or if there is extensive reference to the decisions of the judges below. Since all these versions are dealing with the same general subject matter the incidence of repetition is high notwithstanding the greater flexibility of the language. If the collection is a general collection like the ordinary reports then the incidence of repetition between adjacent documents is likely to be extremely low as compared with statutes. If the collection is specialized, however, like the Commissioners' Decisions on Industrial Injuries for example, the incidence will once again be high.

The precise linguistic structure of law has never been satisfactorily, or scientifically, examined, and one of the byproducts of computer techniques will be the creation of such an analysis. Unfortunately, some aspects of computer development require foreknowledge of the results of such analysis. Thus I was myself once asked by a programmer whether it was likely that non-common words would tend to recur on average within 18,000 non-common words from their place of first occurrence. Of course it was possible only to guess, and because the guess was wrong an inefficient programme was written. However, the example proves another point. Notwithstanding the waste of resources in discovering the correct answer, the information was ultimately obtained and could not have been so economically obtained except by a computer. The conventional alternative of a team of readers recording occurrences and re-occurrences would be more expensive, more soul-destroying and less accurate.

2 SOLUTIONS

It has been seen that case law is enormous in extent and diffuse in form. It has been argued that there is no acceptable way of reducing the bulk of citable authority. How then can relevant authorities best be selected?

First, some consideration should be given to the efficiency of current methods. Despite the direst prophecies in both England and the United States the current systems have not yet broken down. Relevant authorities are still cited to the Courts. Because of the importance in law of retrieving relevant information, the techniques applied have always been highly advanced compared to other areas of knowledge. There is a battery of aids for the lawyer. The publishers produce printed and annotated copies of case reports very soon after the cases have been decided. These reports are also digested and indexed as they appear. They incorporate indexes of all citations made by them, and the publishers provide stick-on labels to attach to reports of cited cases to show in which case they have been cited. Each case report thus incorporates a complete and up-to-date record of where it has come from and where it has gone to. Subject indexes are cumulated several times a year, to constitute a running index, and then annually into the index for the series. The legal periodical literature contains copious reference to recent developments in particular fields, or as in the case of *Current Law* is devoted entirely to this task right across the legal board. In addition there are encyclopaedias of commentary, like *Halsbury's Laws,* and of abstracts, like the *English and Empire Digest,* which present the law in a classified and easily usable form. In specific subject fields there are also specialized encyclopaedias, and of course monographs. These are kept up to date by a combination of supplements, looseleaf additions and frequent new editions.

No other subject field is so well provided for. And yet the research seems to show that this is not enough. In all the experiments which have been carried out it has been found that conventional means alone are insufficient to retrieve all relevant authorities. In my own research the highest recall figure for a group of conventional searches was 83 per cent, and the lowest figure for a group of searches was 24 per cent. The best mean figure for the whole work is probably something slightly under 50 per cent. Similarly, in the American Bar Foundation research it was found that the computer discovered a number of authorities not discovered by a conventional search. This aspect was not systematically tested on account partly of some error in the conduct of the experiment, and partly to the change of emphasis in the presentation of the results owing to the concentration on the explanation of the deviance in judgements of relevance. Nevertheless the final judgement is that the computer is at least as effective as the human being in finding relevant authorities. Since the successes and failures need not coincide the chances are that the computer will find relevant authorities not found by conventional means. This is supported by the American Bar Foundation's figures which after some manipulation can be construed as showing that of the extra cases found by the computer over 40 per cent were relevant.[22] It must be emphasized that all these figures for the efficiency of conventional recall are maximized just because there is no way of establishing with certainty in any sufficiently large-scale test what the total number of relevant authorities is. This experimental work is also supported by common sense and the opinion of most lawyers, if those are regarded as different. No lawyer is ever completely confident that he has found every authority relevant to his case. It is because of such feelings that lawyers are especially suspicious when their search for authority is completely unproductive. This leads to a waste of effort in intensifying or repeating a fruitless enterprise. It may also be partly responsible for the citation of dubiously relevant cases. If the lawyer believed that computerized techniques were likely to add to the relevant authorities discovered by conventional means, and if he believed in the confirmation of a negative result provided by computer techniques, their introduction might be justified on those grounds alone.

Why, with such concentration of effort on the provision of retrieval services for lawyers, should there be such a failure to retrieve all relevant authorities, and such an awareness of such failure? The answer is simple. No lawyer has time to read all the reports, and if he had, he could not remember the details of all of them. He must therefore rely on indexes and classification systems to direct him to the relevant authorities. This is where the difficulties start.

[22] Eldridge, 'An Appraisal of a Case Law Retrieval Project', Proceedings of Computers and the Law Conference 1968, Queen's University, Kingston, Ontario, Table 8 pp. 49–51.

Indexing

Law, and especially common law, is not a neatly and logically arranged static system of concepts, universally agreed by all lawyers. It is unwieldy, inelegant, unsystematic, unagreed and in constant flux. Concepts constantly overlap both horizontally and vertically. Horizontally in that the categories overlap, and vertically in that the level of generality varies. A case in which a negligently drafted prospectus causes loss of profit might be regarded alternatively as relating to company law or to tort, and within either to deceit or negligence, and its elements might be described as prospectus, document or statement and loss of profit, financial loss or damage. To retrieve a reference to this case both indexer and researcher must characterize it in the same way, and the index must be accessible to the researcher.

These conditions are not always met. The first would be more likely to be fulfilled if the terms and categories to be used were standardized, and the practice of ascription to them uniform. Neither is the case. Despite the small number of legal publishers in the United States and Great Britain there is no uniformity of terms or categories. Even companion volumes in the same series sometimes operate on different principles. This is partly because authors often do their own indexing, and partly because in other cases it is usually done by part-time or inexperienced staff with little training or supervision. The result is that each encyclopaedia or general reference work is split up in its own unique way, and each index employs different headings, subheadings and general approach.

Some indexes now adopt a fact-orientated approach, like Bingham's 'All the Cases on Negligence', while others adopt a more highly conceptual approach. In some indexes main headings and subheadings are arranged alphabetically while further subheadings appear in any order, are free and uncontrolled. Lengths vary enormously, thus the All England Reports for the period 1966 to 1971, a total of 18 volumes, and 21,274 pages, compresses its index into 560 pages, or approximately 10 pages of index per 398 pages of text, while the reports of the decisions of the Industrial Injuries Commissioners for the period 1948 to 1968, a total of 5 volumes, and approximately 2,420 pages, spreads its index over approximately 1,713 pages, or approximately 10 pages of index per 14 pages of text. And this comparison totally ignores the larger number of words per page in the All England Reports. It is hardly surprising that different techniques are needed to cope with two such different productions.

Even if all indexes were completely standard and uniform there would still be difficulties. These stem from the fact that indexing normally depends upon the use of the human brain to select the correct terms to characterize whatever is being indexed. As every indexer knows this involves making choices, and there is no guarantee whatever that all indexers will make them in the same way. My own work can again be used to furnish examples of the difficulties that arise. At one time I contemplated using an indexing system in an area of the law where conceptualization was well agreed; this was the issue of the admissibility of confessions in criminal cases. The indexers were given a short finite list of concepts and asked to index part of a given collection of documents by reference to them. Their performance was checked by varying the order of documents and giving each indexer a part previously prepared by another. The correlation between different indexers was very small, and often the same indexer would index the same document in a different way when it was presented in a different context, or perhaps when he was in a different frame of mind. However close the supervision, indexing is inherently inconsistent.

It also gets out of date extremely quickly. The law is in constant flux, and indexing schemes ought to be changed constantly to reflect its latest form. This would mean, however, that all the existing documents would have to be continually re-indexed according to the latest scheme. But this would clearly be ruinously expensive. So a compromise is reached whereby the indexes of new books reflect the latest state of the law, while the indexes of old books remain as they were. But this, of course, simply leads to the anomalies to which attention has already been drawn. A further difficulty for any conventional indexing scheme is that it can only operate upon the main points in the text, and in case law it sometimes happens that a case becomes important not for what it mainly decides but for some tiny point which may well have seemed quite insignificant at the time it was first decided. Here too a subsequent change in the law may indeed create significance for such a point.

In recent years a good deal of attention has been paid to improving indexing techniques. Schemes developed at Case Western Reserve University in the United States concentrate on the roles played by

E*

particular words.[23] Other systems seek to meet the problem of levels of generality and overlapping by a faceted approach.[24] Such techniques seem to work in experimental environments, but it is suspected that they will be found to break down in large-scale practical applications, just because they increase rather than reduce the intellectual demands made upon the indexer, and in so doing slow down the indexing process, make it more expensive and tend to reduce consistency. These problems are exacerbated when the index comes into general use. If it is difficult for indexers to learn to operate one such scheme, it is infinitely more difficult for users to cope with a large number of them, particularly as they have so much less time to devote to the activity.

The question then arises whether some form of automatic indexing might not be feasible. There are a number of ways in which this might be accomplished. One relatively crude way would be to choose a list of terms to serve as the index, and then to programme a computer to scan the text in order to construct a concordance of such terms. Such a system would at least have the support of existing practice since it has been found that in at least some legal materials the entries in the index correspond to the use of the identical word in the text 85 per cent of the time.[25] Such a method would, however, be exposed to exactly the arguments raised above against conventional indexing so far as the selection of the terms to be concorded was concerned. All that could be expected would be that the computer would be more consistent in its operation than a human indexer.

A more sophisticated approach might dispense with the initial selection of terms, and instead allow the computer to select them. This might be done, for example, by having the computer use as its index terms all those non-common words which exceeded a prescribed threshold frequency in the text. Such a technique might have a number of advantages. Being mechanical in operation it would avoid the danger of inconsistency of application. Being wholly dependent upon the linguistic structure of the document it would avoid the danger of reflecting a distorted or outmoded approach. The converse of this, however, would be the inability of such a system

[23] Melton and Bensing, 'Searching Legal Literature Electronically: Results of a Test Programme', 45 *Minn. L.R.*, 229 (1960).
[24] See, for example, the work of D. J. Foskett, no application in law is known.
[25] Fels and Jacobs, 'Linguistic Statistics of Legal Indexing', 24 *Univ. of Pittsburgh L.R.*, 771 (1963).

to identify the golden reference among the dross. Indeed its very consistency would be a disadvantage. Quantity would be its only measure, and unless modified in some way quantity is a poor guide to importance. Such a system would tend to prefer technical terms for which synonyms were rare to non-technical ones for which synonyms abound. Mere accidents of usage might lead to distortion. Thus if a term has a distinct negative counterpart as 'light' has 'dark', it will be less preferred than a term which has no such distinct counterpart and is negated by a circumlocution, as the negation of having a right is simply not having a right. So, too, words with many grammatical variations will suffer compared with those that have few. 'Counsel' being both plural and singular will have an advantage over 'barrister' which is only singular. Some of these difficulties could be cleared up by the construction and use of a thesaurus, but this would reintroduce all the objections which can be advanced against the construction of thesauri in other conventional applications. The main objection here, however, is to the equation of statistical frequency with logical importance. It savours too much of the Bellman and 'What I say three times is true'.

Another indexing approach, only now becoming common in other fields than law, is citation indexing. In this approach a document is characterized not by its content but by its pattern of citation. It can be argued that since, as suggested above, legal citations are not to documents *about* the law, but to documents which *embody* the law, this will have an even stronger validity in law than elsewhere. It may also be argued that the pattern of citation is tolerably regular and systematic. This is clearly a prerequisite for any such approach. In case law also, the hierarchical pattern of the Courts suggests further ways of ordering references. Thus while one searcher might be interested only in references to House of Lords or Supreme Court cases, another might wish to delve more deeply into Courts of Appeal or first instance citations.

There is no doubt that this technique of finding relevant materials by reference to citations is extremely common in the law, no doubt in part for the reasons adduced above. This is reflected in the early development of such methods by lawyers much earlier than in other disciplines, and in the relative sophistication of such systems, especially in the United States. The essence of the method is that one may make any known case a starting point, and move either forwards or backwards from it to other cases which can themselves then be used as new starting points. The advantage of this method is that the intellectual effort is largely left to the original Courts, and counsel appearing before them, once the first starting point has been chosen. The search thus monopolizes on human ingenuity, and yields analogous situations and lines of argument difficult to tap in any other way.

There are, however, some compensating disadvantages. Such a technique depends for finding a case upon its either being cited, or its citing other cases. This is not always true even of reported cases. Thus of the 120 cases reported in 1961 1 All England Reports, sixteen cite no case, and of these no fewer than thirteen seem not so far to have been cited in subsequent cases. The general pattern of citation is such that it now seems unlikely that many of them will ever be cited, and so on a citation basis about 10 per cent of the output of reported cases would be lost.[26]

On the other hand, the citation approach can also lead to the retrieval of large numbers of irrelevant cases. The reason for this is that a case may raise a very large number of issues quite distinct from each other. It may thus be cited quite reasonably as authority in a very large number of cases which have nothing whatsoever to do with a particular point in which the searcher is interested. And this danger is multiplied with each further step in the chain. It is also extremely doubtful whether the overall pattern of citation really is sufficiently uniform for the technique to be accepted as the only retrieval technique required. This view is supported by the practice in the United States where a very good hard-copy version of this approach in the shape of Shepherd's is available, and where while extremely valuable it is by no means the only research tool employed.

Citation indexing should be accepted therefore as a valuable addition to the other methods, not a substitute for them. It will achieve its greatest efficiency where citation practice is uniform and where the materials largely deal with single issues. These conditions hold truer for some series of reports than they do for all reports regarded as a single data base. There can be little doubt that if citation indexing is regarded as desirable, then it is best done by computerized methods. At present, systems can only be kept up to date by frequent editions, supplements or noter-up slips. The first is expensive

[26] This figure corresponds to that obtained by Marx, 'Citation Networks in Law', 10 *Jur. J.* 121, where two of the sixteen cases in his sample could not be discovered by conventional citation methods.

because a new volume is required each year, and even then the only guarantee is that the material is no more than a year out of date. The second can reduce the period to whatever frequency is regarded as desirable, and both economically and administratively possible, which in practice is unlikely to be less than a month. The further disadvantage here is that it involves reference to at least two sources in relation to any particular search, and is wasteful in that the life of the temporary publication is so short. In effect six and a half books are produced each year. Of course it is possible to make the monthly parts non-cumulative, but then by the end of the year a single search involves reference to thirteen different sources. Noter-up slips can reduce delay to about a week, and avoid the necessity of reference to multiple sources. They are, however, aesthetically unpleasing and awkward to handle. Thus the title page of a frequently cited authority becomes completely disfigured, and often these are neither complete nor in proper order owing to the negligence of the usually low calibre labour employed to stick them in.

None of these problems beset the computerized approach. Information can be kept constantly up-dated, and can be retrieved literally at the press of a button. It is hardly surprising to find therefore that such a computerized system has indeed been developed, and is in operation at the Queen's University, Belfast, for citations, both to statutes and cases, made by cases reported in the Northern Ireland Law Reports.

Full-text

A full-text system is here defined as one in which at least all the non-common words in the original text can be directly searched. It may be thought that this omits the further possibility that the text might be characterized by an abstract which could then provide the basis for the search. It might be thought that this is a particularly curious omission in any discussion of the retrieval of case law since the ordinary form of the report of a case contains at least one, and sometimes two, abstracts in the shape of headnotes. This is, of course, true, and such abstracts are used as the basis for such periodical surveys of case law as those contained in Current Law, or such encyclopaedic works as the *English and Empire Digest*.

The reason for not treating abstracts separately as an alternative to indexing or full-text scanning is that while the abstract is indeed a further way of presenting the information in the report, it does not itself provide a different technique for finding it. Abstracts can not be read consecutively to extract information, and even if they could the technique would be identical to full-text scanning except that the data-base would be smaller. In fact, the headnote is itself simply treated as part of the report and access is obtained to it through the ordinary index or classification scheme. This technique has already been discussed, and is equally efficacious whether what is sought is the full-text or an abstract of it. It may perhaps be marginally easier to use a collection of abstracts for browsing than to use an index for that purpose, but once a fairly low threshold of volume has been exceeded this advantage disappears and becomes a disadvantage. Here, abstracts will be considered principally as a reduced form of text for scanning.

Techniques for full-text scanning must now be described in some detail. The general philosophy was broached in the preceding chapter. Here attention will be paid to the special problems presented by case law. In all retrieval systems decisions made at the input stage have their implications for the retrieval stage, implications often crudely expressed in the maxim 'garbage in, garbage out'. Nevertheless in the teeth of this maxim the account which follows is divided into two sections, one dealing with input techniques and the other with retrieval. This is simply for ease of exposition.

INPUT : The first question here is what to put into the system, and the second is how to do it, though they often overlap. The former covers both the selection of the range of materials to be included, and the parts of those materials. So far as range is concerned the above discussion suggests that the widest possible range is theoretically desirable, subject only to limitations imposed by purpose, time, money and machine capacity, and efficiency.

The question then becomes one of deciding which parts to put in. This may well vary according to the nature of the particular reports and the needs of the users of the system. This account assumes that the input material includes the ordinary law reports and that it is intended for general use. It is nevertheless advisable in any large case law project to provide for the needs of classes of different users by the insertion of identification zones which can be used to subdivide the data-base for retrieval purposes. Thus in a system which includes, say, the law of the whole of the United States, it might well be desirable to include a zone specifying the particular jurisdiction so that lawyers may have the option of interrogating either the whole of the data-base immediately or proceeding jurisdiction by jurisdiction.

Similarly, some indication of the date of the report may be used to subdivide the data-base. This will enable lawyers to work their way back gradually if their problem is one which is frequently litigated. The advantage of this procedure is that it enables the lawyer to avoid being swamped by information in which he is un-interested, and at the same time reduces the time and expense of the ultimate search.

This leaves the question of how such texts should be prepared for computer use. By analogy with legislation one might expect some form of automated input direct from the courtroom as the judge-ment is delivered. There are more serious problems here, however, on account of the form of litigation, and in particular its focus upon the disposition of the case before the Court to which considerations of providing an authentic record are rightly subordinated. Many of these will be discussed in a later chapter of this book. It is sufficient to say here that for the immediate future at least the basic material must be in the form either of a written judgement, or a shorthand version of an oral judgement; it will be the report as compiled by the reporter in the traditional form. It is possible that as more and more printers and publishers adopt computerized print-ing processes so more and more law reports will be so printed, and the reports thus made available in computer assimilable form. For those which are not, and for those which already exist, some other method must be used.

At present the most common technique is manual transcription by the use of a keypunch. Such a device has a conventional type-writer-style keyboard, and is fed either by paper tape or by punched cards. These provide a continuous feed of material, and the operator can concentrate on simply copying the report. This technique is subject to a number of disadvantages. The most fundamental is that transcription cannot be exact. The keypunch does not have the same range of typefaces and styles which appear in the original printed version. It is also likely to be deficient in the variety of characters it can supply. For example, an English machine is un-likely to have a dollar sign or an American a pound sign, yet both are likely to appear in reports of cases in the field of Anglo-American trade which will themselves be published in both countries. At one time it was even rare for keypunches to have both upper and lower case versions of characters.

The second main drawback of transcription by keyboarding is that it is expensive, slow and inaccurate. It is expensive because it is labour intensive, it is slow because it is impracticable to have really large numbers of transcribers working in parallel, and it is inaccurate because transcription is so boring that the operators are very easily distracted. Whatever the technique employed, however, there can be no doubt but that data preparation has so far been the least satisfactory feature of all existing systems.

Now, at last, it is beginning to appear that some more satisfactory approaches may be possible. These are still by no means so well developed as to be regarded as having been definitely established as economic and feasible alternatives to the methods outlined above, but they are worth further consideration. For many years machines have been available which use optical methods to transcribe written text into a computer assimilable form. Until very recently, however, such machines have been extremely limited in the range of characters which they are able to recognize, so limited in fact as to require the use of special typewriters or printers, and sometimes even special paper, to prepare information for them. Even so it has sometimes been thought advantageous to use such devices to prepare material, but the advantage of switching from keypunch to typewriter is hardly likely to be ever really significant. But now the versatility of such optical character recognition devices is improving dramatically. They can now read as wide a range of typefaces and styles as is necessary for most law reports. This improvement has been largely achieved by concentration on the programming of computers associated with the scanners rather than on the mechanics of scanning. The costs of such systems are still very high, and as complete systems for legal text they are still in the development stage. If they prove successful a revolution will have occurred in the data preparation phase of legal computer applications.

Whatever system is adopted, however, the end product must be a computer assimilable replica of the original text. The question then arises of what modification will be needed to the text in that form to facilitate the retrieval system. For example, it will be necessary to identify unambiguously the different logical units of which the database is composed. As explained in the previous chapter, a retrieval system based on volume, page, line and word numbers is less useful than one based on document, sentence and word numbers. So the computer must be given some signals to enable it to recognize the beginning and end of such units.

This sort of consideration applies equally to all the other different parts of the document. Thus symbols might be inserted to permit separate identification of such elements as title, Court, date, index terms, headnote, facts, references, names of counsel, argument, names of judges, judgements, order of the Court and names of solicitors.[27] The main advantage of this is to permit the separate search of such elements, and as a corollary to prevent the confusion of such separate parts. In this way the retrieval system can build up its own internal tables of names, citations and indexes. The question then arises of how far these different fields should be subjected to the ordinary rules about punctuation, or whether special rules should be applied to them. Citations furnish a convenient illustration. Suppose the citation is of *R. v. Smith* [1959] 2 Q.B. 35; this is clearly one logical unit and no advantage is gained by storing references separately to each component part. It is clearly better to devise a special way of treating citations whether they are of cases or legislation since exactly the same considerations obtain.

The real point is that the tacit assumption that words and numbers are the only unique units of reference is false for text containing such things as citations or formulae. This may prompt another question. Are citations the only extra units, or should not well established phrases such as *volenti non fit injuria* be treated in a similar way? This is arguable, and depends very heavily upon the particular subject matter. There is, however, this general difference that to treat citations according to ordinary techniques is peculiarly uneconomic since the component parts of the citation are commonly interchangeable, and resemble characters more than they do words. No one would suggest the construction of a concordance of characters since the proportion of references to entries would be too high, and all meaningful retrieval would depend upon the reconstruction of words. The same applies to citations, but does not apply to ordinary phrases, however technical and specialized their meaning. It is not argued that there will never be any advantage in treating phrases specially, simply that is always advantageous to treat citations in this way.

A team of workers at the University of Pittsburgh under the direc-

---

[27] For a different list of the same nature for case law, see the recommendations of The Council of Europe, EXP/Ord. Jur. (71), 9.

tion of Professor Borkowski has devised a technique for identifying any full form citation occurring in a given text.[28] The technique has been tested on an experimental data-base of 191 documents containing over 400,000 words of text and 2,227 full form citations. Of these 2,200 were correctly located, and only three false citations were indicated. Location alone is however not enough, the citation must be correctly identified, that is to say the beginning and the end of the citation must be determined. This was achieved in 1,944 cases. These are remarkably impressive results, especially when it is borne in mind that this was the first full-scale trial of the technique. Already as a result of the trial the specification of the system has been slightly altered so as to give a significant improvement in identification. It would be possible to combine this technique with a table of verified citations such that each could be checked against the table which could itself be automatically up-dated. In the experiment the programming in OS/360 assembler language took fifteen minutes machine time to process the 400,000 words of text. While fast enough for practical use this is too demanding of machine time to be economic at present, as Professor Borkowski frankly admits. In the future, as a result of further refinement both in programming and computers, this could be turned into a most useful asset of any legal information retrieval system.

It will also be desirable for the programmes to be supplemented by the addition of techniques for the identification of short references to cases such as 'The Carrier's Case'. At present it is limited to adversarial cases where 'v' appears in the citation. This limitation would also prevent it from finding cases with titles like 'Re Diplock' or 'In the estate of Park' for example. But these should prove comparatively simple additions. A much more difficult problem is presented by oblique reference, for example by a demonstrative adjective like 'that', or a noun phrase like 'the former'. In a manual or semi-automatic system this can be provided for, but in a wholly automated one the answer still awaits discovery. The best line of approach is not at all obvious since the words in question are so common and so ambiguous. It would just not be feasible to stop each time the word 'there' occurred to determine whether it was an oblique reference to a citation. The only conclusion to be drawn at present is that the human brain must, for the time being, and

[28] Borkowski *et al.*, 'Structure and Effectiveness of the Citation Identifier', 1970 *Law and Computer Technology*, 42, 66.

preferably with the assistance of modern text editing machines and devices, make decisions of this type.

There are a number of further refinements which may be made to the original text in the hope of improving retrieval performance. Some might equally well be considered in the next section as they are concerned with retrieval as much as with input, but as they do bear upon the characterization of the original data in the computer's memory, they are included here.

Two such techniques are first the detection and elimination of words which have little or no information content in themselves and might thus be considered eligible for elimination, and secondly the detection and elimination of spelling mistakes, whether occurring in the original or having been introduced during the transcription process. Such words occur at opposite ends of the frequency spectrum. The uninformative words include auxiliary verbs, conjunctions, prepositions and articles. All of these are of very frequent occurrence. Spelling mistakes in a particular form are usually of rare occurrence. This suggests that one method of approaching the problem would be first to produce a frequency list of unique words. Such a list would incidentally be an invaluable research tool in itself since it would help with the solution of many of the problems confronting those seeking to write programmes for handling legal materials. It is also just the sort of task for which the computer is best fitted. The basic tool might therefore be worth creating. It is much more dubious whether it could really help in the ways indicated, or even that much would be achieved if it could.

So far as common words are concerned it is true that because of their very frequency of occurrence they will be of little value in any retrieval system as such. No one is going to identify a case exclusively by reference to their occurrence in its text. They may, however, perform a crucial role in the construction of phrases and in the modification of the meaning of other words. Other commonly occurring words have importance even though not embedded in set phrases and constructions. Thus the lower cardinal numbers occur very frequently but can yet accomplish a useful retrieval function when read in conjunction with the rest of the document. It might be necessary to find all cases in which a sentence of three years had been imposed for a particular crime. The best way to find such cases would be to search by reference to words characterizing the crime in question, and the words characterizing the sentence, and clearly 'three' would be one such word. It is equally important to be able to distinguish between phrases such as 'trial by jury' and 'trial of jury', or 'no case to answer' from 'case to answer'.

There is the further problem of the common word which is a homograph of a non-common word such as 'will' or 'may', though in the latter case the ambiguity may be mitigated by the use of upper and lower case. These examples are enough to show that the simple elimination from the text of all words exceeding a given threshold of frequency is unlikely to prove an acceptable solution by itself.

So far as phrases are concerned it is possible to locate them by treating them as entities distinct from their component parts, like citations. The difficulty is that only a relatively small number of extremely well established phrases can be treated in that way. These must all have been determined upon in advance, and indicated by the insertion of special symbols at the transcription stage, or by their semi-automatic insertion at some later stage. No established system in law has so far chosen to adopt such a technique. A further possibility is the identification of the phrase by reference to the non-common words which it contains, and to accept the danger of retrieving documents which contain phrases containing the same non-common words but with different common words giving a different meaning. This is the technique usually adopted, if it can be dignified by being so called, and seems not to lead to significant difficulty. But so little attention has been paid to scientific measurement in this field that this cannot be substantiated, and the assumption might prove to be false. In general, however, modern systems are able to eliminate unwanted material increasingly painlessly and efficiently, so this may be unimportant.

For other common words, such as those indicating a negative, and for those with non-common homographs, different solutions must be employed. In the former case if elimination of the concordance entries is considered to be necessary it must be compensated for by the inclusion in any thesaurus of not only synonyms but also antonyms. This will deal with part of the problem of negation, but will not touch other modifiers, such as less or more, to anything like the same extent. It is generally assumed that to do nothing leads to little information loss, and here too it is possible that the assumption is false. The problem of homographs seems insoluble at present, at least in the absence of successful linguistic analysis systems of the type being tried in translation experiments. The only course is to eliminate such words from the list of common words. If this is accepted then the frequency list would be made as a first step only, and would then be subjected to scrutiny by a human editor to eliminate possible homographs. Similar judgements would also have to be made about the treatment to be accorded to other commonly occurring but possibly significant words, like the cardinal numbers.

Spelling correction is at the other end of the frequency scale. Here there seems to be less doubt that the elimination of mistakes is desirable, but more doubt as to whether it is feasible to accomplish it automatically. But a caveat must be entered even as to its desirability. Is it self-evidently desirable that spelling mistakes should be corrected? So far as they are inserted accidentally in the process of transcription they should clearly be prevented from interfering with the retrieval systems. But this might equally well be accomplished in other ways, and there are dangers in automatic spelling correction. The most important of these is that it is unable to distinguish between accidental mistakes in transcription and intentional variations reproduced from the original. Such intentional variations may reflect either geographical or chronological distribution. An American will write 'labor' where an Englishman writes 'labour', a writer in the twentieth century will write cognisance where one in the eighteenth century wrote cognizance. Part of the value of the store of legal writing would be lost by the automatic correction of such spellings. In particular a neat way of restricting a search to place or time would be lost. A better technique would be to treat such variations as synonyms of the word as commonly spelled, unless there were some special reason for not doing so, such as a desire for the sort of restriction indicated above. But even this would not always be desirable. It must not be forgotten that law reports contain, in addition to pronouncements about the law, recitals of the facts to which they relate. It is occasionally crucial to such a statement that a word has been mis-spelled. Thus in the celebrated case of *R. v. Voisin*[29] the issue turned upon the admissibility in evidence of the accused's mis-spelling of 'bloody' as 'bladie'. It is true that such mis-spelling will only very rarely have the slightest significance for retrieval purposes, but it should be a principle of any computerized retrieval system not to induce the loss of information unless it cannot be avoided.

[29] [1918] 1 K.B. 531.

Even if it is decided that automatic spelling correction is desirable, the question arises of whether it is practicable. It has been suggested that most mis-spellings would congregate at the lower end of the frequency spectrum. In most cases this will be true, and in most cases such mis-spellings can be detected and corrected without reference to the original text. But it is not always so, and even where it is, it is not obvious that the computer could be programmed to perform the same function as efficiently as a human being. The first problem is that whilst many mis-spellings may congregate at the lower end of the frequency spectrum, in case law in particular they will not be alone there. They will be rubbing shoulders with all the other low frequency words such as non-recurring proper names and nouns associated with the parties and places involved in a particular case. There would be so many of these that it would be quite uneconomic to have the computer check all words below a certain threshold frequency to see whether they were mis-spellings.

In fact the algorithms for detecting mis-spelling in other areas are formidably complicated. They usually rely upon correspondence with words of higher frequency in all but one or two characters. If deviation in as many as the first two characters is allowed the number of words to be checked, and the number of eligible correct spellings, will be very high. In practice most automatic techniques concentrate therefore on single character mistakes occurring late in the word. This will clearly only correct a small proportion of the mistakes in the data-base, and it may be questioned whether the time and effort of accomplishing such a small improvement is justified. But even if it could be shown to be completely economic to provide comprehensive checks of this type, there would remain the problem of equally eligible alternative spellings. At present the choice between these would have to be made by a human being either on the basis of context, or by comparison with the original. It is conceivable that one day automatic linguistic analysis may have developed to a sufficient extent to cope with the first possibility; the second must remain beyond automatic capability. Exactly the same consideration also applies to the detection of mis-spelling where the mis-spelled form is in fact the correct spelling of a different word. This is a very similar problem to that of the homograph of the common word, and it is very difficult to see how it can be dealt with. One can only hope that it will not lead to significant information loss.

It is suggested that the best solution for the time being is for a human being to scan a frequency list for obvious spelling errors and to resolve these either with or without reference to the original text as necessary, and then to include such mis-spellings or variations as appear in the synonym list in the thesaurus. Of course in the case of the more common variations the whole of the frequency list, and not simply the lower end, will require scanning. At present there seems little scope for automatic spelling correction in the computerization of case law.

RETRIEVAL: So far the selection and form of the information to be stored has been described. The way in which it is stored could also be regarded as an input question, but is so far dictated by considerations of facilitating retrieval that it is here regarded as a retrieval question. Clearly the most important consideration in relation to retrieval is the need of the user. It is therefore perhaps surprising that so little hard scientific information has been gleaned about the needs of the users of legal information.[30] Most commercial development seems to have been guided by lawyers who have relied upon private introspection succeeded by universal extrapolation. It is highly dubious whether this is really adequate. Nor has there been any thorough investigation of this problem in the experimental work.

In the commercial environment the reason may be that sights have been set on what can be sold rather than what is needed, while in the experimental the problem has rather been the necessity for designing experiments of a sufficiently demanding intellectual content as to satisfy both the curiosity of the experimenter and the generosity of his sponsor. With case law no less than with legislation there can be no doubt but that different situations require different approaches, and many of the disputes about the merits of rival techniques really reflect different conceptions of the aims of those techniques. A special difficulty with any new technology is that the availability of the technique itself affects the demand for it. Thus it is of limited use to conduct a poll to discover how many lawyers

[30] Surveys in North America include an economic survey conducted by the Massachusetts Bar Association in 1970 and *Operation Compulex – information needs for the practising lawyer*, published by the Canadian Department of Justice, 1972. In Europe pilot surveys are included in Aitken, Campbell and Morgan, 'Computers for Lawyers' a report to the Scottish Legal Computer Research Trust (1972), and in 'Das Juristiche Informationssystem' the report of the West German Ministry of Justice (1972).

believe that they need direct access to a particular series of reports, or even to engage in a survey of their current practice of reference to that series, since its constant and instant availability will certainly affect the use which will be made of it. In the legislative field this tendency has become very plain. As the new techniques have become available so they have tended to become more and more addictive, and now lawyers who would once have rejected any suggestion that they might use them can no longer do without them.

Even so, there is no real excuse for the dearth of information about the use of research time by lawyers in different environments, and indeed the absence of any developed scheme for distinguishing between the environments. The former defect should be alleviated as the accounting and time-control techniques to be described later come increasingly into use. The latter is a theoretical task which the theoreticians show no taste for tackling. It is nevertheless clear that a general browse through the literature in the hope of discovering a new line of approach to an intractable problem is quite different from a search for the most recent authority on the interpretation of a particular subsection of a statute, and different again from a retrospective search into the development of a particular doctrine. No systematic analysis is attempted here either, but some reference to and allowance for such factors will be made.

This section will not be concerned with the hardware for retrieval whether central processor, mass storage or output device; nor with the techniques of holding large amounts of linguistic data in an accessible form, though something may be said about this incidentally. The main emphasis will instead be on the techniques of searching from the point of view of the user. Since this section envisages the use of a full or amplified full-text data-base, it is clear that the same basic techniques described in the previous chapter must be employed. This means that word occurrence and association must provide the key to meaning. The application of simple Boolean operators like 'and', 'or' and 'but not' also apply here. Occurrence is characterized by reference to document, sentence and word number so that degree and direction of juxtaposition can be indicated. These are the bare bones of a Boolean orientated retrieval system for the retrieval of information from the full-text of legal documents.

Most of the difficulties associated with the employment of such methods occur in relation to case law, and consideration of the refinements necessary to deal with them was deferred. These difficulties arise for two closely interrelated reasons. The language of case law is both more discursive and more diffuse than that of legislation, for the functional reasons described in the previous chapter. There are more words, and there are more different words, without any necessary or corresponding increase in the number of meanings. It follows that the simulation of meaning by reference to word occurrence is rendered more difficult, and some attempt must be made to delineate the problems and possible solutions more precisely. This account accordingly falls into three parts : first, a specification of the problems, and then an account of the possible solutions divided between questions relating to the structure and to the conduct of searches.

Problems: The two basic assumptions underpinning this whole approach are first that the difficulties associated with meaning can be solved by reliance upon word occurrence, and secondly that practising lawyers can so solve them in the course of their ordinary work. Both are questionable. So far as word occurrence is concerned the difficulty is that the draftsman's motto of 'one word one meaning and one meaning one word' quite clearly does not apply to case law. A fundamental problem arises over the definition of a word, for the purposes of measuring word occurrence. A moment's reflection will reveal that the definition cannot be entirely divorced from the meaning. It might be supposed that a word is as the dictionary says 'a unit of language'. But what is to count as a unit? Is the expression 'one hundred and one' four units or less? And what if it appears as '101'? Is right-angle one unit or two? Is 'child' a different word from 'child's', or is it just a different form of the same word? Is 'labour' the same word as 'labor' or 'travail'? Is 'May' the month a different word from 'May' as part of an interrogative start to a sentence, or are they different words with the same form? It becomes clear that meaning and occurrence cannot be easily divorced. Rules must be established to deal with numbers, hyphenation, grammatical variation, spelling variation, whether historical or geographical in origin, foreign words, synonyms, antonyms and homographs. Some of the factors involved in the solution of these problems or in allowing for them where they appear insoluble will be examined later.

The second assumption, that lawyers will in their normal work be able to contribute to the solution of these problems, is also dubious. At present the accurate retrieval of legal information in the field of case law involves the lawyer in matching his characterization of the problem to be solved with an indexer's characterization of the content of a relevant document in an index. The lawyer is assisted by the array of other terms, and fine adjustment can be made by reference to the text at an indicated point, and then back to the index for comparison with other passages. Other books with slightly different schemes may also be consulted, and finally when, and if, original source materials such as reports of cases are consulted, the lawyer may well embark upon a citation orientated search, looking up the cases cited in the report and further opinions in which the report has itself been cited. The most relevant of these may then be checked back with the original books by way of the table of cases to make sure that the ground has been comprehensively covered.

It is apparent that this process involves considerable effort and skill on the part of the lawyer. It might be thought that he would be prepared to expend a similar amount of effort on a computerized search. But this is not necessarily so. The process described above is one which is already familiar to the lawyer. It is what he has been doing all his life, and not only in relation to legal information. A similar process is used in school, university and private life. Professional men are used to referring to books in this way and proud of their skill in doing so. The computer starts with two serious psychological disadvantages. First, the technique of a Boolean search is not precisely the same as the search of an index, and hence the lawyer may, at least initially, feel very uneasy in applying it. Secondly, access is likely to be through a keyboard and to involve the use of mechanical skills and manual dexterity which the lawyer is unlikely to have, and which he probably despises as more appropriate for non-professional aides like secretaries and copy-typists.

These are very real obstacles to the ready acceptance of computer orientated retrieval systems. They can probably only be overcome gradually, and by the demonstration not only of greater efficiency of the computer systems but also that this cannot be achieved without the active participation of the lawyer himself. This is the key factor in the Boolean approach to retrieval from full text. The power of the search compared to a search by conventional means is increased to the extent that the user is freed from the necessity of matching his characterization of the meaning of his problem to an indexer's characterization of the meaning of a document. Flexibility is improved by leaving the lawyer free to specify his search as he chooses,

and to modify it as he chooses. Similarly the source documents themselves will have been subjected to no constraints. Provided that an
idea can be found in them by the human mind, it can, in principle,
be extracted by a Boolean search.

It is perhaps paradoxical that the more sophisticated and computerized the system, the freer the lawyer becomes to reap the fruits
of his human skill and ingenuity. The good lawyer may see a link
between previously disparate lines of authority. Unless an indexer
has also seen it, the chances of assembling all the information quickly
and easily are likely to be very slim in the conventional system.
With a Boolean full-text system there is no greater difficulty in supplying unconventional demands than the most hidebound. Like his
conventional skills, those of using computerized systems are ones
the lawyers will just have to learn. The older and established lawyer
will have to learn by way of formal instruction and subsequent
practice. This will be difficult. But increasingly new young lawyers
will have been exposed to such techniques at their schools and
universities, and by contact with computerized systems as they
gradually infiltrate everyday life in such areas as banking, reservation systems, and credit control. It will eventually become as com-
monplace a factor of everyday life to use a computer terminal as
it is to use the telephone today. In schools and universities there
are already special courses in computing, and soon computing will
become a recognized part of courses in other specialities. Indeed
this has already widely occurred in the United States and in some
other technologically advanced countries.

This increased familiarity will help to solve the lawyer's problem
in having to change his cast of thinking. To some extent these
applications will induce him to think about problems in the ways
prescribed by the use of Boolean logic, but not entirely since the
main problem is created by the application of this logic to free
natural language text. The user of such a system must be induced to
think of meaning in terms of word occurrence. He must learn to
ask not for documents *about* 'involuntary confessions,' but for documents which *contain* certain combinations of words of which 'involuntary' and 'confessions' will merely be two. A difficulty is that
this seems an abnormal way of thinking. The hope is that because
it is possible, it can by repetition become normal. Part of the trouble
lies in our ignorance of our own mental processes. It is not at all
clear whether our brains operate on a basis of meanings or words,

or in some totally different way. In the case of written documents word occurrence is at least a necessary condition for the extraction of meaning, in the sense that the document must be scanned before its meaning can be extracted. But equally clearly scanning is by no means the only element in the extraction of meaning. Until some significant advance is made in our knowledge in this area it seems that one can merely experiment with different techniques in the hope of finding one which becomes easy and effective in use.

A rather less nebulous difficulty experienced by lawyers in the use of a computerized system as part of their everyday work has been the alteration which it has dictated in their ordinary pattern of work. The use of such a system presupposes that a problem sufficiently difficult and well articulated to justify use of the system has been encountered. This articulation and assessment can only be made by the application of the mind of a trained lawyer to the facts of the case, which themselves may be in dispute. A great deal of hard work and ingenuity is required in getting to the point at which a legal information problem can be posed. It is important that the familiarity with the problem generated in the effort of getting to this point should not be dissipated before the answer is returned, because the answer will be in terms of relevant documents to be applied to the resolution of the problem. In the conventional approach briefly described above there is little delay. The books join the primary documents on the lawyer's table, and they are used together to work out the solutions.

Early computer systems interposed a break at this point, not gratuitously but for logistical reasons. Computers which were large enough to answer legal retrieval problems were too expensive for the ordinary lawyer to use exclusively. The only course was to use a central computer shared between a large number of users. This meant that the questions had to be conveyed to the computer, and the answers conveyed back to the lawyers before they could be used by them. This procedure, while interposing a delay between the formulation of the question and the receipt of the answer, had two compensating advantages.

First it permitted a further saving of cost by the use of batch processing techniques. This means that questions from lawyers are not immediately fed into the computer as they come in, but are saved up and put into the computer in a large batch. By good programming this enables very much more efficient use of the computer than by taking the problems one by one. This holds good even if the central computer is dedicated solely to legal information retrieval, but is even more true of larger general purpose computer systems. Such systems themselves have significant cost advantages for legal work, but only if there is a greater volume of use than legal work by itself could expect to generate.

The second advantage is that it provides an opportunity for the centre to check the questions before they are put to the computer, and for the computer's answers to be checked before they are passed on to the user. These are generally known as pre-editing and post-editing techniques. Thus the question posed can be checked by a very experienced user of the computer who does nothing else but formulate computer searches, and if necessary modified after consultation with the original user. Similarly the output can be scanned and some judgement of its likelihood of satisfying the lawyer determined. In this way some element of the browsing process is injected into the computer system. It is also thus possible to utilize similar talents to those which in the conventional environment go into the indexing process. This might be a useful feature in regulating the supply and demand for labour during a period of adjustment to computerized methods in those industries currently involved in satisfying legal information needs, principally legal publishers.

Fortunately these problems need no longer arise. One of the most dramatic recent developments in the computing industry has been the emergence of real-time systems with multi-user capabilities. This means that it is now possible to establish direct links between terminals situated in lawyers' offices and very large central computers. Such terminals can be used both to relay the questions and to display the answers. Because of the enormous speed of both data-link and central computer, the answer will appear to be provided instantaneously, though in fact the computer will be serving a large number of other users at the same time.

This is helpful in a number of ways. Most important of all it enables the lawyer to work through his problem once, and once only, as in the conventional system. It also permits real browsing, just because the system is so fast, and techniques to assist this will be discussed later. It does not allow for the interposition of pre- or post-editing, but this is in accord with the philosophy behind the Boolean full-text approach which is to entrust to the user who is best acquainted with the problem the responsibility of putting it to the computer. Only he really understands its nuances, and only he is in a position to make a really accurate judgement of the relevance of the computer's response. The cost problem is bypassed because the lawyer pays only a relatively low rent for the use of the terminal, and for the computer time actually used by him. Overheads are spread between all the users of the system as with batch processing, but there is none of the delay inevitably associated with such a system. It is not suggested, however, that there is no work in the field of case law which should be done on a batch processing basis. Indeed where there is no great urgency and no need to browse it will generally be the most economic way of doing the job since it will be able to utilize off-peak computer time, and generally make more efficient use of the computer's capabilities. Thus in a mixed system the computer would probably be doing on-line work during the normal working day, and batch processing work during the night.

Structure of searches: The basic philosophy of a search of a full natural language text has by now been indicated several times. Typically it depends upon the detection of documents containing specified words in specified combinations and in specified degrees of juxtaposition to each other. So far there has been little variation in the approaches of the different workers in the field, and all have taken their lead from the pioneering work of Professor Horty at Pittsburgh, notwithstanding that his approach was originally devised for the retrieval of legislation rather than case law. As mentioned earlier, this is not ureasonable, since the difficulty of having a greater range of words to express a given concept in a given case law document than in a legislative document is balanced by the greater frequency of reference to the concept expressed by the words in a case law document.

The most significant feature of such a search philosophy is that it tends to exclude any consideration of the weight to be attached to any word, or to the role which it is required to play. Such a system does not in principle discriminate between 'man bites dog' and 'dog bites man', or if the search is in relation to a bite by a rabid guard dog does not attach special significance to these features. It may be argued that roles can be reproduced by reference to the direction as well as to the degree of juxtaposition. It is true that such a modification would meet the example above by the simple expedient of requiring the word 'dog' to occur earlier in the entrance than the word 'man'. But such an expedient cannot cope with the relatively free arrangement of words in English prose, and would be unable to distinguish for example between 'man bites dog' and 'man was bitten by dog'. It is possible that such difficulties might be overcome by very elaborate algorithms, and in some languages this might be desirable. In English, however, it is thought that the problem is not so serious as to justify the cost of the programming and computing necessary to overcome it.

In a somewhat similar way the problems of weight can be overcome by multiple searching. Thus the first search would require precise concatenation of circumstance; in the example above the word 'rabid' *and* 'guard' would be required to be associated with the word 'dog', and only in the event of the failure of a search so defined would the search be widened to retrieve references to documents containing an association between 'rabid' *or* 'guard' and 'dog', and only in the event of the failure of this to documents simply containing the word 'dog'. This is, however, time-consuming and clumsy, especially in a batch system.

Accordingly, some attention has been devoted to the possibilities of devising new non-Boolean search techniques so as to achieve some reflection of needs like those indicated. Such techniques, it should be emphasized, are not necessarily to be regarded as substitutes for Boolean techniques so much as complements to them. Most proponents of such systems recognize the power of the Boolean approach and seek only to provide an alternative when necessary.

One very simple system, a variant of which has been tried at Queen's University, Kingston, Ontario by Professors Lawford and Latta in connection with the Quic law project, exploits the tendency towards repetition in case law. The user is asked to specify his search terms in order of importance, and references are provided to documents ordered by reference to frequency of occurrence within the document of those terms so specified. Thus the reference printed first will be to the document which contains most such references, or references to the most important terms. Such a technique requires some care to be taken in the selection of terms for search since some terms which are of indubitable importance may occur in far too many documents to achieve any discrimination in retrieval. For such a system to work at all, frequency lists of words within documents must either be stored or be capable of being quickly compiled, and it is necessary to devise complicated mathematical algorithms to calculate the relative significance of different documents in different forms. It will be seen that this system shares with the Boolean approach the initial identification of a document by reference to the words it contains.

A more radical approach is that employed in Unidata, a Swiss firm, whereby the document is not specifically identified by reference to the occurrence within it of specified words. Instead each document is analyzed at the input stage by reference to the words it contains, their relative importance judged principally by their position within the document, and their frequency. A vector expressing this information is then constructed in n-dimensional space, and stored within the computer as the unique characterization of the whole document. The search request is then submitted in ordinary prose, an optional feature also of the Queen's University technique, and analyzed in a similar way with the construction of a vector. This is then matched against the vectors characterizing the documents in the collection, and those which match most closely are selected for retrieval. It is claimed that this fits in better with the mental processes of the searcher and is better adapted to finding analogous documents than a Boolean search. So far, however, the system is still in an experimental stage, though it was demonstrated in Germany in 1970, and relies so far upon too small a data-base for a considered appraisal. It certainly shows a refreshing originality of approach, and provided that it is capable of dealing satisfactorily with the great flexibility of words and formats to be found in common law systems of case law it may well have a considerable role to play in the future.

As remarked, however, the Boolean system can be operated to achieve much the same results, though admittedly at the expense of some ingenuity. The efficiency of any retrieval system reflects the efficiency of the human searcher in grasping the problem, in articulating it in terms of the material to be searched, and in recognizing the right (or wrong) answer when it appears. As the success of the conventional system depends upon these factors so does that of the computer search, subject only to the case of providing automated assistance in the computer search. The structure of the search will be described as having four elements : the expression of the problem in terms of the concepts involved; the choice of the right words to express those concepts; the arrangement of words and concepts by reference to the correct logical operators, taken to include indicators of required direction and degree of juxtaposition; and the specification of unacceptable patterns of retrieval. In systems where the data-base is subdivided, a further element in the structure of the search will include a reference to the portion of the data-base to be searched.

The first of these four elements is common to all types of legal search. In a computerized system, some broad concepts must be used to make gross distinctions, and others to make fine ones. The searcher will avoid retrieving irrelevant information or false drops by the use of the former, and avoid retrieving too much marginally relevant information or over-recall by the use of the latter.

The second element in the computer search is the choice of words by which the concepts are to be expressed. Here there is a fundamental difference between computer and conventional searching methods. In the conventional search, once the concept has been identified it can be looked for directly in the index : in a computerized system concepts must first be expressed in terms of words which may be expected to appear in the text of relevant documents.

The question thus remains of how expansion is to be achieved. There are five main types of necessary addition : grammatical variations, synonyms, antonyms, particularizations, and generalizations. Because full-text is being searched, words may occur in any grammatical form and all must be specified for retrieval purposes since the computer will unless otherwise instructed treat each different string of characters as a separate word. Most lawyers are not linguists and will not be able to call to mind at all easily all the possible grammatical variations of a word in which they are interested. They must therefore be assisted in some way.

One simple possibility is to maintain a list of all the different forms in the computer, say in the shape of an alphabetic list. This is not especially expensive since it is usually necessary to maintain such lists for searching purposes. It should then be possible for the lawyer to extract all the forms he wants. The advantage of doing it this way is that there is no redundancy; forms which have not occurred in the text will not be searched for, and the human brain is being used as the medium for selecting those different forms which are true grammatical variants. It will be obvious that such a method depends for its efficiency upon the concentration of the different forms at one place in the alphabetical list. It could not be applied to irregular verbs like 'go' for example. Such a technique might also be able to provide for minor spelling errors which had occurred in

F

the data-base, subject to the same limitation, namely that the deviation did not occur so early in the word as to remove it too far from
its accurate counterpart in the alphabetic list. Since the technique
depends upon alphabetic listing it is hardly surprising that it has
been suggested that it should be more fully automated.

This would typically be achieved by what is usually known as a
truncation approach. According to this, all words having a specified
number of initial letters in common are treated as if they were the
same word, thus making it possible to catch most grammatical
variations since they differ in their endings. For example, if all the
grammatical variations of 'liability' are required, liabilit. might be
specified. In some systems it is possible to specify how many further
spaces should be filled, and there are many other variations upon
the same basic theme. The difficulty with such systems, like all those
which seek to simulate human judgement, is that they are slightly
less efficient than the human brain. Thus they cannot handle the
irregular verb problem any more than any other solution based on
alphabetic listing.

They are, however, capable of being used to introduce new errors
of their own. It is not always possible to anticipate other words
which may be caught by the truncation approach but which are
unconnected with the original. For example, it is conceivable that
someone interested in a problem involving the law of taxation, might
specify tax . . . , and he would indeed retrieve documents containing
the words 'tax', 'taxable', 'taxation', 'taxes', 'taxed' and 'taxing'. Unfortunately he would also retrieve documents containing the words
'taxi', 'taxidermy' and 'taxonomy', or any version of these or any
other of the seven other different words with these initial letters
listed in the Shorter Oxford Dictionary. Nor does this technique by
itself suggest any simple method of avoiding the difficulty since no
more letters than the initial three can be specified without omitting
the original form itself.

It may therefore be thought that the best solution is simply to
apply the human brain to the problem initially, and to use it to
ascribe particular forms to particular roots. This was the solution
adopted in the case law project at the Southwestern Legal Foundation.[31] This technique has the advantage of allowing the application
of human intelligence at the compilation stage which enables the
problem of irregular verbs and alphabetic isolation to be overcome.

[31] Wilson, 'Computer Retrieval of Case Law', 16 *Southwestern L.J.*, 409 (1962).

It suffers, however, from inflexibility at the stage of application. Thus in many contexts all grammatical variations may be required, but in others only a few. Suppose the problem to involve the legality of 'loss leaders', it would be superfluous to recover references to 'lost leaders'.

At the time of devising my own system no automatic interactive system was available to me, and a clumsy approach by way of correspondence was adopted. This involved the suggestion of grammatical variations to the searchers and their signification of their acceptance or rejection of the suggestions. The suggestions were made on the basis of a list previously compiled by human brain power. This solution would now be much more easily applied in a modern system. The user would simply specify the conventional word in its standard, or indeed any, form, and the system would automatically display all the variations of that word which he could then accept or reject.

This would probably render unnecessary the use of any truncation technique, but if it were decided to employ one for some reason, it too could operate in a similar manner by displaying to the user the effects of any particular truncation in terms of the words which would be caught by it, and the user could then pick and choose among these in the same way. In either case it would be simple to restrict the display to words which actually occurred in the data-base in question. In some foreign languages this is a much more serious problem and requires special treatment.[32] Thus in Hebrew there can be over five thousand variant forms of the same verb in only one of its seven modes. There are further problems in that variant forms are scattered at random throughout the alphabet, and homography is rife. Clearly very sophisticated techniques are required, but even there the basic philosophy has been adopted of using the computer to suggest forms to the user who ultimately chooses by using his own brain.

The remaining four types of necessary addition fall into two pairs, synonyms and antonyms, and particularizations and generalizations. These two pairs have a good deal in common with each other but differ in important respects, and will be discussed separately here though they are not always distinguished.

So far as synonyms and antonyms are concerned, the reason for

[32] Fraenkel, 'Full Text Document Retrieval', Proceedings of ACM Symposium on Information Storage and Retrieval, April 1971.

requiring some such facility is obvious: the computer will unless instructed to the contrary treat 'child', 'minor', 'infant', 'boy', 'girl', 'teenager' and 'adolescent' as separate and unconnected words. It is necessary also to include antonyms since a negative characterization of a concept may be employed for emphasis, precision, irony or simply variety. It might be thought that the problem could be solved by searching for synonyms together with some separate indication of negation. This would indeed be possible were it not for the fact that many systems which exclude common words for retrieval purposes include among their number such common negatives as 'no', 'not' and 'none'. There is an immediate difficulty in that there are no well established conventional legal reference works listing synonyms and antonyms, and many legal terms are omitted from the more common general purpose lists such as Roget and Webster.

Here too, however, something must clearly be done since lawyers cannot be expected to think of all possible synonyms and antonyms unaided, and even if they could the task would be extremely difficult, time-consuming and totally unacceptable. It would also be uneconomic since it would be performed reiteratively both by the same lawyers who could not be expected to remember their previous efforts, and by others since the efforts of one would not be available to the rest. One possible solution would be to eliminate so far as possible synonyms from legal language. This would, in effect, be to apply to case law a more rigid form of the convention that applies within a given piece of legislation. It is unacceptable as an artificial constraint upon judicial freedom which would inhibit the development of the common law which depends upon the ebb and flow of analogy and distinction. This solution is therefore rejected.

A further possibility would be to leave the judges free to cast their judgements in any terms they chose, but to store all references to synonyms under one heading. This might entail the use of a table of synonyms to convert the language of the original text and the language of the search question to a 'normalized' form. In essence it would be the transfer of Wilson's approach to the grammatical variation problem to the problem of synonyms. Such a system is indeed employed by the Supreme Court of Cassation in Rome which translates its data-base into 2,500 such key concepts automatically. The same basic comment may be made here also, namely that such a system is inflexible in operation. It necessarily treats words as being always and everywhere either synonymous or antonymous. This is simply unacceptable since in fact synonymity is heavily dependent upon context. In the example given earlier of the various synonyms for young children it is particularly obvious. For some legal purposes, say the law of contract, 'boy' is synonymous with 'girl' just because there is no need to distinguish on the basis of sex. But in Family Law or Criminal Law these terms are by no means synonymous, nor are they antonymous, they simply belong to different categories. Even more extreme examples of contextual synonymity can be imagined. That words can be synonymous in one context and not in another should come as no surprise. If two word forms are different they are likely to be retained in the language only if they sometimes to some extent perform different functions, and thus have slightly different nuances of connotation. It is indeed doubtful if any two words are always perfect synonyms wherever they appear. Certainly this will be the exception and not the rule. So any inflexible system must be rejected.

It is possible, however, that within particular branches of the law some invariable synonymity might obtain. The Wilson technique could be applied in such cases, and I have myself experimented with such an approach in the field of the law of compensation by the state for industrial injuries. Initially searchers were asked to express all synonyms they could think of, or find with the aid of general purpose works. Then where terms appeared in more than one list the additional terms were suggested to the original compilers. Thus if there were two such lists, one consisting of terms A, B and C, and another consisting of C, D and E, the first compiler would be asked if he wished to include terms D and E, and the second if he wished to include A and B. In this way it was gradually possible to build up lists of synonyms expressing particular concepts in that field. It proved too laborious to complete as a manual experiment. The use of interactive techniques would facilitate the task though it would still involve substantial programming.

Attempts have been made to perform a rather similar task semi-automatically. These have been largely developed by Professors Lyons and Kayton at George Washington University,[33] and although not all the detail has been divulged for commercial reasons it seems

[33] Kayton, 'Use of Digital Computers to Retrieve Case Law', 1965 M.U.L.L. 120; Retrieving Case Law by Computer; Fact, Fiction and Future', 35 George Washington L.T., 1 (1966). These techniques have been adopted by the University of Montreal in their 'Datum' system, see MacKaay 'La crèation d'un Thésaurus bilingue pour DATUM,' 6 R.J.T. 51 (1971) and Schwab 'La réalisation du thésaurus-s et du thésaurus-g'. 6 R.J. T.69 (1971).

to depend very largely upon the use of the association factor as described by Stiles.[34] This is an expensive and complicated technique, and can only be justified by the results it achieves. It depends for its efficiency upon a number of conditions. First, that the area chosen for application is one where synonymity is stable; secondly, that the verbal style of all the documents is similar; and thirdly, that this style is indeed responsive to association techniques, in particular that synonyms are never themselves associated in the original data. It is thought highly dubious that these conditions prevail in any practical legal areas, and in particular that it is indeed characteristic of reports in the field of case law to associate synonyms in the same document for the reasons stated earlier.

It should perhaps be mentioned here that very similar problems arise in relation to mis-spellings, archaic forms and foreign language variants. These can often be treated exactly as if they were synonyms, though of course they are slightly different. Mis-spellings are perhaps the most exact synonyms of all, at least once they have been accurately ascribed to a particular word, and if they do not constitute the mis-spelling of any other word. So far as historical and linguistic variations are concerned it is necessary to be more careful. Legal rules are artefacts, and the terms they employ reflect the structure of the law. Over a period of time and between different systems these structures will differ. Languages too are artefacts and subtle variations of meaning obtain between words, especially those which are older and of a non-technical nature, even though their central meanings are similar. It is partly for this reason that the automatic translation of technical reports tends to be more satisfactory than the automatic translation of poetry. Law may not be poetry but it shares similar characteristics rebarbative to mechanical translation.

The last avenue for amplification to be discussed here is that of the addition of particulars and generalizations. This is perhaps the most difficult and least explored of all linguistic problems in law. It applies both to technical and non-technical words. 'Crime' is a very general technical word, for example, comprehending hundreds of different specific offences. 'Unreasonable' is a very general non-technical word which frequently appears in legal rules and clearly comprehends an infinite variety of different sets of particulars. Legal concepts express levels of generality which are relatively well estab-

[34] 'The Association Factor in Information Retrieval', 8 *J.A.C.M.*, 271 (1961).

lished, and tend to be utilized in the conventional statements of legal rules. They vary in their level of generality according to the purpose of the rule in question. Thus rules intended to establish fundamental principles, like the wide ratio of Lord Atkin in *Donoghue* v. *Stevenson*,[35] tend to be cast in more general terms than a rule intended only to state the liability of tin-kettle manufacturers. In case law, however, the intention of the framer of the rule is not necessarily decisive of the extent of its application. Thus a rule laid down and intended only for tin-kettle manufacturers can by subsequent interpretation and extension become authoritative over a much wider field, for manufacturers generally, for example.

The situation is, of course, different in systems with a controlled vocabulary where there is no difficulty in constructing hierarchical relationships between terms, or in programming a computer system to insert them automatically.[36] Very sophisticated programming might be able to make some contribution in the area of uncontrolled vocabulary. Thus it might be possible to prepare for each word a comprehensive list of other thesaurus groups of synonyms and antonyms which could in some contexts amount to particularizations or generalizations of that word. The computer could then be programmed to display these groups for each of the words specified in the search, and the user could indicate which he wanted included. But even this would probably be too unwieldy since the number and length of such lists would be enormous. Thus some more restrictive scheme limited to particular contexts would probably have to be introduced. But this would add enormously to the complexity of both the preparatory and retrieval phases of the operation, and would still be likely to be unsatisfactory. The trouble is that some words are of such generality that the list of all possible particulars even in a limited legal context would in all circumstances be too large, and conversely some words are of such particularity that they could be assumed under a correspondingly over-large array of generalities. At present it seems that this is a further area where there is no adequate substitute for the human brain. The lawyer must do his best to hit the right level of generality in his choice of words, and then proceed either to increase or decrease it in the light of the response he is getting from the system. At least the more flexible response of modern conversational systems should render

---

[35] [1932] A.C. 562.
[36] This is a feature of many European systems, CRIDON for example.

this a quicker and less tedious exercise in the future than it has been in the past. Here too then the dividend paid by the computer will depend upon the skill of the human user in choosing his terms.

Conduct of searches: As explained earlier, in addition to the intellectual difficulty of framing productive searches, the lawyer is also likely to experience some more practical administrative difficulties in adjusting his work flow to the demands of computer techniques. The first problem here was that if a large central computer were used for batch processing of enquiries the lawyer would be required to deal with his problem in at least two different stages. The first would involve the analysis of the problem and the selection of the search terms, and the second the consideration of the documents retrieved by the computer and their use in resolving the original legal problem. In fact as the batch system is refined so as to make it more efficient, by the use of pre-editing techniques for example, this problem is likely to become even more severe, as between these two stages the lawyer is likely to be approached with suggestions for amending his search terms in the hope of reducing the amount of irrelevant material retrieved. Similarly with post-editing, while it is true that the post-editor may be able to use his own unaided judgement to reject obviously and totally irrelevant documents, he might still do a more effective job if he discusses the principles he is adopting with the original searcher. In the LITE system for example this is commonly done over the telephone. Another method of improving the efficiency of a batch system is to conduct a number of runs over a short period of time on progressively amended versions of the question; this is possible on the CREDOC system for example. But, of course, to be effective such a system requires that the original lawyer should amend his search terms several times in the same day in the light of the system's responses. This will clearly impose a heavy burden upon him. These are clearly unsatisfactory and second-best attempts to overcome the disadvantages of the batch approach from the point of view of quality without incurring the increased cost of an on-line approach.

There are, however, at least two other uses of batch techniques which do not exhibit these disadvantages. The first is a method of attempting to regulate in advance the results of a batch system without further reference to the user. This involves asking him to specify in advance certain statistical criteria which responses must satisfy before they are remitted to him. Thus he might require remission of responses only if they yield less than a certain number of references, or perhaps less than a certain proportion of the total collection. It would be more rare for the lawyer to set a positive threshold that must be attained since the certainty that no documents satisfy a given search formulation is an extremely valuable result in most contexts, and one indeed not readily attainable otherwise than by the use of computerized techniques. It is, of course, theoretically possible for the disadvantages mentioned earlier to be overcome in this way. Thus the lawyer might draft a number of different searches in advance and specify criteria upon which the successive running of them should depend. But this would involve such a level of prior analysis and forethought as to be likely to render the computer application unacceptable.

The second approach is that devised by Dr Luhn of International Business Machines and known as Keyword in Context or KWIC. This involves the use of the computer as an indirect search aid by using it to compile a new sort of conventional research tool, often indeed an ordinary printed book. What happens here is that the compiler of the information selects a number of key terms which characterize the area of law in which he is interested, or which exhaust the interest of a particular data-base. The computer then searches for these terms, and prints out both the terms, in the middle of the page, and a part of the surrounding context. The amount of surrounding text to be printed is variable, and depends upon the needs of the particular compiler, as do questions of whether it is to be measured in characters, words or sentences. In many such compilations the key terms are printed in bold and the context in plain. Usually the key terms are arranged alphabetically and the extracts in the running order of the original text, but all this is optional. The advantage of such an approach is in the integration of the index with the text in effect, so as to permit index reference and a sort of text browsing simultaneously. It is relatively easy and reasonably cheap to compile such documents on the computer, and they are regarded as exceptionally useful by those with access to them in existing systems such as LITE. The main difficulty is that if either the list of key terms or the body of basic data is very substantial they can become extremely bulky tomes whose size alone makes them difficult to use. They could clearly not be contemplated for general purpose case law

F*

systems, but might be useful for giving access to specialized series of reports. They also illustrate the usefulness of some off-line applications for some legal purposes.

No off-line batch processing system therefore completely meets the problem of excessive duplication of the lawyer's work on a case. This problem is, however, completely solved by the use of a conversational on-line system. These may naturally be of many different types, depending upon the particular computer, terminal system and operating system employed. An important difference is that between teletype terminals which operate in a way rather like a two-way telex, and produce output typed on a continuous sheet of paper, and video display units which present the information upon a screen like a television screen.

In general the video system is easier to use, partly because more information can be readily assimilated at any one time, partly because it can be formatted more flexibly for particular uses, and partly because of the use of the visual cursor to direct attention to the appropriate place. This makes it less likely for the user to mistype his information, or at least more likely that he will notice such mis-typing when it occurs, which is especially useful for lawyer users who are not accomplished keyboard operators. A further reason for the greater ease of using the video system is that it makes modification of the question a much simpler operation. On a teletype system some method must be devised for specifying particular characters or words to be amended or deleted, and then of specifying the corrections and what it is they are correcting. With a cursor, or better still a light pen, there is no need for any such elaboration. All that is necessary is the simple over-writing of the incorrect information with the correct information.

So far as the convenience of terminals for conducting searches is concerned, the three different stages of input, modification and output require separate treatment. At the input stage the first task is the selection of the appropriate subdivision of the data-base where the system provides this facility. Next the lawyer must type in the relevant words, abbreviated or truncated as the system demands, and must signify in the appropriate manner the logical or other associations required between them. A further point to be remembered here is that it is at this stage that in the more sophisticated systems the various methods of enriching the question come into play. Once again display on a video screen is vastly advantageous since it permits very fast and precise response without the need for any complicated signalling.

This naturally leads on to the second aspect of the conduct of a search, namely its modification in the light of the provisional responses made by the computer. Here the problem arises of the response which the computer should be programmed to make to search requests, and it is by no means completely distinct from the problem of search enrichment, the only difference being that at the input stage the enrichment takes place *a priori* as it were, and at the modification stage *a posteriori*. The question is what sort of cue the system should provide for the user. Undoubtedly the most common system used at present is a simple count of the number of documents which satisfy the search criteria as originally specified. This is useful since the user can add further terms if the number is unacceptably large, and eliminate them if it is unacceptably small.

A further alternative is for the user to operate the system in reverse as it were. He might know of one case on his topic but wish to find other similar ones. In some systems, like that of Unidata for example, he could do this directly by simply requesting all cases similar to a given one, whereupon the vector technique would come into play and the degree of similarity could be precisely prescribed. In the more common systems this is not possible directly, but some degree of indirect simulation of that technique can be managed. Thus the user might first request the display of the full text of the case he has chosen as his model, and might then underline certain words with a light pen for example, and the system might be able to formulate the search for him by detecting the logical pattern exhibited by these terms in the given case. This would, however, require very complicated programming except for the most simple searches, and it would probably be better to leave the logical and associational combination to the user to determine in the ordinary way. Thereafter the search could be modified in the way described earlier.

Thus the system can be used to help the user by giving him a choice of further words to use to amplify his search at the input stage, or by indicating the number of documents provisionally re-trieved at the modification stage with the further facility of displaying the text, or part of the text, of any such documents. Could anything more be done? At present it is not easy to give an answer to this question, in law at least, since so little research seems to have been directed at the problem. In principle a number of possibilities seem open.

One difficulty is that a display of the number of documents retrieved by itself gives no clue of the likely variation in the event of any particular modification of the search pattern. This, at least, should be capable of being remedied. If too few documents have been retrieved, it should be possible for the computer to indicate how the numbers would change with the elimination of any particular conjoined terms. Suppose a search were conducted to retrieve documents containing a combination of word groups, A, B, C and D and the result was that no documents were retrieved as containing words from all four groups. The computer should be able to inform the questioner that A, B, and C would yield a hundred documents, A, C and D eighty, and B, C and D perhaps five. This would clearly give some assistance in deciding upon the best modification. It ought also to be possible, though the programming might be more complicated, to do the same for variation of the scheme of logical or other relations. The advantage of all such techniques would be that the user would be presented with more useful information in the light of which to modify his search than he could get from unaided introspection. Any such techniques could, of course, operate in conjunction with modification in the light of scanning the original output.

It should also be possible to combine citation indexing with schemes for modification. In such a system the user might first formulate his search, receive his responses, verify that they were indeed relevant, and then ask for further cases in which the response cases were cited, or which themselves cited the response cases, and these could then be displayed for a decision as to their relevance. Similarly, where the full text has been amplified by reference to works of authority or commentaries, and if these are also held in displayable form, then they too could be listed, and if necessary displayed, for the user. With such facilities the terminal system would really come close to simulating the facilities likely to be used by the lawyer in the library, in addition to providing the services which only the computer can supply.

A further possibility lies in the re-use at this stage of the enrichment facilities described earlier. Thus it was suggested that it might be possible to arrange for the user to be prompted in his original search formulation by the listing of, for example, synonyms of the terms originally chosen. It would be possible for the computer to search on the basis of such synonyms even though the user should not have requested them, and suppress the results until they were asked for at this stage. Such a scheme could also operate on the self-monitoring basis described above in connection with the different logical and associational criteria.

Some use might also be made of the system of subdivision of the data-base in this connection. Suppose that the data-base is divided by reference to geographical and jurisdictional subdivisions like the states in the United States. It would be possible to associate the subdivisions in an interlocking way. Thus on a crude geographical basis contiguous states might be linked. The effect of such linking might be that if on the self-monitoring basis described above the state subdivision actually requested were giving a deficient response, say on Ohio case law, then the computer would, if it found Indiana and Pennsylvania were giving a better result, keep on searching these, and would be in a position to display these results if the user were interested. There would clearly be many different ways of combining such subdivisions.

It should also be possible to develop a self-regulating system for search modification. Thus the computer could gradually build up a store of successful modifications of particular search patterns, and also of unsuccessful ones. Such a store could also be used to suggest possible modifications of the original search to the user. Indeed this is really only an amplification of the technique already suggested for the enrichment of the original input terms.

There are doubtless many other and more sophisticated systems which might be suggested, though it is thought that the list sketched out above would add greatly to the power and acceptability of any system so far operational. Unfortunately it has not yet proved possible to test such a belief by hard experiment, and in its absence this must remain a matter for speculation. One further and final point is that any such techniques depend for their point on making things easier for the user, and they should be kept under constant review so that they can be changed both in response to the views of users, and even more important their practice in using an operational system.

Finally there is the question of output. In some cases the teletype or video display will prove sufficient. But to the extent that one of the reasons for adopting a computerized system is a desire to expand the lawyer's range of possible reference this may not be enough. Indeed one criterion for putting data into the system may be that it is in demand, but cannot be made generally accessible so cheaply in any other way. It would be exasperating for the lawyer to be given the citation of such a relevant authority and nothing more. For this reason it is desirable to have some device associated with the terminal for producing a hard copy version of the information displayed. The main disadvantage of this is that it is an uneconomic use of the terminal to have it occupied with the provision of hard copy print-out if there are a large number of long cases to be produced in full-text versions. An alternative system is for the provision of micro-form versions of otherwise inaccessible materials to the user. In some systems, though none are yet in use in the legal field, these versions can be linked automatically with the terminal so that the micro-form version can be displayed on the screen. One advantage of such a system from the point of view of the computer system is that it relieves it of the necessity to store the full-text for display purposes. Indeed it is this sort of saving in storage which dictates its use in the scientific environment, though there the saving is greater since the computer system will only be storing an indexed version of the original, whereas in a full-text legal system the minimum store is of a concordance of the non-common words. From the lawyer's point of view, however, there is still the difficulty that in such a system the terminal is being used uneconomically for display purposes. Here, however, there is a simple solution. It is to provide the office with a cheap and simple micro-form viewer as well as a computer terminal. In batch systems there is no difficulty in this respect since the central computer can either be used to drive a very fast off-line printer, or alternatively, as in the CREDOC system, copies can be provided by means of the ordinary commercial copying devices if required.

6

Computers and case law: experiments

This chapter will consider some experimental testing of the theory advanced in chapter five. It will first set out some of the difficulties which confronted the early workers, and will then go on to consider experimental design and results, largely in the light of my own work, for the reasons which will be given.

1 EARLY DEVELOPMENTS

There are, of course, many possible aims of research in the field of case law. In the early years, the period up to about 1967, it was relatively novel to think of applying computers to non-numeric tasks, and the main aim of the work was simply to demonstrate the feasibility of using computerized methods to retrieve legal information. In such experiments it was necessary to devote a great deal of effort to programming work. These difficulties were exacerbated by the limitations of the computers upon which most of the researchers were working. The central processors were by modern standards extremely slow and small, and without the benefit of mass secondary storage in random access devices or any sort of facilities for on-line operation. It is surprising in the circumstances that so many of the views expressed and attitudes taken at that time seem still valid today. The result, however, was the expenditure of a disproportionate amount of time, energy, money and ingenuity on simply making the system work. It should also be noted that at that time the manufacturers were completely unable to supply the packaged programmes in these areas which are now so much in evidence. This in its turn led to the adoption of very low level programming languages as the programmers tried to wring the last drop of capacity from the computers. All this has now changed, and continues to change progressively. Each development feeds the next. The central processors have become increasingly more powerful, and have indeed tended to outstrip the demands that users can make of their facilities. They are supported by very fast and immense secondary storage which can handle virtually any amount of data required. The manufacturers have developed operating systems which allow simultaneous use of the computer to a variety of users engaged upon a variety of tasks. The programming languages are infinitely more sophisticated and reliable, and there are specially written 'packages' of programmes which will perform many of the tasks lawyers demand of the computer with the very minimum of modification. All this has freed the experimental worker from the bondage of devoting most of his resources to making the system work. That is now assumed.

Even in the earliest work there were of course some further aims, albeit limited, since they were legal experiments and not just experiments in non-numerical computing. In general the aim was to compare the performance of the existing conventional systems. This remains an important part of modern experimentation, but has become more sophisticated in the range and subtlety of the comparisons made and in the comparison of different computer approaches. It is now broadly accepted that computers can be used to find relevant authorities, and enquiry has switched to discovering which techniques are most efficient and acceptable, and to measuring these criteria more scientifically. The main change has been a recession from the rather crude global attitude that something valid can be said about the general efficiency of universal computer techniques for all types of legal information retrieval in every different area of law, towards the isolation of different variables, and a more intensive examination of their effects.

An enormous amount still remains to be done, indeed the surface has been little more than scratched, largely owing to the practical difficulties which have so far impeded experimental work. The greatest practical obstacle has not generally been the inaccessibility, or even the enormous expense, of computing facilities, since in the university environment at least these tend to be readily available and at no, or nominal, cost. It has rather been the inaccessibility of the legal data-base in a machine assimilable form. Legal materials had never been prepared in a way amenable to computer assimilation for the very good reason that computers had not been invented for most of the time, and for the rest their use had not been anticipated. Even now few legal publishers see either need or advantage in so preparing their publications. Thus the greatest practical difficulty for the early workers was the conversion of the conventional legal data-base into a machine assimilable form. This factor itself made indexed or keyword systems more eligible since the volume of transcription required was vastly less than in a full-text system.

Transcription typically took the form of keyboarding the relevant text on to punched cards or paper tape. This involved the employment of a good deal of unskilled clerical labour, and very diligent checking to make sure that the text was accurately transcribed. The administration of this side of the work tended to absorb a further disproportionate amount of time and ingenuity. It is a great tribute to Professor Horty that in the very earliest days he was far-sighted enough to see that these problems were worth overcoming in the interest of long-term advantage. But for him, the technique of full-text applications might never have been pursued, but left to founder in a morass of financial and administrative difficulties. Here too in more recent times there has been a progressive reduction in the degree of difficulty involved. Once a given data-base has been satisfactorily prepared in a computer assimilable form, it is a relatively cheap and easy matter to copy it, so any new research should have no difficulty to that extent by making use of the work which has already been completed. In any event the task of transcription has been eased by the development, first of devices able to perform optical character recognition of a limited range of typefaces, which permits greater speed and simplicity in the process of transcription, and latterly of devices able to perform optical character recognition of a greatly extended range of fonts so as to permit some legal text to be assimilated straight from the printed page. Possibly more important still has been the development of computer typesetting techniques which will make it increasingly likely that a corrected original tape of legal materials may be available for use for research workers. At present such tapes are not available in the field of case law to any significant extent, but legislation is increasingly becoming available in this form,[1] and there is every reason to suppose that case law will eventually follow suit. Thus for the research worker of today, or tomorrow at the latest, who does not wish to expend a high proportion of his research funds and time in the production of

[1] Federal legislation in the United States is already available in this form, and the British Stationery Office has similar plans for statutes.

his own data-base, there are three possibilities : he can copy an existing data-base, he can conduct an optical character recognition operation on archive material, or he can use a tape prepared for typesetting new material.

2 EXPERIMENTAL DESIGN

The question then arises of how the research data-base is to be selected and prepared. This must clearly depend upon the aim of the particular experiment in question, and the way in which it is proposed to conduct it. As an example of the sort of questions which arise in the design of a legal information retrieval experiment in the field of case law I shall use my own work, not because it is in any sense a model but simply because it is best known to me. Other workers will naturally be concerned with different problems and will need to deal with them in different ways, but many of the questions and decisions are likely to be sufficiently similar for it to be worth spending a little time in describing the process of designing this particular experiment.

Data-base

Its aim was rather ambitious, almost certainly over-ambitious given the limitations of the technology in the early 1960s when it was devised, and of the budget within which it had to be financed. It was generally concerned to measure the efficiency of computerized legal information retrieval as compared with conventional techniques, and further to test whether this efficiency depended, and if so to what extent, upon the type of case law data-base selected, or the particular form of the text. For this reason the data-base was divided into two contrasting parts. The first was a general series of reports of decisions in the High Court, the All England Law Reports. The second was a series of administrative decisions in the field of insurance claims for industrial injuries, the Commissioners' Decisions. The choice of these two particular series was dictated by a number of factors connected with the aims of the experiment.

The main consideration was that they were at opposite ends of the form spectrum. The All England Reports is a very typical general series. It comprises a selection of decisions at every level by every type of higher Court and in every area of law. The individual reports tend to be discursive, but subject to that general characteristic are relatively heterogeneous in form, including lengthy reports of decisions in the House of Lords with a multiplicity of judgements and brief notes of decisions by a single judge sitting without a jury in the Chancery Division. The general format is, however, the same for all, namely title, telegraphic abstract, headnote incorporating references to Halsbury's Laws, and the text of the decision, sometimes with the facts stated separately and sometimes in the judgements. This set of reports does not include reports of the arguments of counsel. The Commissioners' Decisions are quite different. They all deal with the application of a very limited range of statutory provisions, and are almost all decided by specialist judges who deal with nothing else. They tend to be very homogenous in form, and that form is much more concise than that of judgements in general case law, perhaps because all the questions do arise on the construction of limited provisions. Their general format is, however, similar to that of the general reports except that the telegraphic abstract is much shorter, and is indeed occasionally omitted altogether, and there is generally only one judgement divided into numbered paragraphs, though the numbering has little significance and is indeed no longer unknown in general case reports. Quite apart from these general differences there were two specific points of contrast of special importance from the point of view of the retrieval experiments.

The first has been already indicated implicitly. It is that the vocabulary of the general set of case reports is much larger than that of the specialized decisions.[2] As stated, the cases deal with all types of law and all types of jurisdiction. The decisions are taken from the tiny segment of industrial injuries. The result from the information retrieval point of view is that in searching the former, using a natural language or free vocabulary approach, the danger of ambiguity is especially great, particularly between legal concepts. Thus in some cases 'election' might relate to a parliamentary election, as in a case dealing with an election petition, whereas in others the same word might signify the equitable doctrine of election, as in a case arising on the construction of a will. There is further in the cases a greater chance of ambiguity between a proper name and a legal concept. Thus one of the parties to a case might be called 'Wills'. There is the further possibility that a given set of facts might appear in any one of a number of legal contexts. Thus a motorcar

[2] From this point on, 'cases' refers to the general series, and 'decisions' to the limited series.

accident might be reported in the context of criminal law, the law of torts, or the law of insurance. Thus a search based simply on the specification of the factual elements in the situation would be unlikely to be sufficiently discriminating. These features of case law maximize the danger of retrieving irrelevant documents on the basis of the occurence in them of such ambiguous search terms. The danger is much less in the decision reports, partly because only one major area of law is involved so both legal and factual searches are unlikely to be ambiguous, and partly because the tone is more impersonal with the decisions numbered rather than titled and the parties referred to by occupation more often than by name. These factors do not eliminate the danger completely, but they do reduce it substantially by comparison with the case reports.

There is, however, a compensating danger with the decisions. Just because the vocabulary is limited and all the decisions are in the same basic area, there is a chance that unless extremely meticulously drafted the search will retrieve far too many remotely relevant documents. This danger will arise largely because of the choice of search terms of too high a degree of generality, and the consequent appearance of these terms in far too many documents in the data-base. This is clearly not so great a danger in relation to the general case reports since it is highly unlikely that anyone would search by reference to terms sufficiently general in such a collection; they would need to be at the level of 'legal remedy' for example to be in danger of having comparable effects. These considerations tend to suggest that the best chances of success are likely to be achieved in the case reports by searches employing legal terms, and characterizing legal concepts, while in the decisions it might be preferable to choose words expressing fine factual distinctions.

The second principal difference between these two data-bases relates not to the data itself but to the means of securing access to it. The general series of reports is, of course, indexed both for the volume in which it is bound and for the general series in which it appears. The general index is cumulated each year by the addition of the volume indexes for the volumes which have been published in that year. The index terms are in fact taken from the telegraphic abstract printed beneath the title in the main body of the report. The cases are also, like most other legal materials in the field of case law, indexed by reference to their citation of and by other cases. These are conventional indexes maintained by the publishers. In addition, and much more importantly in practice, access to the reports is secured by their use as authority in textbooks, encyclopaedias and periodicals. It is a curious feature of such books, especially those intended for practitioners, that the text is in effect an extended index to the primary sources which are cited as authority for the propositions contained in the text. The reason is that those citations are to materials which are accepted as primary sources, and do determine the outcome of litigation. The textbook is *about* the law; the materials it cites in justification *constitute* the law. In practice the cumulative indexes to series of reports as produced by the publishers of law reports are used very little, and certainly exhibit a number of defects.

The indexing of the decisions is, however, very different. The volume of material is very much less for one thing. The preparation for the computer of twelve years' output of decisions amounted to no more than one million text words, while one year's output of the All England Reports amounted to very nearly two million words. The decisions are not indexed by individual volume except in the most cursory way, but instead a loose-leaf index is maintained as the decisions multiply. This is an extremely detailed and thoroughly cross-referenced index, reproducing indeed a very high proportion of the original headnotes. It is also very heavily orientated towards the factual situations occurring in the problems on account of the considerations mentioned earlier. This index is used by practitioners and has a relatively high reputation. It should also be mentioned that the topic of insurance claims for industrial injuries benefits is one which is not very fully covered in the ordinary encyclopaedias and textbooks, so the amount of indirect indexing in those ways is, by contrast with general case law, extremely limited.

These two features largely dictated the choice of data-base for the experiment since they accentuated two important variables for retrieval purposes: the comparative efficiency of conventional methods and the comparative effects of different vocabularies.

Evaluation
Experiments test hypotheses. Here the hypothesis was that computerized searching of the full natural language of the text of case law by questions cast in free form was a feasible method of selecting cases for reading with a view to citation. The somewhat lame conclusion was dictated by the limited technology available at the time,

and in particular the unavailability of video display facilities or on-line operations of any sort. Had these been available the research could have aimed at the real end of the enquiry situation, namely the selection of cases to cite.

Two special features of case law were of some assistance in designing the conduct of the experiment. The first is the practice of the internal citation of authority which is characteristic of common law jurisdictions. This had been a factor militating strongly towards the selection of case law as the data-base for the experiments. Case law is an environment in which retrieval is constantly being carried out in real life by conventional means, and where the results are easily discoverable. The advantage of this is that artificially contrived experiments and arbitrary judgements for the purposes of the experiment can be largely eliminated. It was possible to select as experimental problems situations which had actually occurred, and for which there was documentary evidence of the results of an independent conventional search. This enables two dangers to be avoided. The first is the selection of problems which are orientated excessively towards the research which is being carried out. Thus in the area of statute law research for example, in some experiments questions were framed in such broad terms that it was hardly surprising that conventional research could not find all the relevant provisions, nor that so few of the provisions found by the computer were irrelevant. There is no dishonesty in this. It is just that specifically statutory research is rarely undertaken, and when it is, only by a very special sort of lawyer whose knowledge is such that the questions he might ask would probably not be at all suitable for experimental purposes. The consequence is that the research workers have to make up their own questions, which are inevitably somewhat artificial and tend to reflect their own approach which is also reflected in the design of the computer system, and thus the system starts with an unfair advantage. The second problem, which is reduced by choosing case law for the experiments, is that of determining the relevance of the materials retrieved. This assumes much less importance. The acute difficulties in arriving at an objective judgement of relevance within the purely research environment is well illustrated by the results of the joint American Bar Foundation and International Business Machines experiment.[3] There the differences in evaluation were critical. The four evaluators differed in

[3] Eldridge, 'An Appraisal of a Case-law Retrieval Project', Computers and the Law Conference Proceedings, Kingston, Ontario, 1968.

almost two-thirds of the cases submitted to them,[4] and in over one-tenth of such cases[5] each evaluator gave a different one of the four possible grades. In fact the evaluators were able to agree on a positive grade in only about 3 per cent of the cases submitted to them.[6] It is interesting to note that in that experiment the two dangers were regarded as mutually dependent in that the differences of evaluation were related to a bias in the choice of questions towards the sphere of only one-half of the panel of evaluators, because all the questions were taken from practice whereas two of the evaluators were not practitioners but academics.

The method chosen to minimize these difficulties in my own work was to select the data-base from a period in the then recent past, near enough to the present for most of the law to remain in force but old enough for subsequent cases to have been reported which cite cases in the data-base. Such subsequent cases were then isolated, and their facts used as the sample problems. It was thus known that they were real problems which had actually occurred, and it was known that relevant material existed in the data-base, because it was assumed that if a case were cited in another then it was in fact relevant to it. The converse assumption, that if a case were not cited it was not relevant, could not of course be made without assuming conventional research methods to be infallible. Thus to that limited extent it was necessary to court the dangers of evaluation encountered by the American Bar Foundation experiment. In fact the assumption that a cited case is relevant to the case in which it is cited is true only to the extent that the facts of the citing case clearly raise the issue upon which the case is cited. In the experiment it was found that a number of problems had to be re-drafted to cater for this situation. By accident a further and still more reliably relevant group of cases emerged in the course of the experiment. It transpired that within the data-base itself, and especially the decisions segment since it covered a period of twelve years, there was a certain amount of internal citation, so that in some instances the case which was used as the basis of the problem not only cited a case on the data-base but was itself to be found in the data-base. In other words the searchers were in such cases being asked to find the case upon which the problem had been based.

The second major feature of case law which was of assistance in

---

[4] 464 out of 706 i.e. 65.7 per cent
[5] 51 out of 464 i.e. 11 per cent
[6] 21 out of 706 i.e. 3 per cent

designing the experiment was the internal division of the format into three sub-categories, namely the telegraphic abstracts, the headnote and the full-text. This allowed comparison between computer retrieval performance in the three categories, and the hypothesis that full-text will give a better result to be tested. However, two comments should be made about this. First, neither the telegraphic abstract nor the summaries in the headnote were originally prepared with retrieval operations in mind. It is true that the initial terms in the telegraphic abstract are a partial exception to this. But they are designed for retrieval only through the medium of the classified index which they help to constitute, and not independently. The rest of the terms which appear in the telegraphic abstract are intended only to indicate the content of the main document once the abstract has been found, and not to provide a means of getting access to the main document. Similarly the headnote has no other function than to summarize the full-text, and would no doubt have been organized and arranged in a different way if intended instead for retrieval purposes. These factors were exacerbated in the experiments because for reasons of time and expense it was not possible to provide searches orientated specially towards keyword or summary formats, and such comparisons as may be made between results in respect of the different formats must be understood with this reservation in mind. It is possible that searches drafted with a view to a keyword data-base would have been quite differently structured. Thus the telegraphic abstracts have no sentence structure, and hence many of the refinements of the full-text search become meaningless in that context. This is much less true of the headnotes, and comparisons between results based upon them and upon the full-text are probably valid. Headnotes do have a sentence structure and a free vocabulary like the full-text, and it is difficult to imagine what major differences of approach could be adopted for searches specifically orientated towards them. The second necessary comment is that here too if an experiment were being designed today it would probably not stop short at the full-text level, but would also include the sort of further information indicated earlier as appropriate additional material to constitute an amplified full-text version. In a sense the telegraphic abstract and the references to Halsbury's Laws in the All England Reports amount to a primitive form of amplification, since they, and indeed the headnote, are added to the original text by the publishers. It was not, however, possible to make any special use of these additions in the experiments, and in any systematic work a much more thorough and sophisticated pattern of additions would need to be provided.

The main outlines of the experiment will now be apparent. The detailed planning was devised so as to impose as few constraints as possible upon the participants. The participants had first to be selected, then instructed, and finally set to work. Ideally, great care should be devoted to the selection of participants, but practice often falls short of perfect. Here it would be best to have a large number of participants from different backgrounds with different levels of legal and technological skills. The valuable information on evaluation standards yielded by the American Bar Foundation experiment is wholly attributable to the care with which the evaluators were selected from such different backgrounds. The practical difficulty is that participation in such experiments is a time-consuming and often unsatisfying task. Research funds rarely permit the payment of sufficiently lavish fees for participation to compete with the rewards offered by their ordinary work to those in professional practice. The inevitable result is that the director of research is left with a self-selected band of good-natured and enthusiastic volunteers, who whatever their other admirable qualities are unlikely as a group to exhibit the statistically desirable mix of qualifications and abilities, backgrounds and training.

The degree of instruction which is necessary will, of course, vary according to the aims of the particular experiment, the method it is proposed to employ to carry it out, and the abilities of the participants. In general, so far as lawyers are participating as a control group by conducting conventional searches, they should be allowed to use normal methods subject only to modification so as to prevent any distortion in the comparison of their result with that achieved by computerized techniques. Two examples may be given of the sort of distortion which can occur as a result of defects in instruction to participants. In a pilot study for my own work, I took a very limited sample of the data-base, one volume of the All England Reports in fact, and asked the participating control group doing the conventional searches to indicate which of the cases reported *in that volume* were relevant to the problems. The mistake here was to direct the attention of the searchers to the particular volume. It was true that the computer was only searching that volume, and it might thus seem only fair that the conventional searchers should do the same. But the computer search of one volume will not differ in principle from the computer search of any number of volumes, and certainly will not if the drafters of the search are given no indication either of the fact that only one volume is to be searched and of the techniques likely to succeed better in that context. But a conventional search changes its character completely if the segment of data is so narrowly specified. Thus in this case the conventional searchers were able to browse through the index to this particular volume in a depth which would certainly be unattainable in any larger volume of data. To correct this in the main experiment, participants were given no indication of the whereabouts of the chronological sample included in the data-base, and were thus unable to concentrate their searches unfairly.

A second example of the sort of difficulty that may occur, though here as a result of under- rather than over-instruction, is that conventional searchers should not be allowed to read the materials retrieved so as to form a final judgement on its relevance, even though this would be a normal practice, unless some comparable facility is allowed to the computer searchers. In my own work, which was conducted in a batch-processing mode, there was no facility for the computer searchers to edit the output of the machine, and therefore the conventional searchers were cut off in their research at an earlier stag than normal. Nevertheless, since this was a stage which they would in the ordinary way pass through, it was not thought to be a major flaw in the experimental design. As remarked earlier, the existence of more modern retrieval systems should prevent this from being a problem in future work. A further point which may be relevant here, at least for the near future, is that it is highly unlikely that any of the participants will be as skilled in the use of computer techniques as in the conventional ones which they will have been using all their professional lives. It is unlikely that a crash course in computer methods complete with practical hints on how to achieve the best results will entirely redress the balance. This is all the more true since so little work has been done in this area that such hints are likely to be little more than guesswork. Nevertheless it is difficult to see what else can be done at this stage of development. The only further step which must be taken is to allow for this factor in any dispassionate consideration of results.

The precise control of participants during the experiments must again depend upon its aims. In my own work, for example, I was not concerned to compare the cost or time of using computer and conventional techniques so it was not necessary to set up elaborate schemes for measuring these elements. Indeed in the early stages of experimental work it may well be better as a rule to allow participants to work in their own way without too much external control. Their methods may indeed make a significant contribution to the work by suggesting new lines of enquiry which can then be more rigorously tested in future experiments. For the same reason it is often useful to solicit suggestions from participants about the organization of the work, and in particular any suggestions which they might have for how it might be made easier and more acceptable to them. At first participants are likely to turn for help to the director of research for suggestions, but they should soon be able to manage without much assistance. The one essential of experimental method, however, is that any difference of technique adopted by individual participants should not be so significantly great as to impair the general comparison and accretion of results.

3 RESULTS

Once the experiments have been planned and conducted, the only remaining task is the compilation and presentation of results. Here once again the precise method chosen must depend upon the aims of the particular piece of work attempted. There are, of course, some general principles of statistics which must be applied to the presentation of any series of experimental results, but they will not be rehearsed here. All that is necessary is some elucidation of the two basic concepts which dominate the presentation of the results of experiments in information retrieval, and then in the light of these some attention will be paid to particular features of the results achieved in three experiments in the field of case law : my own, the American Bar Foundation's, and Professor Fraenkel's in Israel.

Precision and recall

The two basic concepts are precision and recall, or if looked at from the point of view of impediments to the success of retrieval, noise and silence. The former terms are more commonly applied in English-speaking countries, the latter in French-speaking countries. The concept of precision connotes the consistency of quality of documents retrieved. It is measured as the proportion of the documents retrieved by the system which satisfy given criteria to the total number of documents retrieved. Thus if ten documents are retrieved of which six satisfy the criteria, typically of relevance to the problem, then the figure for precision is 60 per cent. It will be seen that in this example four of the documents retrieved did not satisfy the given criteria, so the figure for noise is 40 per cent. The aim is naturally to secure as high a figure for precision, and consequently as low a figure for noise, as possible. There is, however, a countervailing factor, and that is the need also to secure as high a figure in respect of the other factor, recall, as possible. The concept of recall connotes the efficiency of the search in retrieving relevant documents. It is measured as the proportion of documents retrieved by the system which satisfy given criteria to the total number of documents in the collection which satisfy the criteria. Thus if six documents are retrieved which satisfy the criteria, typically of relevance to the problem, and there are ten such documents in the collection, then the figure for recall is 60 per cent. It will be seen that in this example four documents in the collection which did satisfy the criteria were not retrieved, so the figure for silence is 40 per cent.

To summarize, precision measures the performance of the system in avoiding the retrieval of irrelevant documents, or noise; recall measures the performance of the system in not failing to retrieve relevant documents, or silence. The aim of the system is to retrieve all the relevant documents, and only relevant documents. Both aims must be kept in view. It would be possible to maximize recall by retrieving all the documents in the collection, because in this way it would necessarily follow that all relevant documents in the collection had been retrieved, but the user would be no better off than before he started. Similarly it would be possible to maximize precision by retrieving only one relevant document no matter how many there might be in the collection so long as no irrelevant documents were retrieved at all, but here too except in very rare situations the user would be entitled to be dissatisfied. In most circumstances a balance must be struck between precision and recall. In general the two concepts tend to move in inverse relation to each other, as precision increases so recall tends to fall, and as recall increases so precision tends to fall. In each subject field, and in relation to each purpose within that field, separate judgements must be made of the relative importance of these factors. In law it seems feasible that greater importance should generally be attached to recall since it is very difficult for the lawyer to manage without all the relevant materials, while it is relatively easy for him to sort through and reject irrelevant materials, if he can be sure that all the relevant material is present. This is, however, only a general tendency, and does not hold good at the extremes. The amount of material retrieved must be of manageable proportions so as to enable it to be sifted through, and if there are a hundred cases illustrative of a particular point it will probably not be too serious if one slips through the net, and is not retrieved. Different types of search will even so require different balances. The search for a particular statutory provision obviously requires complete recall, the search for a lead into a problem requires only very low recall.

It is necessary to make three further points about the measurement of these concepts. A first general point relevant to both is that in the typical retrieval experiment a number of different searches are carried out each with its own individual result. A decision must then be made on whether the results are to be expressed in terms of an overall average, or in terms of an average of the results of the individual searches. Suppose that three searches are carried out. In the first two there is only one relevant document in the collection, and it is retrieved in each case, but in the third there are ten relevant documents of which seven are discovered. The recall figures for the three searches taken individually are therefore, 100 per cent, 100 per cent and 70 per cent, and the average of these is 90 per cent. Overall, however, nine relevant documents have been retrieved out of a total of twelve, and the recall figure calculated directly is only 75 per cent. It is necessary to bear this possibility in mind in comparing the results of different experiments since different principles might easily be applied. Provided the searches are expected to be of relatively uniform character there should be little divergence between the two approaches. In my own work the second approach was adopted in order to minimize the effects of a run of freak high or low scores by different individual searchers.

The other two points which are related to each other concern the reliance to be placed upon the exact figures calculated for recall and precision. So far as recall is concerned, the problem chiefly arises from the difficulty of establishing a reliable base figure for the total number of relevant documents in the collection upon which the percentage recall actually achieved can be calculated. It is true that by establishing either a very small data-base or an extremely stringent and totally objective criterion of relevancy this can be overcome, since in these cases it is possible to establish with some confidence what the total number of documents satisfying the relevant criterion really is. But neither is a wholly satisfactory expedient. The trouble with the first is that the smaller the data-base the less statistically reliable the results obtained by using it, since the aim is to arrive at sufficiently statistically valid results to permit the extrapolation to a wider range of case law. For such purposes the data-base must be larger than is convenient for the establishment of a universally agreed criterion of relevance to every different search for every doucument contained in it.

The second alternative is more attractive, and has great utility, especially as a check on the pattern of results obtained by the use of less stringent criteria. The difficulty is that if objectively valid criteria are exclusively employed, then the computer's ability to find further authorities which are relevant but which do not satisfy such criteria is not measured. To rely simply upon results thus calculated turns the experiment into a barren exercise in computer gymnastics, and makes no allowance for the qualitative aspects of the computer's performance. Indeed the situation is worse. The computer is not merely not rewarded for finding further relevant material by getting better scores, but is in fact penalized by getting worse. The reason for this is that if only objective standards are applied not only will such further relevant documents not be counted as being *relevant* for the purpose of raising recall, but will indeed be counted as being *irrelevant* for the purpose of depressing precision. To avoid this problem it is necessary in any complete assessment of the computer's performance to go beyond formal criteria, and to make some qualitative assessment of the relevance of all the authorities which are retrieved. But if the data-base is as large as was suggested above to be necessary, the difficulty of establishing a base figure for calculating recall is revived. It will be impossible to establish the total number of documents in the collection which satisfy such qualitative criteria in relation to each separate problem with sufficient precision.

The best that can be done is to make an approximation upon the basis of the results which are achieved. Thus a common technique is to treat as the basic figure for the calculation of recall percentages the sum of the numbers of those documents satisfying any objective or formal criteria and of those satisfying qualitative and subjective criteria whether the latter were initially selected by computer or by conventional techniques. It is true that such a figure may err on the low side, and will thus tend to exaggerate recall percentages, but it gives a sufficiently accurate relative measure of computer and conventional performance, even though it may be deficient as an absolute standard.

A somewhat similar point has to be made in relation to the calculation of the figure for precision. Here too all depends upon a qualitative judgement of relevance once objective and formal criteria are rejected as the sole standards for the reasons given above. The adoption of subjective standards is, however, fraught with difficulty, as illustrated by the experience of the American Bar Foundation experiments. There, judgements of relevance were made by a panel of four lawyers with different backgrounds. It was decided that evaluation should be absolute rather than relative, that is to say the panelists were asked to make a judgement about each individual document considered by itself, and were not asked to rank the documents by reference to their relative relevance to the problem. This decision was based on previous experience of the unreliability of such ranking lists when the numbers to be ranked exceeded about two or three, and this judgement seems sound.

So far as the individual decisions were concerned the panelists were asked to use a four letter scale. An 'a' case was one which 'could be used by itself to dispose of the issue raised in the question'; a 'b' case was one which 'is not dispositive of the issue, but ... could form a part of the disposition of the issue raised in the question'; a 'c' case was one only 'in the same general subject matter as the question'; and a 'd' case was one which 'has nothing to do with the question raised, could not contribute to its resolution, and is not in the same general subject matter'. The divergence between the panelists in applying this scale has already been mentioned. It is significant that the panel was in complete agreement in only 242 cases out of a total of 706, or 34·3 per cent. Of even greater significance is that in 221 of those 242 cases, or 91·3 per cent, the sense of the agreement was that the case fell into category 'd'. The difficulty therefore was principally in distinguishing accurately between the three positive grades. It is interesting to note further that in the presentation of some of the results the American Bar Foundation itself abandons the four letter scale in favour of a simple division between 'a' or 'b' judgements which are counted as useful, and 'c' or 'd' judgements which are counted as not useful. In that experiment no objective or formal criteria appear to have been used at all.

In my own work such criteria were supplemented by the adoption of a three-point qualitative scale. The three points were defined as cases which were relevant without any doubt, cases which were of doubtful relevance, and cases which were irrelevant without any doubt. The panelists were asked to work fast and to make liberal use of the doubtful category. The principle was that if they had to think at all the case was to be placed in the doubtful category, the other categories were reserved for situations in which certainty was complete and immediate. It is not claimed that error was thus eliminated, but concurrence of judgement was obtained to a larger extent than in the American Bar Foundation work, though it must be confessed, not so rigorously tested. The use of the doubtful category also enables the presentation of results in the alternative, with the doubtful assimilated either with the relevant or the irrelevant classes. In the results of the Israeli experiments documents are categorized as relevant or irrelevant, but no explicit information is given of the method of evaluation employed. There is, however, some evidence that it was carried out by an independent panel, and in one case the comment indicates that documents in the same general area were not regarded for that reason alone as relevant documents.[7]

The Oxford experiment
It is now possible to give some indication of the results obtained by different experiments in this field. It will be clearest if the presentation is principally of my own results since all the relevant figures are available to me, but these will be compared where appropriate with results obtained elsewhere.

First of all attention should be directed to those cases where it was possible to establish criteria of relevance completely independent of the subjective evaluation of anyone connected in any way with the experimental environment. These are authorities which were themselves cited in the reports chosen as the basis for search problems, or exceptionally were themselves references to those very reports. Thus in the latter case the searcher was given a set of facts taken from a report in the data-base and asked to frame a search to find reports relevant to those facts. One would in such circumstances expect 100 per cent recall. As explained, this situation was

[7] Fraenkel, 'Full Text Document Retrieval', Proceedings of ACM Symposium on Information Storage and Retrieval, April 1971.

more common in the decisions sector of the data-base, and in fact occurred in relation to twenty-two decisions, but the recall figure was only eighteen or 82 per cent by conventional means, and seventeen or 77 per cent by computer. Even together these methods missed one reference, and the combined recall figure was thus no better than 95 per cent. This may be compared with the consistent figure of 100 per cent recall achieved in the Israeli experiments where the data-base was of comparable size and the criteria of relevance were presumably much less easy to satisfy.

This then was the least questionable criterion of relevance, and the one which should have been most easily satisfied. The failure to achieve better than around 80 per cent success by conventional means can by itself be regarded as a complete justification for the experiment. Whether the improvement of that figure to 95 per cent by the addition of computer methods can be regarded as a justification for their use is more arguable.

The next category of objectively established results is that obtained in relation to cases where the authorities in the data-base were cited in the reports chosen as questions. If these are added to the previous class, and the figures totalled for both parts of the data-base, it is found that there were 120 such items of which fifty-one were found by conventional methods giving 43 per cent recall, fifty-three by computer techniques giving 44 per cent recall, and seventy-five by both techniques taken together giving 75 per cent recall. These figures are surprising for a number of reasons. First, because the recall figures for such indisputably relevant documents are so low, especially for conventional methods. They are so low that it would be worthwhile to duplicate the experiment using different conventional searchers, but it is nevertheless spine-chilling that any group of fully qualified lawyers should achieve such poor results. The second observation is that as the American Bar Foundation discovered, computer techniques seem to work at about the same level of efficiency as conventional techniques so far as recall in these categories is concerned. A vitally important factor, however, is that the two methods tend to fail in different places. Overall, twenty-two references discovered by conventional methods were not found by computer, while computer techniques discovered twenty-four references not found by conventional methods. Thus the hypothesis that the drawbacks of the two methods tend to be complementary is supported by these results. The problem with conventional techniques

G

lies in handling indexes, and with computer techniques in assembling the right combinations of words. It is, of course, possible that further experience with computerized techniques, which these participants were largely using for the first time, would lead to improved performance and might elevate joint recall performance to a more satisfactory level.

It will have been noticed that no precision figures have so far been given. The difficulty is that with exclusively objective criteria of relevancy of this sort they are bound to be unreliably low for the reasons advanced earlier, namely that even documents which anyone would agree were relevant are counted as irrelevant if they fail to satisfy the objective tests. However, this should not impair the comparative figures for conventional and computer techniques, provided not too much notice is taken of the absolute levels. Thus overall in these categories, conventional methods attained a precision figure of 47 per cent while the computer managed a meagre 10 per cent. Computer techniques retrieved in all 440 references not found by conventional techniques, but of these only twenty fell within these limited criteria of relevance. Conventional techniques found forty-one references not found by computer techniques, and of these nineteen fell within these criteria.

To gather a more realistic figure for precision it is necessary to advance at least to the next criterion of relevance which is the first of the qualitative levels, namely where the evaluators had no hesitation in regarding the documents so found as relevant to the problem. Here it is useful to distinguish between the results in the two segments of the data-base, since the judgements in respect of the cases are slightly more reliable than for the decisions, since the borderline of relevance is there more sharply defined. Thus fifty-two out of twenty-six relevant decisions fell into this category, or 54·2 per cent, while only twelve cases out of 110, or 10·9 per cent, fell into it. The reason is quite simply the homogeneity of the items in the decisions data-base, and the heterogeneity of the items in the cases data-base.

Of these fifty-two additionally relevant decisions twenty-two were found by conventional methods, and forty-nine by computer, giving recall figures of 42 per cent and 94 per cent respectively. The figure obtained by taking both together was fifty-two, and recall 100 per cent. This is, as explained, a conventional figure since other decisions in the data-base could not be evaluated independently for each problem, and it was assumed for the purpose of calculation that all additionally relevant decisions had been discovered. In view of the results for the objective criteria of citing and cited authorities where the whole data-base could be checked, this assumption was clearly wrong. It is virtually certain that there were other documents in the collection which would have satisfied these criteria, as was indeed stated to be the opinion of one of the evaluators. The distortion consists therefore in an exaggeration of the recall figures for both techniques. The relative balance between the two is probably little affected, but the greatest care should be taken in any comparison of recall and precision figures since here, by contrast with the limited objective area, the precision figures are likely to be at about the right absolute level.

The most significant figures are obtained by combining the figures for relevant documents to include both those satisfying the formal and objective, and qualitative and subjective criteria. These are summarized below.

	Decisions			Cases			All		
	No.	Rec.	Prec.	No.	Rec.	Prec.	No.	Rec.	Prec.
Conventional	57	58	85	43	39	100	100	49	92
Computer	77	80	37	67	61	22	144	70	29
Together	91	96	39	84	76	27	175	85	32

Table 2

Commentary

A number of comments may be made about these results. The first is that the most striking feature is the disparity between conventional and computer precision figures. Indeed the extent of the contrast is to some extent masked by the use of percentages rather than gross numbers. Thus overall the computer techniques retrieved 496 documents of which only 144 were relevant, compared with the 109 retrieved by conventional methods of which 100 were relevant. Thus computer techniques retrieved 352 irrelevant documents compared with only nine retrieved by conventional methods. This may seem too high a price to pay for the extra forty-four relevant documents, though improved searching and filtering techniques might be thought likely to lead to an improvement in the precision figure. In fact it was possible to test two such techniques to some extent in the experiments. The first was the adoption of a low threshold of response for the decisions so that only searches by computer where the total number of documents retrieved was less than 2·5 per cent of the data-base were counted, and the second was the substitution of a better for a worse set of computer searches in case law where two participants overlapped. The effect of these two devices was to improve computer precision by 6 per cent, but this was balanced by a drop in recall from 70 per cent to 61 per cent. It is evident that more sophisticated methods must be applied.

The precision figures may be compared with other experimental results. As previously remarked, the Israeli recall figure was an astonishingly high and consistent 100 per cent. The figures for precision quoted here are calculated from the eleven runs on the full data-base. In those eleven runs forty-six relevant documents were retrieved, and 183 irrelevant, giving an overall precision figure of 20·1 per cent. The American Bar Foundation project has not presented its results in a precisely comparable way, but if the unanimous decisions are divided into useful and not useful and then added back to the summary tables, it appears that the precision figure, in terms of useful to not useful citations, was 13·2 per cent, or 374 out of 2,824.

In assessing these extremely and uniformly poor precision figures it should be remembered that all three experiments operated on a batch basis which is likely to produce poor precision figures, and that to counter this both the Israeli and Oxford workers plan to use conversational techniques in the future. It may also be significant that if the criteria for relevance are further relaxed by allowing dubiously relevant documents to count in my own work, or category 'c' documents in the American Bar Foundation experiment, there is an apparent improvement in precision. It can, of course, be argued that such documents are not really worth counting, and that they are unlikely to contribute much to the resolution of the particular problem posed. But it is not completely inconceivable that in some sorts of situation where the lawyer is casting around for a new line of enquiry such documents may be valuable in furnishing a pool of possibilities from which the indisputably irrelevant have been filtered out. On this basis, in my own work conventional techniques achieved 99 per cent precision with 35 per cent recall, while the computer techniques achieved 45 per cent precision and 73 per cent recall. Computer techniques found 153 such documents not found by conventional techniques, and missed thirty-four which the conventional techniques discovered. In the American Bar Foundation experiment the computer precision figure also rises to a roughly comparable 42·7 per cent, or 1,207 out of 2,824. So for some types of search at least the precision figures for computer techniques may be mis-leadingly low. On the other hand, there can be no doubt on the basis of the results of these experiments that the human brain is a far better instrument than the computer for achieving precision, and this is a further reason for the eligibility of conversational systems which permit the use of the human brain to perform that function in the most useful and appropriate way within a computer system.

While not so dramatic, the second most significant feature of these results is the consistently better performance of computer techniques so far as recall is concerned. Thus in relation to both cases and decisions there was a 22 per cent advantage in terms of recall. This advantage held good in case law whatever criteria of relevance were selected; in the decisions it only appeared when the qualitative and subjective criteria were added to the formal and objective ones. The reason for this was undoubtedly the difficulty in selecting the most relevant decisions from among the many similar ones in the same area, the very factor which led to abnormally low precision figures for conventional techniques on this basis. In other words, the figures in that limited area and on that limited basis are funda-mentally unreliable because the extrinsic standard, while indeed formal and objective, is also thoroughly unreliable; decisions ex-cluded by it may well be as relevant, or more so, than the decisions it includes. The general advantage of computer techniques in respect of recall is, however, most significant. For the lawyer, recall is more important than precision since the human brain can be used to eliminate irrelevant material; it cannot find further relevant material. This is especially important in view of the advent of conversational systems which may be expected to improve precision without affect-ing recall. A further interesting feature here is the complementary effect of conventional and computer techniques so far as the im-provement of recall is concerned. When they fail, they fail in different places and for different reasons, so the results for the application of both techniques together are invariably better than for either considered alone. In principle it should be easier to improve computer techniques than conventional ones if only because they are at so much earlier a stage of their development, but it is clear that further intensive research is necessary into the best way to do it.

The amount of work remaining to be accomplished in this field is virtually unlimited, and it is hoped that further experimental results will be reported. The Israeli work is currently being extended, and further results can be expected there with some confidence. Advanced work is also under way at Queen's University, Kingston, Ontario and at the University of Michigan, in both cases using conversational techniques, so that much needed information should be gathered of the precise effects of such approaches as against the older batch-processing techniques used by the experiments described here. In addition, several centres on the continent of Europe can be expected to publish results in the near future. It is, however, expected that for the time being research is unlikely to provide final answers, but rather to supply a stimulus for further work as the full range of possibilities opened up by new techniques gradually becomes apparent.

7

Computers and case law: operational systems

This chapter will describe in necessarily brief outline some practical applications in the field of case law. Full descriptions cannot be given, partly for reasons of space and partly because the main aim of such systems is to make a profit or do a job rather than to furnish information, and published material is sometimes accordingly scanty. To offset this, addresses of organizations are given. For purposes of exposition these applications are divided into those which are, and those which are not, made by governmental bodies. The main reason for making this distinction is that in the latter, financial considerations tend to dominate whereas in the former more account can be taken of less tangible factors like social need and national interest.

1 NON-GOVERNMENTAL APPLICATIONS

Most of these have so far taken place in the United States though one well established European system will also be included. The general reason for the earlier attempts in the United States is simply a reflection of the normal lead held there in the application of advanced technologies. Computer applications are a particularly good example of this, and computer applications in law no exception to it. In part it is due to the pioneering efforts of Professor Horty, in part to the vastly greater problem which the retrieval of case law presents to the lawyer in the United States, in part to the organization of the profession, in part to a more hospitable reaction to technological advance, in part to the greater wealth of the United States, in part to the initiative of the American entrepreneur, in part to the closer connections between professional, academic and business worlds, in part to the anti-trust laws encouraging diversification, and in part to a desire to spread the costs of computer systems developed for other purposes. These factors will have operated to different extents and in different proportions in relation to the different applications described below, but whatever the reason the fact remains that the United States has so far given rise to more widespread and determined efforts to apply computerized case law techniques in a commercial environment than the whole of the rest of the world put together.

Some of the applications described here may by now have been discontinued, revived or modified. They are described in the form which is best documented. The first three applications, Law Research Incorporated, Autocomp Incorporated and CREDOC are index orientated systems, while the last, that of OBAR is full-text orientated.

Law Research Incorporated

One of the earliest commericial ventures in this field was started in New York in 1964 under the direction of a New York lawyer, Elias Hoppenfeld. He took the view that the growth of case law in the United States was reaching such proportions that some computerized system for dealing with it had become essential. At that time he felt that the only economically feasible approach was by way of indexing or the use of descriptors, and for the large body of law he had in mind this was clearly an accurate assessment at the time. He also regarded the descriptor approach as theoretically more desirable since he felt that the human brain had traditionally performed the task of indexing, that lawyers were used to having such inter-mediate preparation of materials, and that it was by no means established that full-text methods would do as well. It is interesting that he took the same view in relation to legislation despite the work of Professor Horty which was by then well established and documented. It should be emphasized, however, that he recognized the value of full-text for the lawyer once retrieval had been accom-plished, and his system indeed provided a micro-form version of the full-text as part of the service. His view was simply that retrieval was best accomplished by using descriptors.

At first, searches were conducted with three human phases inter-vening between the user and the supply of material to him. The user filled in a form specifying the nature of his problem in his own words with some indication of any background material and a designation of the area of law concerned. This form was then sent to the computer centre where it was passed on to a search editor for that area of law. The editor then framed a computer question in terms of the descriptors which he knew were used in the system. Thus there are here two aspects of human intervention. First there is the general stage at which the raw material is characterized by words and phrases selected by a human indexer, and then at the retrieval stage a further human being translates the question into the appropriate words and phrases. There is clearly some sense in this double approach since it is essential that data and question match, and one of the deficiencies of a conventional system is overcome in that the danger of differing interpretations of words and phrases between indexer and user is avoided. The new danger is, however, introduced that the editor who translates the problem into words and phrases to put to the computer may misunderstand it. The third point of human intervention in this system occurs at the output stage. The computer produced list of case names and references which was then scanned by a human editor to select the four which seemed to him most relevant to the original question. The full-text of these decisions was then micro-filmed and posted off to the enquirer together with a full list of the citations produced by the computer from which the four had been selected.

The original cost for this service was 25 dollars per search, and at this price it was claimed that the majority of law firms in the state of New York became subscribers.[1] It was found, however, that lawyers wanted more direct access to the computer. Consequently the system was modified to permit the elimination of the question editing stage. Instead law firms were given the option of renting on-line teletype terminals for 18 dollars per month which they could use to formulate their questions directly. To assist them in this it was necessary that they should be provided with lists of the words and phrases used as keywords in the system. These were sold in hard copy versions divided up according to subject matter and jurisdiction and showing the appropriate numerical codes.[2] The elimination of the editing stage allowed the price per search to be reduced to 10 dollars plus a line charge of 2 dollars, though of course the rental of the terminal and the purchase of the thesaurus should be taken into account in making any comparison with the original system.

Plans were made to extend this system to other states and indeed

---

[1] Hoppenfeld, 'Law Research Inc.', *Modern Uses of Logic in Law*, 46, March 1966.
[2] Seventeen volumes for the federal jurisdiction, and eight for each state.

G*

other countries, but the service suffered a number of setbacks and became involved in protracted litigation which seems to have prevented it from achieving all that was hoped.

The danger points in a service like this seem to reside in the choice and allocation of descriptors, the quality of the editing, the absence of any techniques for automatic enrichment of the search, the relative poverty of the facilities for combining and modifying descriptors, and all of these magnified by the absence of any conversational facilities despite the use of on-line teletypes.

Autocomp Incorporated[3]

This is another American company active in the field of case law, though in this case only as one among a number of related activities. The company was founded in 1966, mainly to develop and combine full-text retrieval and photo-composition techniques, and its initial effort was in the preparation of a sophisticated package of photo-composition programmes, RECOMP, which were employed in the printing of a number of legal and other publications. The main impetus towards the expansion of the case law retrieval side of the company's operations was stimulated by a merger in 1969 with Autocode Incorporated which then became a subsidiary of Autocomp. Autocode had been an organization specializing in services to lawyers in the field of municipal law. This is very important in the United States where in addition to the federal and state governments there is a market of nearly forty thousand other governmental units with some legal services which require support. Autocomp provides a wide range of services for such bodies, including the preparation and printing of legislation, especially legislation in codified forms, assistance with the preparation of applications for federal assistance and grants, and the searching of legislation in particular areas relevant to the interests of municipalities, such as legislation relating to the preservation of the environment.

In the field of case law the major endeavour has been the establishment of a service known as MUNICOMP which stands for Municipal Law Computer Search and Retrieval System. This service was inaugurated in 1970, initially processing some forty thousand decisions of American Courts at all levels, federal state and local, in the field of municipal law. It was planned to add to this further

[3] Further information may be obtained from Autocomp Inc., 1367 Connecticut Av. N.W., Washington D.C. 20036.

materials commenting upon and annotating cases taken from such secondary sources as journals and periodicals. This is, like Law Research Incorporated's, an indexed system. Each case is assigned a code number, and then indexed at three different levels. The primary term reflects the principal issue in the case, and may express either a legal or factual concept. An alphabetic list of such terms constitutes the main structure of the data-base. Then for each case the primary term is qualified by reference to a secondary term which itself may express either a legal or a factual concept, and which is designed to focus more specifically upon the particular point decided by the particular case. There follow a number of tertiary terms which make the issue even more specific, and give a reasonable impression of the content of the report of the case. In addition each entry is annotated by cross-reference to further primary terms which might be of assistance in relation to that particular entry. A further feature is a thesaurus which has as its entries the whole range of terms which lawyers might use, and relates them to the relevant primary terms or terms under which a search should be conducted.

It is envisaged that the service should at first be organized on a remote batch basis, that is to say that enquiries either in ordinary language or by the specification of search terms should be sent to the computer centre in Washington to be processed, and then the computer's responses consisting of citations and summaries of the relevant cases should be sent back to the user. It is hoped that ultimately the system should be made available to municipalities to run on their own computer systems, and that it should be transformed into an on-line system.

The major point of difference between this system and that of Law Research Incorporated is that Autocomp specializes in one particular branch of case law. This is significant in that it is reasonable to assume that lawyers working in the same limited area will be able to agree on a vocabulary for indexing, and to apply it consistently. It also permits a greatly reduced data-base and consequently more intensive coverage of it by the terms chosen. A further advantage is that the users of this system, being themselves specialists in the area, should be able to draft their questions with considerable expertise, and thus the need for editing questions and responses should be eliminated. It is also the case that in this field the pace of litigation is somewhat slower than in many others, and the delays inherent in a remote batch system more easily tolerated. From the commercial point of view there is the further advantage that these specialist users invariably have access to public funds to finance their searches, and are able to take a broader view of the value of their searching than might perhaps be possible for a purely private lawyer representing an individual client. They are also more likely to be familiar with the advantages of computer techniques as a result of seeing them in operation in other aspects of local government, and especially from seeing them in operation in the legal sphere in the preparation of local legislation as described in the previous chapter.

As yet no reliable information about the large-scale operation of this system has become available, and it is thus not yet possible to assess its success. Perhaps it major drawback is that as it is intended for experts in a limited area it must analyze the materials to a depth beyond that of conventional methods, or include materials in its data-base which are inaccessible by such methods, and it is not entirely clear that this has been achieved.

Credoc[4]

This is a system developed in Belgium, and although unlike the two previously described it is not planned as a profit-making enterprise, it is a private body and is intended to cover its own costs, and to that extent at least is governed by financial considerations. It was originally introduced on account of the special difficulties experienced in the retrieval of legal information by conventional means in a small country. In large countries the impetus for computerized legal information retrieval systems is generated by the inability of conventional methods to cope with the enormous volume of material which appears. The difficulty is in handling the information. In small countries the volume of material is certainly capable of being handled by conventional methods, but the problem arises on account of the smallness of the market for conventional services in the form of encyclopaedias, citators, indexes and the like. These are costly to produce and the overheads such that they need to be spread over a large number of subscribers to make them economically feasible. In small countries, and especially in periods of rising costs, this is often impossible, and the result is that the practitioners are starved

[4] Further information may be obtained from CREDOC, 34 rue de la Montagne, B1000, Brussels.

of the services, and if anything worse off than their counterparts in larger countries where some conventional services, flawed though they may be, are provided. To meet this problem in Belgium the profession, both lawyers and notaries, established a study group on computer applications, and as a result CREDOC was set up in 1967 with the active support of the judges and of all the Belgian universities.[5]

The primary aim of the system is to provide a service for practising lawyers in Belgium, and for this reason it aims to give a complete coverage of Belgian law including those parts of international law which have an effect in Belgium. This covers all sources of law, extending far beyond case law to encompass in addition treaties, legislation, commentaries, parliamentary materials and even such miscellaneous sources as standard form contracts and collective agreements. As it has proved impossible to prepare all this data at once priority has been given to new legislation and those topics most in demand by practitioners. When the system became operational in 1969 the total number of documents included was over 25,000; by the end of 1969 it had risen to more than 35,000, by the end of 1971 it was 85,000, and the forecast for 1972 was 150,000 which will exhaust the backlog and should have achieved complete coverage of Belgian law. A special feature of this system is that it operates in both the official languages of Belgium, and partly in German.

This system is similar to the two American systems described earlier in being based upon an indexing philosophy. It uses about 5,700 descriptors and about 500 modifiers which gives a total of about 30,000 different complete concepts. Relationships between concepts within the same document can also be expressed. These descriptors are not inflexible either in their content or in their relationship with each other, and a weekly conference is held to decide upon possible additions or alterations.

The user of the system pays a fixed annual fee irrespective of the number of searches he performs, thus encouraging use of the system which is now running at about 40 searches per day. Like the system of Law Research Incorporated there is pre-editing of questions at the computer centre by the CREDOC staff. The user formulates his search in natural language, and the machine search is then framed by an editor. The questions are currently run in batch

---

[5] Compare the almost identical impetus and support for the creation of the Scottish Legal Computer Trust.

mode, but as CREDOC has its own computer and is able to conduct several runs in the same day some limited simulation of conversational techniques is possible. Thus if a search should yield a nil response the search terms can be enriched and the question re-run before the results are sent off to the subscriber. The descriptors are held in the system in the form of four digit alphanumeric codes with an associated table of French and Dutch words expressed by the codes. This allows the centre to search the same data-base for terms expressed in either language, and makes it equally easy to supply the responses in the language of the question. The response is in the form of a list of citations, or on request abstracts of documents, or in the case of legislation in the form of the full-text of the relevant provisions. If the full-text of case law is required as a response this is supplied by the use of conventional copying techniques.

It seems that this system has proved very effective in supplying the needs of Belgian lawyers, though it is recognized that it might be still further improved by, for example, the introduction of on-line and conversational techniques though these are at present beyond the limited financial resources of the enterprise. It would also be desirable to introduce more sophisticated syntactical relationships between the descriptors than are at present provided, and this is likely to be done in the near future.

Ohio Bar Automated Retrieval (OBAR)[6]
This is without doubt the most advanced of all the commercial systems in current operation. This in part reflects the fact that it was the latest on to the field, only coming into use in 1969 though the basic system had been devised some time earlier. It is also in part due to the willingness of the promoters to make continuous improvements to the system on the basis of an extensive research and development programme rather than to seek to maximize profits at as early a stage as possible. The system was introduced because a committee of the Ohio Bar Association set up to investigate the possibilities of computerized legal information retrieval between 1964 and 1967 recommended that none of the systems then in existence quite filled the lawyer's need, and that Ohio should accordingly develop

---

[6] Further information may be obtained from OBAR, 33 W. 11th St., Columbus, Ohio. And see 'McCabe, Automated Legal Research', 54 *Judicature*, 283 (1971); Harrington *et al.*, 'The Mead Data Central System of Computerised Legal Retrieval', 64 *Law Library J.*, 184 (1971).

its own system. This was achieved in cooperation with what is now Mead (Data Central), a subsidiary of the large American conglomerate Mead Corporation.

The importance of this system is that it is the only full-text system in active commercial operation anywhere in the world. It has the largest full-text data-base yet established, and it employs the most advanced techniques. It is better financed and supported by its parent organization than any other venture in the legal field, and accordingly seems to have the greatest prospects of ultimate success.

The data-base currently includes all Ohio case law in full-text going back to 1832 together with Ohio legislation and some federal law. The Ohio Supreme Court segment of the data-base alone runs to more than 240 million characters. As the system is introduced into other states so the data-base is expected to grow at a spectacular rate. The full-text of the documents is stored sequentially within the system so as to enable the display of portions of the text in their ordinary form for lawyers to read. In addition, for retrieval purposes a common word list of about a hundred words is used to distil an inverted concordance file of non-common words which is divided into alphabetically ordered segments and available for fast random access. This is one of the keys to the success of the system. The information is also subdivided into a large number of fields to provide for extremely economical searching and display.

The system uses remote terminals situated in the lawyers' office with a dial-up telephone link to the main computer. It can accommodate a wide variety of terminals, but is probably used most conveniently in conjunction with a video display unit coupled to a device for producing hard copy. Very modern devices are available with such facilities as those for a multi-colour display which is remarkably effective in speeding the browsing process.

The method is basically that described earlier in connection with the searching of full-text. The user keys in the words he wishes to use in the search, and the logical and associational connection between them. There is a facility for providing plural and singular forms automatically while other grammatical variations can be attained by the use of standard truncation techniques. The automatic provision of further enrichment of the question by means of a thesaurus is currently under investigation. The initial response of the system is to indicate the number of documents satisfying the search as originally formulated. The formulation is then modified until the number of documents seems to be about right, and then the system will display citation, headnote or full-text of the documents as desired, and the search can then be further modified in the light of this output until the user is satisfied with the selection with which he has been provided, whereupon he can if he wishes have a hard copy version printed out.

At first the system was only available with teletype terminals, but these were found to be rather slow and unsatisfactory. Even now the system is under constant scrutiny with a view to making further improvements, especially in its ease of operation. It is reported, however, that use of the system is increasing in Ohio, and a great expansion is planned for the near future both within Ohio and in other states.[6a] The strategy for this expansion is modelled upon the initial plan in Ohio where there was very close cooperation with the state bar association. At present the operation is undoubtedly unprofitable by itself, but one of its strongest features is that the retrieval system is in no way tied to case law, or even law, but can be, and indeed is, used in a very wide range of applications, thus enabling the enormous cost of producing such a system to be spread over a very large number of users.

If the promise of this system is fulfilled it will become the standard by which all other legal information retrieval systems will have to be measured.

2 GOVERNMENTAL APPLICATIONS

At this end of the spectrum of applications the United States does not occupy quite so dominating a position vis-à-vis the rest of the world as it does at the commercial end. There are a number of reasons for this. Many of them reflect the obverse side of the reasons for the general dominance of the United States noted above in relation to commercial development. The general problem is smaller in European countries, the private entrepreneur seems less willing to take risks, the profession is neither so wealthy nor so well organized as to be so conducive to marketing such a service on a commercial basis and the money to finance such development is simply not forthcoming from private sources to anything like the same extent. A further factor is the generally greater activity of European governments in the commercial sphere, and in particular their greater

[6a] Agreements to introduce the system in New York and Texas have already been made.

authority over the whole range of case law on account of their unitary constitutions. In the United States there is no government with exclusive and complete authority in relation to the case law operative within the area governed by it. Every citizen is subject to different systems of law, that of the state and that of the federal government. These are both very extensive, and both have their own independent system of case law. It would be supererogatory for the federal authorities to computerize the state system, or for a state government to computerize the federal system. The result is that very little has been accomplished here by state governments; in the field of computerizing state case law the initiative has come almost exclusively from private enterprise. Even the federal government has made only limited incursions in such fields, as tax with the RIRA system, some bodies of administrative decisions through the LITE system and documentation with the Department of Justice in the JURIS system. It is interesting that in the field of case law it is the federal government which leads the state governments, whereas in the field of legislation the positions are reversed.

In Europe, however, some governments have taken more forthright steps, largely because unless they were to do so, nothing would be done at all. Even so these steps have generally so far been small ones, although they are likely to constitute the basis for further progress for those who have made them, and to be copied by others. In this section therefore, by way of contrast to the last of the five applications to be very briefly described, three are European and only two American. Here too the list is intended to be illustrative only, and is known not to be exhaustive. These five have been selected, first because they are in actual operation and secondly because they utilize different approaches. Thus the Italian Court of Cassation has a semi-automatic indexed approach, that of CEDIJ in Paris an amplified full-text approach, the Swedish Insurance Court a conventional indexed approach, and the RIRA system, while also conventionally indexed, has to deal with a set of very special problems. As in the previous section space forbids lengthy treatment, and details are given of further sources of information.

Italian Supreme Court of Cassation[7]
This system was devised by the indexing Office of the Court, which

---

[7] For further information see Laporta, Borruso, Falcone and Novelli, *Sistema de Ricera Elettronica della Giurisprudenza*, Rome, 1969.

has since 1924 been responsible for the conventional system of information retrieval in the field of case law. This has always involved the drafting of short summaries of Court decisions. These are given a title, a number representing the area of law involved on the basis of a prescribed classification system, and a text of approximately two hundred words. Twelve thousand such abstracts are produced each year. It was felt that while necessary, the classification plan was not alone a sufficient method for locating these summaries. This was mainly on account of subjective, and occasionally arbitrary, decisions as to the location of a particular summary, the complexity of the system which made it unsuitable for conventional use, and the rigidity of the frame of reference so provided. Accordingly in 1966 it was decided that this corpus of information constituted an ideal data-base for an automated retrieval system.

It was felt that such a system would only be economically viable if some system of indexing were incorporated. One possibility which was actively considered was the adoption of a freely assigned set of descriptors, but this was rejected as being likely to be inefficient on account of the difficulties of controlling the indexers, and uneconomic as it would entail the continuous employment of large numbers of highly skilled, and thus highly expensive, indexing staff. For these reasons the Italians adopted a unique semi-automatic indexing scheme. This involves keyboarding the entire text of the summary together with its title and in all thirteen separate items of bibliographic information in coded form, most of which can be used as independent search criteria. This includes such items as the area of law involved, the number and reference of the decision, the composition of the Court and the names of the parties. Two items which should be specially mentioned are first the 'title', which is in fact a coded representation of the classification number according to the established system, and is useful as an additional search parameter, and secondly the citation of any legislation referred to in the decision, in particular sections of the codes, which are available for the same purpose. The text itself is first reduced by the elimination of common words, just as it would be in any ordinary full-text system.

The crucial operation here, however, is the next, in which the text is translated into a formalized vocabulary. This vocabulary consists of some three thousand Italian words selected by human beings as the basic elements of the Italian language, from which all more complicated concepts can be synthesized and to which they can be reduced. It has been designed as an atomic linguistic system, and is based upon a study of ordinary dictionaries of the Italian language. These terms express both legal and factual concepts, and are the keywords of the retrieval system. This formalized vocabulary is implemented by the use of a thesaurus. In the thesaurus all Italian words likely to appear in the summaries are listed together with the keywords which represent them. This thesaurus doubled in size from twenty thousand words in 1968 when the system was devised to forty thousand in 1970 when it had been in operation for two years and some six thousand summaries had been processed. Three-quarters of this increase occurred in the first year, however, when only fifteen hundred summaries were processed so the rate of expansion is clearly diminishing sharply, and the number of terms will probably never exceed fifty thousand. This method of representing the text eliminates all problems of grammatical variation and synonyms. Where homographs occur, both keywords are included. The process is not simply one of verbal substitution, however, since the programmes allow the representation of phrases by single keywords. The result of the two stages of eliminating common words and then formalizing the vocabulary is a reduction of the original text by approximately 80 per cent. Comparison of this figure with the reductions achieved by common word elimination alone indicate the degree to which the phrase translation programmes are relied upon. The thesaurus programmes are specially designed to allow for the problems of generic and particular terms, whether legal or factual, and related terms.

At the retrieval stage the user can either formulate his question directly in the keywords of the system, or presumably his request can be translated into such keywords by the automatic thesaurus. The usual Boolean operators are available, and also specification of order of appearance of keywords in the abstract. In addition the user can, as noted above, limit the output by reference to the internal citation of particular legislation, or the area of law indicated by a particular classification code. These devices also help to offset one of the disadvantages of the semi-automatic indexing approach, namely that in the case of homographic ambiguity both keywords are included, thus guaranteeing in all such cases that one of the keywords by which the summary is characterized is wrong.

The system is intended for use by the Italian judiciary, and is still in an experimental stage, though an advanced one. There are, however, no plans for any fundamental revision of the philosophy of the system, so presumably the sponsors are satisfied with the results they have achieved so far. It is dubious whether such a system could be adopted in common law countries since it would be difficult to reproduce such satisfactory controls as those furnished in this system by the well-established classification system, and the reference to sections of the codes. These provide a much more secure logical framework than could be found in any common law system. Similarly, it is dubious whether the importance of case law within a common law system could be sufficiently sensitively reflected by the use of such a limited number of keywords, nor would it be easy to find anything really comparable to the summaries used in Italy. There may, however, be special areas of law in such systems where such techniques could be profitably applied, and the progress of this system will repay careful observation.

Centre de Developpement de L'Informatique (CEDIJ)[8]
Lucien Mehl, a member of the Conseil d'Etat, was one of the first Europeans, if not the first, to make public his interest in the computerization of law.[9] As a result of his industry and inspiration the Conseil d'Etat has helped pioneer one of the most advanced operational systems for case law to exist anywhere in the world. This system, which also handles other sources of law, has a number of interesting features. It seems destined to become the nucleus of a national legal retrieval system in France, and through its close contacts with the Commission of the European Economic Community, perhaps also in Europe. The system was devised in 1965, tested in 1968, and became fully operational in 1970. It is unusual in the field of case law systems in relying heavily for its software upon the International Business Machines package known as the Document Processing System (DPS). This has enabled it to devote its programming resources to the intensive study of the special problems associated with legal documentation rather than dissipate them on more general problems involved in handling linguistic data. Its special

[8] See Breton, 'DOCILIS ou la Documentation Souple', *Law and Computer Technology*, December 1969, 26 (English translation appended). A full report on the system for the French government is in the course of preparation.
[9] Mehl, 'Automation in the Legal World', *Symposium on the Mechanization of Thought Processes*, National Physical Laboratory, United Kingdom, November 1958.

contribution has been to the resolution of the problem of enriching the responses made by the system so as to improve recall performance especially.

The first subject areas which were treated by CEDIJ were those of fiscal, commercial and civil law. At first a keyword system was tried, but this was subsequently abandoned in favour of a full, or free, text method. The workers at CEDIJ were among the first to appreciate that indexing and full-text were complementary and not competing approaches.[10] The case law segment of their data-base amounted to 4,500 judicial decisions per annum between 1967 and 1970, but it is expected to build this up to about 250,000 by 1975. These decisions are prepared from abstracts of about five hundred characters each, representing a 10 per cent reduction of the full-text version. The most interesting feature is the stress on the bibliographic data which is added to ease the operation of the system. There are no fewer than fifty-three different bibliographic headings, and they have been carefully selected so as to be capable of being applied with only the most minor alterations to each of the various different sources of French law. In case law five different types of information are distinguished, that identifying the work in which the document appears, that characterizing the document, that indicating the position of the document in the work, that identifying the names of the judges and lawyers, and finally that giving cross-references to other documents. The first includes title, author, origin, publisher and subject of the work. The second gives the date, names of the parties, stage within the legal process and nature of judgement delivered. The third gives all the information necessary to locate the document within the general work such as the page or document number. The fourth is, in French law, relatively unimportant and in most cases gives only the names of the Rapporteur and the Commissaire du Gouvernement. The fifth gives a reference to other texts, and expresses the precise relationship between them in terms of a very elaborate coding system.[11] In the interests of economy and efficiency the team has also compiled a standard system of abbreviations for the major French legal institutions and periodical citations known as SNORTEJ.[12]

[10] See, e.g., Breton, 'Indexation par mot-clés ou texte intégral ?', *Law and Computer* December *Technology*, June 1969, 24 (English translation appended).
[11] Breton 'DOCILIS ou la Documentation Souple' *Law and Computer Technology*, December 1969, 26 at 33 (French text only).
[12] Système de références normalisées aux textes juridiques.

A feature of the system is that all these bibliographical headings can be used in the control of retrieval. In essence DPS is an ordinary full-text system of the type previously described. As modified and applied by CEDIJ, however, it has had built into it a most impressive array of techniques for enriching the retrieval process. This is accomplished by the incorporation into the system of lists of the various meanings of homographs, of grammatical variations, of syntactical variants, of synonyms or conceptual equivalents, and of more remotely connected concepts, hierarchical and associational, which might assist in any conversational system. The first four of these are already included in substitution lists within the DPS system which means that their incorporation in the retrieval process is purely automatic.

The system also permits the use, in addition to the usual operators for natural language concepts chosen by the user, of an IF operator which limits the selection by reference to specified bibliographic data such as cases decided only after a certain date. Truncation facilities are provided. The degree of association can be expressed in terms of words, sentences, or more unusually, paragraphs. Finally there is also provision for weighting the search terms used, and for retrieval to be specified in terms of relationship to a numerical threshold thus enabling the number of documents retrieved to be more effectively controlled.

These devices will prevent many of the causes of failure in overall performance, but some further manual devices have been found to be helpful. None of these automatic devices, for example, can meet the problem of defective reference to the original, such as the use of a pronoun in place of a full form, and in these cases the text is completed before processing by adding the appropriate word or words into the text between a pair of asterisks. It has also been found necessary to construct hierarchical dictionaries outside the system in order to deal with the problems of generalization and particularization. It is estimated that at present the system is able to achieve 85 per cent recall at a precision level of 50 per cent.[13] These results are a remarkable testimony to the efficiency of the system, and it will be most interesting to discover how far they can be maintained when the data increases in the proportions envisaged.

[13] Answer to questionnaire circulated by the Council of Europe (EXP/Ord. Jur. (71)1 Prov. p. 193).

Swedish National Court for Social Insurance[14]

This system is included as a typical example of a small-scale application in a limited field. It was developed entirely within the Swedish Court for Social Insurance for its own purposes, and out of the annual budget provided by the state. Because Sweden is a relatively small country, and because the area of social insurance law is also rather strictly confined, the volume of material is manageable at small cost. In 1969 when the system was implemented the total number of decisions processed into the system was no more than 1,550; this had grown to 1,700 by 1970 and is expected to go on expanding at a rate of about 5 per cent per annum. This is obviously a readily manageable body of data, and in this system it is treated in a thoroughly economical manner with one card used to hold all the coded data necessary to identify the decision and to characterize its content. In most cases only one index term is found necessary, and the overall average is no higher than 1·4 terms per decision. This is made possible by the use of a decimal classification system which has been developed to characterize the field of law. In this sort of area there are immense advantages in such an approach. It is, *ex hypothesi,* always an area of a purely statutory origin, and this makes it possible to use the statutory framework as the basis for the classification system.

Thus in Sweden the primary classification is by reference to the particular law dealing with a particular class of benefit. These statutes are carefully planned in advance since they tend to be instituting complete schemes, and not codifying already developed rules. This gives a logical foundation, well suited to computerization. In the Swedish system this classification system is developed far enough to encompass all generic and specific features of both law and fact which may be required. The structure of the classification system which also performs the function of a thesaurus is under the control of the president of the Court. Again the small number of judges involved has the advantage that the system is understood and can be interpreted in a common sense, and this is fortified by the distribution of printed copies of the thesaurus among all those involved with the working of the system, and all those coming into contact with it as applicants or as advisers. This common agreement on interpretation allows conventional methods of indexing to be used in a com-

[14] Further details may be obtained from L. Granqvist, National Court of Social Insurance, Sveavagen 13–15, Fack, 103 04 Stockholm.

pletely satisfactory way, and removes the need for sophisticated search techniques to amplify either questions or responses.

This system is a very good illustration of what can already be achieved in special limited situations, and there may well be more of these to be exploited than is generally realized. It is not always necessary to think in terms of giant universal systems with their inevitable complexity and expense. Where there are self-contained and well-defined small areas of this type, the advantages of a simple and inexpensive approach are manifest, and this Swedish system shows what can be achieved.

Reports and Information Retrieval Activity (RIRA)[15]

This system was developed by the United States Internal Revenue Service in the early 1960s for immediate use. For that reason it was necessary to make it simple enough to be applied very quickly to the enormous mass of data which the Service handles, and also for it to be capable of being handled by the somewhat primitive equipment available at that time. There were, moreover, a number of special difficulties with which this system had to deal, and indeed for which it was devised. The system was primarily designed to help the 650 lawyers employed by the Internal Revenue Service in their day-to-day work. Half of these lawyers are distributed in thirty-five field offices in large cities throughout the United States. At any one time they are dealing, in conjunction with the remainder of the lawyers situated in Washington, with about 14,000 pending cases. The most pressing problem was to secure uniformity of approach by these different and widely dispersed lawyers. This is especially important in tax law since the whole system of administration of the country depends upon the regular collection of taxes, and this in turn depends upon the willing cooperation of the taxpayers. The payment of taxes is always, and inevitably, unpopular, and suspicion that it was being operated unfairly might have serious consequences. One of the best ways of avoiding any appearance of unfairness is for a uniform approach to be adopted to similar problems throughout the country. Thus a unique feature of the RIRA system is that it was primarily designed to operate in relation to cases while they were still in the negotiating stage, and thus much earlier than in any other legal retrieval system described here. The aim was to keep all the

[15] See Link, 'RIRA', 43 *Taxes* 231 (1965); Cohen and Uretz 'RIRA', *Law and Computer Technology*, Sept. 1968, 2.

lawyers engaged upon the negotiation of tax cases for the government, informed of the progress of similar negotiations in other parts of the country. But it was not only important to ensure that all the lawyers were saying the same thing, it was also necessary to ensure so far as possible that what they were saying was correct. This entailed entering into the data-base, not only details of all pending cases but also, and more conventionally, details of all the established rules of law laid down by statute, administrative rulings made by the department, and decisions of Courts and tribunals.

There are further special difficulties in tax law systems on account of the complexity of the law involved, the frequency with which it is changed (sometimes these are major structural changes) and the time lag involved in litigation. That tax law is complicated is partly due to the fact that here, more than in most areas, litigation takes the form of formal conflict as the culmination of a series of steps deliberately taken and carefully calculated with the ultimate litigation in mind. It is more like an eighteenth-century battle than a modern one. It is not a matter of establishing the legal consequences of a chance event such as much of the law of the tort. In tax things do not just happen, they are deliberately made to happen in full knowledge and awareness of the rules in order to exploit quite deliberately any inconsistencies, ambiguities or loopholes. Thus litigation is heavily concentrated on fringe situations. Large sums of money are usually involved, so the very greatest legal ingenuity can be purchased on both sides, and a high proportion of tax cases go right through the system to the highest Courts. About half the time of the House of Lords in England is spent on tax appeals. When the decision on a particular point is unacceptable to the government of the day, it is often necessary to pass fresh legislation to remedy the situation. Such legislation is often of minute complexity so as to apply precisely to fill the gap which has been revealed. The law thus builds up a layered structure as the cycle of legislation, avoiding action, litigation and fresh legislation continues. Apart from such detailed changes there are occasional revolutions when a whole tax is abandoned or a new one introduced, such as the abandonment of Selective Employment Tax in Great Britain, and imposition of the totally different Value Added Tax. It is interesting to note that such changes are frequently delayed just because the Revenue officials find it difficult to cope with the extra work involved in introducing them into the existing system. These difficulties are exacerbated by time lags in litigation. Some of these are inherent in the nature of the subject matter, as receipts must come in and accounts be made up before the assessment process can begin. Then since this is so critical plenty of time has to be allowed on both sides for preliminary consideration and negotiation. A dispute may well thus not come on for ultimate disposition until some years have elapsed since the year of account to which it relates. In that time the relevant rules of law are likely to have undergone a number of changes. Here more than anywhere else therefore the retrieval system must be designed so as to permit the representation of the law as it was at any given moment of past time.

However, there are some compensating advantages. The most significant of these is that the tax system, like the social insurance system, is very closely tied to the statutes imposing the relevant taxes, and this statutory format can be utilized to provide an indexing and classification scheme. Thus RIRA uses the section numbers of the Internal Revenue code as the basic unit, to which are added two further code numbers to represent two further levels of subdivision within the code. The number so formed is used as part of the information held on tape by which a particular unit of information is identified. This system allows the individual lawyers to index their own cases with a considerable degree of uniformity, and the system is made flexible by allowing a short natural language descriptor of up to fifty-five characters to follow the code number, and also by allowing a range of numbers unrelated to the code for concepts which are important but not adequately expressed by reference to a particular section of the code. This permits retrieval by reference to concept where the code number is not known, but this is a relatively rare situation. Here the users understand the area of law well enough to be able to articulate the problem precisely in the terms of the code; their problem is simply that they need to know of current activity elsewhere in relation to that area. The system also uses another eleven-digit code to identify each particular case in such a way as to store together only transactions relevant to one particular Court appearance while permitting access to the records of other stages either precedent or subsequent. These records are compiled with the assistance of a standard questionnaire, and to assist the lawyer in its compilation he is provided by the computer with a complete record of all previous transactions in that case whenever he makes a new entry. The main use of these records is to permit the reproduction of regular monthly lists of pending and closed cases. These are compiled directly from the taped records, and present the identifying information ordered by the legal concepts as expressed in the numerical coding derived from the code numbers. Thus each month the lawyer in the local tax office receives a list of all pending and closed cases on each minute sub-provision of the Internal Revenue Code. In order to make this list of practical use to the lawyer, it is also necessary to provide access to the materials referred to in it. This is done by the use of a simple and inexpensive microfilm system. When making the report on his case the lawyer is also required to prepare an abstract setting out the facts and the positions taken by each side. This is regularly up-dated as changes take place. The abstracts are microfilmed, and a running number given to each page of the abstract reproduced on each reel of film. In this way a micro-film access number is created which is printed on the monthly listing of cases. Cartridges of film are held in each regional office of the Internal Revenue Service so that access is cheaply available where it is required when it is required. It takes only about five seconds for a hard-copy version to be produced from the microfilmed version.

As with the Swedish social insurance system, though to a lesser extent, the system is feasible because it has a relatively rigid and well-agreed structure so as to permit successful indexing, because the indexers and users are a common group with comparable backgrounds, training and needs, and because of the regular contact between them. In such circumstances an indexed system has many advantages, not least in cost, but unfortunately these characteristics do not obtain, and cannot obtain, for the whole field of legal information, and whole range of situations in which access to it is needed.

Juris[16]

This system has been developed by the United States Department of Justice for its own internal purposes, and is intended to help its employees with their legal research. One of its aims is to prevent the unwitting duplication of effort. The computing system is largely based upon 'RECON', a sophisticated on-line terminal-based retrieval

[16] See Kondos, 'JURIS: Remote Terminal Legal Information Retrieval at the United States Department of Justice', 4, *Law and Computer Technology*, 147 (1971). A fuller account, to which this summary is particularly indebted, is contained in a speech made by B. W. Basheer to the First National Conference of Automated Law Research held in Atlanta in March 1972.

package, itself originally developed by the Lockheed Corporation and improved by NASA. This is a second generation application in so far as the Justice Department was able to economize by taking over an existing system, and could concentrate its own effort on adapting it to its particular requirements. It was thus possible to add special desirable features from other systems, and to end up with a final version superior to any of the component parts at a fraction of the cost. The special position of the Federal government in relation to research which it has itself financed of course carries with it privileges not vouchsafed to private organizations.

The data capable of being handled by this system is very catholic, both in content and in from. It mainly comprises briefs and other documents generated by the Department, the US Code and similar public documents, and evidentiary materials. These can be entered in full-text, as key words or phrases, or in coded form. There is a correspondingly wide variety of possible output.

The system operates on-line, and performs three main retrieval functions. First it gives the usual retrieval facility based on Boolean operators, for example a combination of the SELECT and COMBINE commands is equivalent to Boolean 'and'. It has the further useful features of a LIMIT command which restricts the search to a specified time segment of the data-base, comparable content limitation being achieved by the insertion of a coded prefix to the SELECT command, and a KEEP command which enables the user to accumulate material in an interim store for display later.

A more unusual and obviously valuable function is the facility for assisting the user in the conduct of his search. One command EXPLAIN does just that, and helps the user by displaying a description of the system whenever he is in doubt about it. An EXPAND command assists the enrichment of the search. It can do this in a number of ways. One is by giving a display of words in the data-base which are closely associated alphabetically with the original search terms. This helps to cope with the problem of grammatical forms. Another utilizes hierarchies which have been incorporated into the system. One of these employs the West key-number system. The entry of a search term may thus be followed by the display of terms given at the next inferior level in the hierarchy. This constitutes a welcome, and overdue, recognition of the problem posed by generalizations and particulars, and constitutes an interesting attempt at a solution. A further useful facet of this technique is that the expansion terms are accompanied by an indication of the number of different documents in which they appear. It is possible for the user to obtain a complete log of the operations which he has conducted by the use of the command STATUS. Finally in this connection there is a DISPLAY command which provides a large number of formats, pre-set or user determined, in which documents can be presented. A particular feature here is the possibility of using a variable KWIC display of any number of terms in the same document which should be an invaluable aid to browsing.

The third function is to record search results. Three commands accomplish this, TYPE which causes a document to be printed in its entirety, in a KWIC form, or a citation or micro-fiche reference to it, at the remote console, PRINT which performs the same range of functions but on a high speed line printer situated at the central computer installation, and SPECIFY FORMAT which permits the varia-tion of output formats.

This is a fascinating and advanced system which embodies many of the techniques advocated in this book, though it does not, as yet, incorporate a thesaurus as such. It is at present far too early to evaluate the system since it was only due to become fully opera-tional at the end of 1972, but its progress should be followed with the very greatest interest.

8
Computers and litigation

Legal rules have not only to be made, they have also to be applied
where they are, or might be, relevant. Such applications may be made
privately by a member of the public or an official in ordering his
affairs in one way rather than another in the light of the rules. In
more doubtful cases the advice of a lawyer might be sought. In a
tiny minority of instances the further step of testing this advice by
litigation might be taken. The testing can itself take many forms,
such as arbitration or administrative decision as well as litigation in
the ordinary Courts. Litigation is also inseparably connected with
the process of the criminal law since in most countries punishment
cannot be inflicted upon an accused person without giving him the
opportunity of trial. The activity of litigation, therefore, constitutes
an important and necessary part of any legal system, and it too can
be assisted by the use of computer techniques. At present such techniques lag behind those employed in the activity of legislation, for
a number of reasons. One of the most important is that those involved
in the conduct of litigation are generally not so closely involved
with the allocation of the resources of the community as those involved with legislation. They are also insulated as far as possible
from close connections with government so as to preserve both the
reality and the appearance of independence and impartiality. This
results in their having less easy access to such facilities as state-owned
computers installed in government departments. A further factor is
that litigation is mainly conducted by private individuals who are
themselves often assisted by lawyers in private practice who operate
either individually or in relatively small groups. This too is hardly
conducive to the widespread employment of highly capital-intensive
plant such as computers.

It was noted in a previous chapter that legislative rules tend to be cast in general terms so as to limit the need for frequent revision. The corollary of this is that litigation must be left to resolve the inevitable problems of application. This makes good economic sense since litigation is normally decentralized and distributed between a relatively small number of decision-makers whereas legislation is centralized and tends to require a relatively large number of participants. For these reasons the process of any one piece of litigation involves the expenditure of less total resources than the creation of any one piece of legislation.

1 PREPARATION OF LITIGATION

This section will deal first with the application of computer techniques to the interviewing of clients in prospect of litigation which may or may not ensue, and the preparation of any necessary preliminary documents. The second section deals with the use of systems to organize the material which builds up both during this phase, and during the trial itself. Both will be very short, partly because not much is being done, and partly because the techniques involved do not differ significantly from those described in other connections.

Client interview
The starting point for almost all litigation is the first interview between the lawyer and his client. It is at this stage that the utmost delicacy is required so as to establish personal relations upon the best possible level so as to maximize harmonious cooperation and enhance the prospects of success. The lawyer must trust his client, and the client must have confidence in his adviser. To suggest that a computer should intrude at this stage seems to countenance the worst sort of Orwellian foreboding. Indeed in an ideal world the computer might well be banished from this stage of litigation. Unfortunately the world of legal advice is far from ideal. In Great Britain report after report condemns the defects of the current services, and in particular the unmet demand for legal assistance caused principally by the inaction of those needing advice and the scarcity of advisers to give it. The gap is only partly filled by voluntary services. In the United States a similar situation has led to the development of the concept of the Neighbourhood Law firm, partly under the auspices of the Office for Economic Opportunity. The situation requires examination. What are the reasons for it? What

are the consequences of it? Can computers help to ameliorate it? The scarcity of lawyers is partly a reflection of their general scarcity, but sharply focused by the unremunerative nature of much of the work currently left undone. The inaction of potential clients is partly through simple ignorance of the need to secure legal advice, and partly through suspicion of the conventional legal profession, recruited as it is from a different class of society, and associated most closely in its professional activities with the traditional adversaries of these potential clients. The consequence is that most of the need is unmet; and such as is met, is met only by inexperienced or unqualified advisers able to offer no more than a relatively low standard of relatively restricted services. This in its turn serves only to aggravate the suspicion responsible in part for the original problem. Seen against this background the computer takes on a different aspect. It introduces a capital intensive approach so permitting more productive use of the existing qualified manpower. It can be used to supplement the knowledge of the unqualified helpers. And in so far as it is substituted for the lawyer, so far from hindering the establishment of warm and friendly cooperation, it averts the risk of cold hostility. In short, many of the currently unassisted poor might well prefer a classless, impartial and knowledgeable machine to their conception of the average legal adviser. The possibility of computer application must therefore be examined.

It may be felt that even discounting the question of personal interrelation, the initial interview is so formless that it requires the use of a highly skilled human being to perform the intellectual processes necessary to conduct it successfully. The task of the interview is to establish the nature of the client's problem, to give appropriate advice, and to initiate any practical step to ameliorate it. The first is in many ways the most difficult. The lay client, and especially the ignorant and uneducated lay client who is currently so often unassisted, is frequently confused, inaccurate, unchronological and irrelevant in his statement of his problem. His adviser must first translate this rambling monologue into an orderly sequence of events. He must then consider the possible legal implications, and usually pose further questions to elicit relevant information. Only then can he go on to the further step of tendering advice or drafting documents. This process is indeed completely unsuitable for the computer. Even if audio transcription devices were perfected, the transcript of the client's story as told by the client would be far beyond the capacities of any known technology to deal with. A completely different approach must be employed in which the information becomes structured at an earlier stage. The most advanced work in this field is that carried out by Professors Chatterton and McCoy at the University of Wisconsin under the auspices of the Legal Services Division of the Office for Economic Opportunity. So far, however, this has not been developed into a completely comprehensive system, but concentrates rather on specific areas of great importance and frequent recurrence. The account which follows, while partly inspired by this work, does not purport to describe it, nor still less predict its future development.

In most legal advice offices at present the client first sees a receptionist. It is not envisaged that this will be different in the computerized office. In the conventional system the receptionist then refers the client to a qualified adviser. In the computerized system the client will be referred to one of a number of advice assistants. They would not normally be professionally qualified, but would be of similar calibre to the staff currently employed by Citizens Advice Bureaux, or as higher grade clerical assistants by lawyers. Their task would be to listen to the client's initial story with a view to deciding upon the main area of law involved. This process could itself be computerized, but for the present it is probably more sensible to retain human brain power at this stage. Nevertheless the client can even as early as this be introduced to the computer for the preparation of a new file. The pattern might be that adviser and client sit together in a position in which both can see a video screen and operate a keyboard. At first the adviser will operate the keyboard in response to cues from the system which appear upon the screen. Thus the first caption to appear might be 'Client's name?'. The adviser will ask the client his name, and key in the response. Other formal details will follow, and it may be expected that the client will gradually begin to answer the question as it appears on the screen, rather than wait for its repetition by the adviser. When these details have been completed, and the relevant area of law selected, the computer can be reintroduced.

In the Wisconsin work the client is encouraged to do as much as possible for himself, though the system will contain many directions to him to seek the assistance of the adviser. The essential element is that the appropriate legal area has been structured in such a way as to direct the client's responses into an orderly sequence

H

by way of the questions which appear on the screen. The structure has two main functions, to inform and to elicit information. It informs the client about the use of the machine and about the general principles of law in the branch in question, and where necessary may include the possibility of providing a hard copy print-out for future reference. It elicits information by means of the answers to the structured series of questions. These questions follow the general principles of learning systems, and allow sufficient flexibility for the computer to adapt itself to the background knowledge and speed of learning of the individual client.

In the case of any difficulty the adviser is on hand to help. For example, an illiterate client will need to have the screen read, and the answers keyboarded in. Even the partially literate client may need assistance in the latter respect, though the employment of multi-choice answer systems can go some way to reducing the necessity for this. The computer is throughout this process collating the information supplied by the client with a view to providing personal advice at the end of the interview. It is conceivable that no further human intervention should take place, but for the present it is probably still best for the adviser to make the final explanation of the situation to the client, just to make sure that it is thoroughly understood. As a result of the structured build-up of information and with the expertise built into the system, it should certainly be within the competence of even the professionally unqualified adviser to give good advice in the straightforward case, and to be able to detect which cases are not straightforward, especially as the adviser gains experience of using the computer system with an increasing range of clients each with his own individual variation of the basic pattern. In the non-straightforward case the client will naturally be referred to a fully professionally qualified adviser, whose skills will then be being used in the most economic way.

This is not the whole of the usefulness of computerized interviewing techniques. There are also a number of incidental advantages. One which has been averted to automatic file creation. The chore of summarizing interview notes into a coherent statement is completely eliminated, as are the largely mechanical tasks of filing and indexing. Both of these become completely automatic. Already many firms of lawyers are using computerized accounting systems, and the approach to client interviewing described above fits in well with such a development by allowing much more accurate time control, and billing. The computer will automatically record the time spent on any interview, and enter it into the billing system.

The most important ancillary advantage, however, and the most characteristically legal, is the facility which is provided for the automatic drafting of documents. This is basically similar to the automatic drafting of legislative documents described in a previous chapter. Here, however, there is if anything even more scope for its application. These techniques can be used for the compilation of everything from the most simple forms to complicated precedents for wills or conveyances. So long as there is some common material, it is immaterial that the precise concatenation of parts is unique. It is interesting that the work in Wisconsin began from the automatic drafting of wills, and only later extended into client interviewing. But the two are clearly intimately connected. From the point of view of the parties there is little difference between an interview for general advice and an interview to draft a will except that in the latter case the precise orientation of the will is established earlier. Where litigation is advised the interaction may be very close. The system may indeed itself be based upon the plan of a statement of claim which is drafted as the relevant answers emerge. This is clearly a very logical way to arrange the interview. The final end product may be the creation of a statement of claim, particulars and supporting proofs of evidence, and the advice will be tailored to this end. In the case of some of the more simple forms it will often be possible to draft without recourse to the usual question and answer format, but instead by automatic reference to information already held in the file. Names and addresses can be treated in this way, and their display can be either eliminated or used as a check for accuracy only.

It should be emphasized that these techniques are not yet completely established. They have been found successful in a theoretical environment but require much more testing under real-life conditions. They may come under strain in a number of places. The clients may not adapt easily to the use of the mechanical devices, some will be unable to read or spell, and very few will have any facility in using a keyboard. It may be found extremely difficult for the professionally unqualified advisers to select the most appropriate set of instructions, and this seems hardly to have been tested at all at present, largely because of the very limited range which have yet been constructed.

It is suspected that the most vulnerable aspect of the system will prove to be the compilation of the logical trees to express the different areas of law, and still more the maintenance of these trees in the fluid environment of the common law. Certainly the best hopes for success are in the more formal and rigid branches of law, but to be wholly successful the systems must extend to all areas where advice may be sought. It is possible that the law is more complicated and less certain than such systems allow. The main disadvantage of all learning systems is a tendency to over-precision and dogmatism. Contrary to popular belief the law is remarkably free of these vices, and it would be unfortunate if any computer system were ever to militate in their favour. So far no significant work seems to have been done on the automatic up-dating of algorithmic learning systems of this type. The problems seem formidable but not completely intractable. It will be necessary for them to be solved before whole-hearted support can be extended to really extensive computerized interviewing and drafting services. Nevertheless the case for using them in relation to selected topics to which they clearly suited such as the drafting of wills, or perhaps small claims litigation as envisaged by JUSTICE is very persuasive.

Documentation for litigation

As indicated above the computer can be used to create files in connection with litigation, to draft documents and to prepare accounts. In all these cases the computer is itself generating the documentation. But a great deal of the documentation used in the process of litigation is not generated by computers. It consists of the evidence of private transactions and will consist of things such as entries in private diaries, letters, notes, certificates and book entries. These have all to be handled by the lawyers. If the firm is not so highly mechanized as to use computer systems for the tasks mentioned earlier there will also be a mass of interview notes, proofs of evidence and accounting documents. This must all be handled efficiently, and it is clear that modern methods offer considerable advantages.

Litigation has its own special features which demand some specialized attention. For one thing the documentation can be immense. In *US* v. *United Shoe Machinery Corp.*[1] 6,000 patents were considered, 5,512 exhibits ran to 26,474 pages and the transcript itself totalled 14,194 pages. It is hardly surprising that over five years

[1] 110 Fed. Supp. 295, 299.

elapsed between complaint and judgement, and that apart from the time spent in taking 47 depositions amounting to 2,122 pages, the hearing lasted for 121 days.[2] In England in the criminal case of *R.* v. *Bloom* the documentation was estimated to run into tons of paper, and it was expected that the proceedings would last for a year.[3] To prepare efficiently for such cases a way must be found to deal with such volumes of paper. What is primarily required is an efficient indexing system so that references to specific documents can be assembled quickly. Most of the information is unlikely to have any permanent value once the case is over, and the expense of preparing the full-text of all the documents in a computer readable form would almost certainly not be justified. Nor would such a system be well adapted to the primary purpose of the rapid location of the relevant original documents.

More importantly, this is not necessary since the volume of documentation while immense can be related to a relatively few precisely defined issues upon which the outcome of the litigation depends. These concepts will be not only precise, but agreed and well understood by all the users, namely the lawyers involved in the litigation. The relatively confined boundaries of one piece of litigation avoid many of the problems associated with indexing vast ranges of material. Both selection of indexing terms and consistency in their application are enhanced. Liberal cross-reference is also possible. There are many ways of approaching this task. Conventional methods tend to rely heavily upon typed lists of documents relevant to particular points. This involves the selection of the points, the relation of each document to its appropriate point or points, and often the allocation of a code number to the document.

In many cases this is sufficient, but in especially complicated cases it may be desirable to split the issues down into rather more different points than can be conveniently handled by such lists. The cheapest and most simple equipment for dealing with this situation is the use of edge-punched cards. Such cards have numbered holes around the edges. The first step is to give each point in the case a number corresponding to one of the holes on the cards. A card is then used to represent each document in the collection, and for each point dealt with in it the relevant hole is extended to the edge of the card. Thus at the end of the indexing process there is a deck of

---

[2] Figures from Freed, 'Machine Data Processing', 6 *Practical Lawyer*, 73 (1960).
[3] In fact they were abruptly terminated by a plea of guilty.

cards corresponding to the number of documents in the collection, each document having one or more notches at its edge. A simple mechanical device can then be used to select the card representing documents relevant to a given point. Similarly, if the search needs to be more refined and only documents dealing with combinations of points are required, this can be easily accomplished by using the same technique. The facility for making such combinations clearly gives much greater power to the indexing since any number of complex notions can be easily constructed. Exactly the same sort of technique except that it operates by light passing through holes in special cards is also often applied to achieve the same results.

If a case is extremely complicated, or if the body of documents is abnormally large, it may be necessary to consider different techniques. One possibility is the use of standard punched cards. These are especially useful as they can be prepared in a form which renders them readable either by the machine or by the human eye. This is useful if the cards themselves are required in Court where there may well be no facilities for mechanical reading. Here a possible technique would be to allocate each card to a document and then to punch it with the identification of the document and the points dealt with by it. The cards could then be sorted on a mechanical sorter to assemble those dealing with a particular point, or combination of points. So far there is little advantage over the less sophisticated methods described above, except that it remains efficient for a much larger volume of documentation.

A further advantage, however, is that this technique permits the creation of new cards for special purposes by the use of associated computers which need only be very small. Thus an inverted file can be created automatically from the original cards in which each card represents a concept rather than a document, and the entries are document and not concept numbers. Similarly printers can be used to prepare the lists of documents relevant to given points or combinations of them. In any practice where computers are used for client interviewing, drafting or accounts, it would be worthwhile to apply computerized methods to document handling, since the extra computing would be minimal and the same apparatus and machines could be used for data creation, thus spreading overheads more widely.

2 COURT ADMINISTRATION

The previous part dealt with the preparation of an individual case and the preliminary work necessary to prepare it for trial. In this part the focus changes to the actual arrangements for trial. This entails a shift in emphasis from the individual case to consideration of the mass of cases considered as a whole, and from the work of the lawyer to the work of the Court administrator. This part is divided into two unequal sections, the first and longer concerned with the general administration of the system for enabling cases to be brought to trial, and the second and shorter dealing with arrangements relating to the conduct of the trial.

General administration

Here then the concern is with the facilities provided by the state for the conduct of litigation. This involves the provision and organization of judges, courtroom accommodation, and ancillary services, and the financing of all of these. Such provision is invariably the prerogative of the government since the private disposition of justice died out as an organized and comprehensive system in England as early as the reign of Henry II. In this respect, therefore, Court administration has something in common with legislation. The resources of the state can more readily be brought to bear on the problems, and it is reasonable to expect faster progress here than with the systems discussed in the previous part. A further reason for the more advanced state of computer application in relation to these problems is their acute nature, which is so spectacular that it can not be ignored. Since it is patently the province of government to solve these problems, and since the problems cause difficulty and resentment very widely in the community, there are obvious political advantages in solving them and, perhaps even more important, serious political disadvantages in failing to solve them. It might be thought that only a small proportion of the community, and a politically inarticulate section, would be affected by such problems as the long delays in bringing criminals to trial or in enabling victims of accidents to recover compensation, and that there might even be positive advantages in having an inefficient system for the recovery of traffic fines. But this would be to overlook the fact that inefficiency in the organization of litigation affects many more people than the parties to the litigation, that inefficiency always costs money, here it costs public money, and to that extent every member of the community is affected. It is therefore greatly to the advantage of any government to provide a speedy, efficient and cheap system of trial, and it is for these reasons that computer applications have been canvassed.

Here again most progress has so far taken place in the United States,[4] and for reasons which will have become familiar. Certainly the problems had assumed quite terrifying proportions there, in the total volume of litigation, in the size of the backlogs which had been allowed to build up, and in the times taken to bring a case to trial and achieve a hearing. In Cook County, Illinois, the Circuit Court alone is presented with over $3\frac{1}{2}$ million new items of litigation each year, of which over half involve motor vehicles.[5] The United States as a whole has to handle over 100 million parking offences each year.[6] In the United States District Court in Philadelphia the backlog of tort cases increased from 3,000 to 5,000 over the period 1961 to 1966, while the Superior Court of Los Angeles had in 1963 a backlog of 25,000 civil cases. Naturally such backlogs lead to commensurate and increasing delays in securing a hearing. In Los Angeles the average delay increased from twenty-one months in 1963 to twenty-four months by the following year.[7] But these are by no means maximum figures for the Courts in the United States. An analysis of civil cases in the Suffolk County of New York found that of 475 cases refered to an auditor for hearing in 1960, 401 were not referred until a year after they had been filed, and of these 313 waited for a further sixteen months for a hearing, and no fewer than 172 were still waiting after forty-five months, and had thus spent more than five years in the pipeline.[8] Similarly in the Court or Common Pleas in Allegheny County, Pennsylvania, the average delay in civil proceedings from the moment of filing was approximately $4\frac{1}{2}$ years in 1963[9] In England the problem is much less acute

---

[4] World of Peace Through Law Center Pamphlet 8, 'Uses of Computers and other Automated Processes by the Courts' (1968) lists 59 separate projects of which 57 are in the United States. In 1969 48 out of the 75 municipal Courts in California were using automated processes. Kleps, 'Computers and Court Management', 53 *Judicature*, 322 (1970).

[5] Johnen, 'Data Processing in the Circuit Court of Cook County, Illinois', 53 *Judicature*, 291 (1970).

[6] Halloran, 'Judicial Data Centres', 53 *Judicature*, 156 (1968).

[7] Higginbotham, 'The trial Backlog and Computer Analysis', 44 *F.R.D.*, 57 (1968).

[8] Spangenberg, 'Data Processing: A modern tool to help improve Judicial Administration', 50 *Mass. L.Q.*, 31 (1965).

[9] Ellenbogen, 'Automation in Court', 50 *A.B.A.J.*, 655 (1964).

with only 6,915 civil cases disposed of by the High Court in London or on Assize in 1967, and the longest average waiting time for any category of case, that of non-matrimonial cases tried in London, being no more than nine months.[10] Even this was considered thoroughly unsatisfactory by the Beeching Commission.[11] Of course individual cases can also exceed the average by a substantial margin. Thus in *Ford* v. *Lewis*[12] the events occurred in March 1960, the writ was issued in 1963, and the first hearing only came on in July 1970. It has now been referred back for re-hearing, and will so drag on still longer.

It must also be remembered that these problems occur within the context of a system which is seriously starved of resources on acount of competing demands, and in which the response to particular problems is invariably delayed. Thus even if expense were no objection, it is just not feasible to double the judiciary at a stroke of the pen to deal with an accumulated backlog of cases, at least not if the backlog is evenly distributed throughout the system. Trained manpower is extremely scarce and the period of training is long. Thus to double the size of the judiciary would inevitably mean draining the bar, and this could easily lead to still more serious problems. Similar difficulties exist in regard to all the other resources which the Court system needs. Clerks, shorthand writers, bailiffs, jurors and witnesses are all in limited supply, and must be used in the most economical way. Given the variety of constraints upon the system, and the enormous number of diffused resources which have to be coordinated into an efficient system, the case for the application of modern methods is virtually unanswerable. In the subsections which follow some examples will be given of the various points at which modern methods have so far been tried. It must be emphasized that this is no more than an illustrative list based upon accessible documentation. In particular, no attempt is made to delineate the sort of fully integrated system which might be developed to encompass all these applications, and no doubt many more.

STATISTICS : Most countries regularly publish official statistics of judicial business. They are, however, commonly regarded as of ex-

[10] Royal Commission on Assizes and Quarter Sessions (1969) Cmnd.4153, apps. 1 and 8.
[11] *Ibid.*, paras 65, 66.
[12] [1971] 2 All E.R. 983.

H*

tremely limited scope and range even for the purposes for which they are required.[13] Thus all serious research into the working of the judicial system has to be conducted on the basis of specially commissioned studies since the information in the official publications is invariably too meagre, and sometimes even misleading.[14] Even so general and straightforward a study as that of the Beeching Committee into the working of the Assize system had to be based upon a special statistical survey to determine the answers to such questions as how long cases have to wait for a hearing, the reasons for postponement, and the nature of variations between the ways in which different Courts deal with cases.[15] The basic difficulty here is that the documentation associated with the preparation of a case for trial is orientated towards the most efficient disposition of that case, and not to its aggregation with documentation for other cases so as to permit the compilation of mass statistics. This is itself dictated by the demands made upon the manpower currently available for clerical tasks within the Court system. Because the staff is so hard pressed, the information has to be prepared in the most simple way for disposition, and this makes the task of aggregating it more time-consuming and even more clearly beyond the regular capacity of the clerical labour. It is for this reason that the official statistics are so sketchy. The poverty of the system first creates the problem, and then impedes its solution. This is another situation in which the introduction of computer methods is the best way of determining how far computerized methods can be applied. One of the most valuable features of computerized systems is the mass of otherwise inaccessible statistical information which is generated. This can be enriched and re-presented with great ease, at great speed and at very low cost indeed. While conventional methods take approximately equal amounts of time to prepare and present the same set of statistics for each different form in which they are required, the computer can perform each subsequent manipulation of the data in a fraction of the time and at a fraction of the cost of the initial operation once the data has been prepared. As noted, it is just such enriched and re-ordered information which is needed for statistical purposes, and especially for those aimed at improving efficiency.

[13] See the recent reports of the Committees on Criminal (Cmnd. 3448) and Civil (Cmnd. 3684) Statistics in Great Britain.
[14] See e.g. Report of the Committee on Statutory Maintenance Limits (1968), Cmnd. 3587, and McGregor *et al.*, *Separated Spouses* (1970).
[15] Cmnd. 4153, app. 2.

It may be necessary to record some extra details in the first place for these purposes,[16] but the time taken in doing this will be more than compensated for by the savings in the time needed for subsequent compilation of statistics, and hopefully in improvements in the system made possible in the light of the information provided by such detailed statistics.

SIMULATION : A particular, and rather sophisticated, application of such statistics to improve the system of Court administration is in their use to create a computer model of the administrative system. The use of similar computer models is already a common feature of administrative planning in other areas, both public and private. It is, for example, extensively used by defence departments who simulate the international military situation for the playing of 'war games', and by economists and demographers who use models of the national economy or population. These models mirror the existing situation, and then illustrate the consequences of changes in the possible variable factors. The use of the computer permits the construction of very complicated structures, and an infinite array and number of combinations of such factors. The system of Court administration is very eligible for such treatment since it is suitably complex and there are many possible variables. So far there is little documentation of works in this area though it may be expected to expand in the future. Thus the Department of Justice in the United States has instituted a programme at Notre Dame University which will construct such a model of two different courts in Indiana. Similar techniques also seem to have been employed by scientists at Imperial College, London University, in connection with the work of the Beeching Commission, but not using computers. A somewhat simplified model has also been applied to the United States District Court for the District of Columbia.[17] In all such models the first essential is to describe the system to be simulated in sufficient detail for the model to work effectively, and for this it is necessary to have minute statistical information about the details of its working which is too often unavailable at present. In the District of Columbia system it was necessary to prepare special records of the numbers of defendants in criminal cases, their characteristics in terms of the offences committed by them, the pleas they made, the

[16] The Suffolk county questionnaire required twenty-nine different items of information about each case. Spangenberg, *op. cit.*
[17] Navarro and Taylor, 'An Application of Systems Analysis to Aid in the Efficient Administration of Justice', 51 *Judicature*, 47 (1967).

procedures they chose, details of disposition in terms of the number and length of the various stages in the trial process and the intervals between them, and the ultimate pattern of sentencing. The next features to be considered are the constraints upon the system in physical terms, such as the availability of accommodation, numbers of judges, lawyers, jurors, witnesses and administrative personnel, and in legal terms such as the impermissible forms of trial for particular offences and required intervals between different stages of the process. When all these details have been assembled it is necessary to write the programmes which will allow the computer to calculate the effects of the interaction of the variables. Since the information will have been derived from a working system an objective check of the efficiency of the programmes is available. Thus the programmes should, when programmed with all the observed variables but one, calculate a figure for that, equivalent to the observed value. Once this has been established for all variables the model can be used to test possible modifications, and especially modifications of the existing constraints since these are most likely to be capable of control in practice. Thus the effects of providing extra courtrooms or extra judges, or of changing the rules relating to the prescribed forms of trial for different offences, can be calculated precisely. In the District of Columbia criminal system, for example, it was found that half of the adult felony cases were taking over six months before their initial disposition, and thirty-six days of that time was spent in waiting for a grand jury. The model was applied, revealing that the provision of one extra grand jury, one full-time attorney and one full-time clerk would reduce that period to eight days without any significant increase in waiting time after arraignment. This was the most significant reduction revealed by the model, but by indicating a large number of other possible further savings it was calculated that the average delay in bringing criminal offenders to trial could be roughly halved.

Such techniques can be applied to any aspect of Court administration and can be expected to yield similarly impressive results. If they are also applied to the financial management of the Courts it is quite likely that they will pay for their costs in direct financial savings.[18]

CALENDARING : The production of a smooth flow of work keeping judges, courtrooms, lawyers, jurors and court officials fully occupied is an exceedingly difficult undertaking. There are so many variables

[18] Johnen, *op. cit.*

to be considered, and so many unforeseeable impediments which may occur. Whatever system is employed, it is clear that the ideal of full and steady occupation for everyone will not be achieved, but the application of modern methods can nevertheless be expected to bring about a considerable improvement upon current performance. This was one of the earliest areas for the application of automatic data processing in the United States, where twelve Courts had such systems in operation as early as 1965. In some areas, such as traffic Courts, calendar preparation is relatively simple since the lengths of cases are reasonably predictable and the volume of cases high. But for ordinary civil and criminal Courts where there is more variation, it is necessary to devise more sophisticated systems.

One of the most advanced examples of such a system is to be found in Philadelphia, where it operates for both Common Pleas and Municipal Courts and for both criminal and civil business. The aim of such systems is to secure as smooth a flow of work as possible, and by first detecting and then eliminating possible areas of conflict of work, to speed up the whole process of litigation. Thus in the United States District Court for Eastern Pennsylvania it was found that 8 per cent of the backlog of cases in 1961 involved longshore-men, and that by 1966 this proportion had risen to 23 per cent. It was calculated that unless some action were taken there would be a further rise to 60 per cent by 1972. Further investigation revealed that the cause of this increase was a concentration of work of this nature among too few firms of attorneys who because of their existing obligations were falling further and further behind. When this was discovered and such cases were re-assigned to other lawyers, more such cases were terminated in the ensuing two months than had been terminated in the preceding two years.[19] It is widely believed that postponements of hearings on account of overwork by the most popular lawyers accounts for a very high proportion of the delay in litigation in the United States. The civil system in Philadelphia is primarily orientated towards the solution of this problem. Information about each case is entered into computer storage, stating the present status, type of trial requested, Court term and number, date of certificate of readiness filed by the lawyer, and a host of other details. When the certificates of readiness are completed the case is entered on to a file of cases available for trial. Each afternoon the computer produces a list of the top 250 cases, 125 jury

[19] Higginbotham, *op. cit.*

and 125 non-jury cases. This list assesses priority by reference to the date of the certificate of readiness or any special factors, and then weeds it out by eliminating conflicts of obligation between lawyers. These lists are then published in the local legal newspaper and are delivered to offices on the following day. Lawyers who are engaged in the top twenty cases in each list have to appear in a call-room at 9.30 in the morning of that following day, and are expected to be ready to go to trial since a case takes approximately five days to work up the list into the top twenty, allowing ample opportunity to seek a postponement. Indeed this may be the most important improvement facilitated by the system. By eliminating last-minute postponements it has been possible to secure a much better use of courtroom and judicial resources. As lawyers become engaged in cases their names are entered on an engaged file, and this is used to edit the list of available cases so that a case will not appear on it if one of the lawyers is otherwise engaged. This list is also published daily and circulated to the lawyers whose names appear on it. In addition a list is produced each month for every lawyer in the system showing all the cases in which he has been retained. The judge is provided with a print-out of relevant data in his case and fills in disposition data so that the records are automatically kept up to date. This data also allows a wealth of statistical information to be gathered about the pattern of work and disposition of cases in Philadelphia. The same data-base is further used to produce listings of cases by lawyers, names of parties, names of judges, by courtroom or in whatever way is useful for a particular purpose without any additional clerical labour. The system has recently been improved by the use of a number of video terminals situated in convenient places for even speedier up-dating and display of information in a required form.[20] The criminal system is not so highly orientated towards the elimination of conflicts in the work pattern of individual lawyers, but otherwise operates in a similar way, producing daily lists of cases, documentation for the grand jury, district attorney dockets, arraignment schedules and even witness and defendant subpoenas.

A further problem of calendaring which occurs in some places arises on account of the juxtaposition of a large number of indepen-

[20] Blake and Polansky, 'Computer Streamlines Case-Load at Philadelphia Common Pleas Court', 53 *Judicature*, 205 (1969); 'Data Processing in the Courts of Philadelphia', IBM Application Brief.

dent Court systems, with the result that lawyers may practice in any number of them. There are fifty such systems in the San Francisco area for example. At present each operates independently of the others in its scheduling of cases with the result that frequent conflicts of engagement occur.[21] It is clear that the use of a large modern computer could achieve coordination of these calendars, and could indeed cope with the calendaring for the entire state, and at the same time achieve enormous economies in the use of clerical labour currently employed in all fifty areas.

RECORD KEEPING : It is clearly necessary to make and keep records of all litigation in any Court system. It should always be readily available for up-dating and accessible to users. In most current systems the documentation is compiled by hand; indeed many different hands since much of it consists of copies of documents compiled by judges or the parties' lawyers. It is generally filed by reference to the case to which it relates, and is not readily accessible for other purposes. One judge has estimated that in his system, if he knows the names of the parties and the number of the case, he can assemble most of the records in about twenty minutes, but if he wants an absolutely complete set he needs twice or three times as long. If he knows only the names of the parties then it will take him half as long again, and if he knows neither the names of the parties nor the number of the case, then his only hope is to find someone who can supply those details as a result of recognizing his description of the case in which he is interested.[22] Within a computerized system this sort of problem can be completely eliminated.

Indeed it is possible to avoid many such problems by adopting very much more simple forms of automation. A typical and early example is the Probate Court at St Louis which instituted a punched card system as early as 1962. The Court then handled about 3,500 estates at any one time, and each was active for about nine months. The work of the probate court is somewhat repetitive, and it was found that 98 per cent of the business could be expressed in terms of 365 different minutes of Court action. These were coded, and pre-punched on cards so that there was a stack of such cards for each minute. As an estate entered the system it was allocated a

---

[21] Davidson and Davidson, 'Computerised Court Calendaring' 54 *A.B.A.J.*, 1097 (1968).
[22] Hayden, 'Computers and the Administration of Justice', Proceedings 1963 Fall Joint Computer Conference.

number and a master card was prepared. Then as each action is taken the master card and the appropriate pre-punched one are put into a punching machine which first transfers the estate number on to the pre-punched blank, and the clerk then keys in the cost of the particular transaction. The minute card is then used to generate the mailing of a note of the transaction to the representatives of the estate, to provide a list of transactions for printing in the local legal newspaper twice daily, and to up-date the accounting system. The minute card is then added to the file on the particular estate. This is an extremely simple system, but it has enabled considerable economies to be made while at the same time increasing efficiency. Because all the various records are generated by the same card, opportunities for error and delay in transcription from one record to another are eliminated. It ensures that all the records are automatically kept together, and available to the judge whenever he deals with the estate. It has simplified the accounting to such an extent that whereas before the introduction of the system only 150 accounts could be submitted for payment each week, it is now possible to submit all 3,500 as frequently as desired without any additional effort. All official records such as Court minutes, settlement notices and accounts are generated by the same cards, and it is possible also to use them for the compilation of statistics about the Court's business. This has enabled an accurate prediction of the effects of a proposed change in fee structure, which before the introduction of the system would have entailed considerable extra administrative expenditure on clerical checking of records held in the old forms.[23]

For Courts with more varied procedures and jurisdiction a more sophisticated computer based system may be necessary to achieve comparable results.[24] But the basic principle is the same, namely to produce all the records on the basis of one entry of data into the system, to up-date them automatically and to provide access by reference to any part of the data held in the files. This enables routine accounting, record keeping, addressing and publication to be handled with ease, and also provides facilities for special searches and statistical examination of the data held.

JURY SELECTION: In the United States especially, jury selection is

[23] Hensley, 'Punched Cards produce Progress in Probate Court', 48 *A.B.A.J.*, 138 (1962).
[24] See e.g. Ellenbogen, 'Automation in the Courts', 48 *A.B.A.J.*, 138 (1962).

a tiresome and time-consuming process. In Union County, New Jersey, for example, the conventional system first involved sending out jury questionnaires to every resident in the county. These were then scrutinized, ineligible persons eliminated and the remainder filed. For each session of the Courts three thousand potential jurors had to be selected, and divided into panels, and sub-panels. The first step was to type out in full all three thousand names complete with addresses and occupations. These lists were then screened, and any who had been eliminated were replaced. Each name was given a number, and a jury selection into panels and sub-panels took place by drawing discs with corresponding numbers. The whole process took a day and a half, and involved the participation of about eight people including a judge. The next task was to type up panel and sub-panel lists, again with full names, addresses and occupations. Then subpoenas, payroll ledger sheets and name slips had to be typed, amounting in all to about two months' work for one typist.[25] It will be seen that this is a thorough and impartial process, but highly repetitive and time-consuming, and clearly susceptible to automation.

Indeed in many cases it is possible to start from an electoral roll which is already in computer readable form. This can be automatically reduced by running against it records of those who are ineligible for some reason, such as criminals, lawyers or parties to the cases to be heard. The reduced list can then be subjected to an automatic random selection procedure which will produce lists of names grouped or presented in any or all of a number of different ways. The same output can be used to generate any further documentation which may be required, such as addressed envelopes, subpoenas and accounting records. The great advantage of automation is in speed. The New Jersey system, for example, takes only an hour to accomplish all the tasks which were described at the beginning of this section. Such savings in time are matched by savings in cost, and it has been estimated that in another of the early systems, that for Dutchess County, New York, the saving amounts to 1,000 dollars a week.[26] It is, of course, necessary to design the system carefully so that the selection of the jury really is random, and that incidental factors do not accidentally distort the

[25] Wagner, 'Jury Selection by Computer', 2 *Law and Computer Technology*, 6 (October 1969).
[26] Halloran, 'Judicial Data Centres', 52 *Judicature*, 156 (1968).

result, as has occasionally happened on the introduction of such systems. In New Jersey, for example, an early punched card system failed because the final sort of the cards was by reference to the third letter of the street name in the address, and this was found to throw together people from the same neighbourhoods, and thereby, given the ghetto pattern of distribution of population in that area, of the same ethnic character. However, such problems are easily avoided once there is awareness of them, and particularly if computers rather than punched card equipment are employed.

A further possible advantage of employing computerized methods is that the process of jury selection will strain the Court's administrative personnel less, with the result that it can be completed earlier in relation to the date of the trial. This will allow more time for claims of exemption, and for replacement for other reasons to take place. It will be further assisted by the use of computerized lists right up to date at the time of selection. Under the existing system an out of date list is often searched at the last minute; the computer can overcome both difficulties at once and so make the system much smoother in operation.

TRAFFIC SYSTEMS : The single most common application of automatic data processing to Court administration in the United States is almost certainly in respect of traffic offences. By 1968 about two hundred traffic Courts were applying for such techniques. The reason is simply that in urban centres there is so much work for such Courts that there is no other way of handling it. In Chicago there are about 2½ million parking offences each year, and about half that number of moving traffic offences. Every day the Courts deal with four to six thousand cases.[27] Such volumes of work clearly generate very large sums of money in fines, and the computer system can be paid for by the saving of interest on outstanding sums by speeding up collection, and making it more thorough. A feature of the Cook County system in Chicago is that both moving traffic offences and parking offences are cross-related to each other, and with further computerized records held by the police department and the vehicle licensing department. Thus if a man who appears in Court on a moving traffic offence has a number of unpaid parking fines these will be dealt with at the same time, since a simple automatic procedure put such information on to his file. Similarly, if such a person applies for a new vehicle licence, it can be made a

[27] Danaher, 'Computers in Court', 3 *Law and Computer Technology*, 128 (1970).

condition for obtaining it that he has first paid all outstanding fines. It has been found that by giving publicity to computer application in these areas, a significant deterrent effect has been achieved, and that the incidence of early payment has shown a dramatic increase, thus easing further congestion in the administrative process. Similarly in Suffolk County, New York, the automatic integration of summonsing and licensing procedures has been estimated to have reduced the incidence of non-appearance on summons from 60 per cent to 15 per cent.[28] The adoption of such measures in Cook County has tripled the revenue of the Traffic Division while at the same time permitting a reduction in the number of personnel employed, while in Suffolk County, New York, a computer system costing 25,000 dollars a year has replaced forty-five clerks costing 300,000 dollars a year.

A feature of the Cook County system is that the judges themselves compile the forms in relation to the disposition of traffic offences, and these are then entered on pre-punched disposition cards. The use of the computer system makes it possible to integrate the Court's accounting system very closely with these records. The cash registers at the Court are themselves required to tally with the running totals calculated from the cards, and dispositions must tally with the books of tickets issued to policemen. This ensures the system so far as possible from the danger of embezzlement and corruption. Here too there are the by now familiar advantages of automatic record keeping and publication of the various returns required of the traffic court.

Conduct of the trial

One of the perennial nightmares of the computerphobe is trial by computer in which the machines, with or without wigs, take the place of the judge. It is true that suggestions are sometimes made that this might occur in special situations where the facts fall into familiar patterns, such as traffic offences.[29] In fact there is not the slightest chance of this happening without some developments in computer technology so completely different from anything under current investigation as to be totally unimaginable. But automation cannot be excluded from the courtroom altogether in a more modest

[28] Orchanian, 'Effective Use of Computers in Government', 1 *Rutgers Journal of Computers and Law*, 98 (1970).
[29] Allott, 'Law and Language', Inaugural Lecture School of Oriental and African Studies.

role, and it may one day extend to some low level of computer application.

COURTROOM RECORDING : One of the bottlenecks in the judicial process at present is the difficulty of securing transcripts of proceedings speedily enough for appeals to be heard promptly. In the case of the 'Oz' conspiracy trial[30] in Great Britain, for example, bail was exceptionally allowed pending the appeal because there was likely to be a five-month delay before the transcripts were available. This delay is largely caused by the difficulty in securing an adequate number of shorthand writers and transcribers. In the United States it is common for Court reporting to be done on special stenographic machines, and one solution which has been investigated by the Aspen Systems Corporation is the development of programmes capable of transcribing the stenographic tape automatically into computer readable tape, whereupon transcripts could be produced on a high speed printer without any delay at all. There are, however, considerable technical difficulties in accomplishing this, and stenographers would be required to adopt much more uniform practices than obtained at present. The system would also, of course, still be limited by the supply of stenographers.

A different solution is to use tape recording techniques in the courtroom instead of employing shorthand writers. This solution has been adopted in a number of American states,[31] and has been introduced on an experimental basis in some Courts in the United Kingdom.[31a] In Alaska the system has been in operation exclusively for more than ten years with considerable success.[32] In that system the judge is responsible for the production of an accurate record, but the key figure is the clerk. He acts not only as clerk, but also as a sort of reporter. His most important function is to maintain a full and accurate log of the proceedings so that the tape can be interpreted. Such a log will start with the title and number of the case, and the names of the judge and the lawyers, and the nature of the hearing. Then as proceedings start the clerk enters the name of each speaker and the number from the tape counter so as to indicate who is speaking at each point. Similarly, entries are made

---

[30] R. V. Anderson [1972] 1 Q.B. 304.

[31] Alaska, Indiana, Tennessee and Virginia.

[31a] 37 courts at the Royal Courts of Justice and 19 County Courts. Report of a Working Party on Recording Court Proceedings (1972) para. 4. 2.

[32] Reynolds, 'Alaska's Ten Years of Electronic Reporting', 56 *A.B.A.J.*, 1080 (1970).

for extraneous events such as the production of real evidence, or a change from examination in chief to cross-examination. This log is kept in duplicate, one copy for the file and another for the Court journal. The tape is then transcribed by an audio-typist, who need not, and probably will not, have been present in Court. The use of the log makes this possible. When the transcript is completed it is then checked for accuracy, and entered in a folder on the cover of which are cross-references to any other reports of the same proceedings.

When this system was being introduced it was carefully compared with the conventional system to check its accuracy, and it was found to eliminate a number of different types of inaccuracy, such as unconscious correction of grammar and syntax, omission of questions and answers apparently deemed irrelevant by the reporter, failure to hear and transcribe words accurately, and the interpolation of passages of interpretative narrative when things went too fast. One difficulty with the Alaska system was occasioned by the use of a single-track system with six microphones, since it was very difficult to distinguish what was happening when more than one person was talking at once. This difficulty can be eliminated by the use of multi-track tapes, one track for each microphone. Then in this situation each track can be played back separately to resolve the confusion. It should be noted that the conventional reporter will in this situation fare worse than the tape recorder since he will tend to hear and write down only one of the contributions being made, since the human brain cannot in such situations perform the complicated logical operations involved in understanding several contributions being made simultaneously. Hearing is, like all sensory perception, an incredibly demanding task for the brain, and involves the coordination of a very large number of different rules. The relative failure of audio input systems for computers is the counterpart in the realm of hearing to the relative failure of optical character recognition devices in the realm of seeing. The translation of sounds into words and sentences taxes the brain when one person is speaking, and defeats it altogether when there are a large number. The use of a single track tape gives some advantage to the transcriber in that it can be replayed over and over again, and at reduced speeds, so as to enable each strand to be followed separately whereas the shorthand writer hears everything at once and only once. There can be no doubt that the multi-track tape offers the best solution.

There are some technical difficulties in siting microphones, but improved wireless microphones can be expected to meet some of the difficulties created by lawyers, who in the United States especially seem to enjoy moving around the courtroom.

The advantages of using such recording systems are first that the transcription tends to be more accurate, and perhaps even more importantly, that in the event of a dispute as to its accuracy the tape can be played back for the Court to make up its own mind about this. Such a procedure incidentally permits many audible but non-verbal aids to interpretation and evaluation to be used such as tone of voice, timing, hesitation, emphasis, and accent. These can be invaluable in situations where there is potential ambiguity, and might be further enhanced if a visual record were combined into a complete system. It has been found in Alaska that the facility of playing back the recording has considerably reduced the number of disputes, and the incidence of cases where an appeal by way of a trial *de novo* has been requested. The second great advantage is in the speed of production. The tape itself can be copied extremely quickly, and as an interim or emergency measure copies can be supplied to lawyers or judges within minutes of the end of the day's proceedings. The log can be equally quickly photo-copied and there is thus a complete working tool as soon as it can possibly be required. Similarly, transcription can be speeded up since it is not necessary to have it done by the reporter who originally made the record. It can be done by ordinary audio-typists, and thus by dividing tape and log between a number of different transcribers can be accomplished extremely quickly, and even during the proceedings themselves if the early parts of tape and log are removed for transcription at appropriate intervals during the day.[32a] A further cause of frustration and delay is also avoided here in that the transcription is no longer dependent upon the continuous availability of a particular individual. In conventional systems if the original reporter is unavailable on account of illness or death it is sometimes extremely difficult to provide adequate transcription at all. The third major advantage is in the saving of cost occasioned by the combination of functions of clerk and reporter, and the employment of less highly paid audio-typists for transcription. It is estimated that Alaska has thus saved a quarter of a million dollars per annum out of a total

[32a] Though the British working party recommended the retention of shorthand writing for this purpose. *Op. cit.* para 6.3.

budget of four millions, while another estimate is of saving of two to five thousand dollars per courtroom per year where the system has been introduced.[33] A further possible improvement might be the use of a film of the proceedings in the courtroom by the use of a simple camera which could be synchronized with the tapes to assist still more with interpretation. Such a system could also be used for depositions, or any other occasion when evidence has to be given remotely from the courtroom.

It is appreciated that such a system has little current scope for computer application. It is, however, conceivable that one day audio input devices will reach a sufficient degree of sophistication as to achieve direct transcription, and by the use of computerized logging and matching the two outputs, the clerical labour element might be further reduced.

INDEXED INFORMATION : Much of the information which is indexed and stored in the sorts of computer system so far described may be useful to lawyers or judges during the actual trial of a case. Thus the accused's previous record might be useful in those jurisdictions where use can be made of such information, or records of other cases in which one of the parties has been involved, or a particular plot of land, or road, or details relating to jurors on the jury panel. Once such records are automated, access to them is made easier and the trial process can proceed much more smoothly. A particularly dramatic example of the use in a trial of computerized, though not legal, information involved an action for negligence brought against a hospital.[34] The plaintiff called a doctor as an expert witness to testify that the treatment given for a rare disease had been defective. The defence lawyer was then able to go to the local hospital where the records had been recently computerized, and check through $6\frac{1}{4}$ million treatment charts to find the only twelve cases which had occurred there, including one which the plaintiff's witness had prepared. This showed that he had himself failed to diagnose the disease, and had indeed proceeded in much the same way as the hospital in the instant case, and his evidence was thus completely neutralized. The lawyer was quite sure that he had been able to find this vital document only because the records had been computerized, which made it possible to complete the search in less

[33] Martin, 'Electronic Courtroom Recording', 50 *Judicature*, 262 (1967).
[34] Morris, 'Hospital Computers in Court', *Modern Uses of Logic in Law*. March 1963. p. 61.

than half an hour. In the trial environment it is likely to be this reduction in the time spent in searching for material which sharpens performance. It is easy to translate this example from hospital to Court records, and to see how much more effective trial practice may become.

9

Prediction of judicial decisions

In this chapter the applications of computerized methods to the prediction of judicial decisions will be very briefly discussed. First, some consideration will be given to the reasons for the use of computerized methods to perform this task, then some of the different methods will be mentioned, and finally a short evaluation will be made.

1 REASONS FOR THE APPLICATION OF COMPUTERIZED METHODS

Lawyers have always attempted to predict judicial decisions. To do so is an essential part of their duty to their clients, who cannot without some such advice choose sensibly whether to litigate or not, or at what level of settlement they should aim. Hitherto, however, it has normally been conceived as essentially a matter of applying human judgement to a consideration of the evidence and the likelihood of proving certain facts, and on the basis of such facts to apply the relevant legal rules. On appeal the former task is usually eliminated, and it becomes merely, but by no means trivially, a matter of forecasting what rules of law are likely to be applied and estimating their probable effect on the facts as found by the trial Court. This traditional approach assumes that the Courts will seek to apply the existing rules, and that they will be applied consistently and impartially. In other words it assumes the principles of *stare decisis*. Such an approach might concede the utility of computers to find the relevant rules of law in the ways described in the first part of this chapter, but, once they had been found, would tend to see little further scope for the application of computers.

It is only if it is assumed that *stare decisis* does not apply in the way envisaged by the traditional theorist that the opportunity for computer application begins to emerge. If the judges are not deciding cases according to the existing rules alone, but are instead changing them, or are not applying them consistently or impartially, then any prediction of the decisions which the judges will reach must be made upon some other basis. The view that judges were indeed motivated by other, and unavowed, considerations than those expressed in their judgements was one of the cardinal tenets of the jurisprudence of American legal realism.[1] Similarly American legal realists enthusiastically endorsed Justice Holmes's dictum that 'predictions of what the Courts will do in fact, and nothing more pretentious, is what I mean by the law'.[2] For the American legal realist one of the fundamental tasks was the prediction of the decisions of the Courts on something other than the rules of law expounded in the reports. The range of factors canvassed varied from the state of the judge's digestion to his intuitive reaction to certain combinations of circumstances. This approach has always been most popular in the United States, and it is interesting to note that the leading exponent of a somewhat more moderate version of the theory in Great Britain, Dr Goodhart, is himself an ex-patriate American. There are good reasons for this phenomenon. Among the most important are the greater political role necessarily played by the Courts in the United States, and especially by the Supreme Court of the United States. The Constitution requires the Court to decide ultimate questions of interpretation which can hardly avoid being political, and this power has been interpreted as applying also to general oversight of the systems of the several states. In the states themselves many of the judges are elected, and appointments to the Supreme Court generate intensive political lobbying, as shown in the recent Haynsworth and Carswell nominations. In this atmosphere, and given this role, it is inevitable that the Supreme Court should permit itself to change its course from time to time, and accordingly it has never applied a strict policy of always following its own decisions. The

[1] For an early Realist expression of this view see Haines, 'General Observations on the Effects of Personal, Political and Economic Influences on the Decisions of the Judges', 17 *Illinois L.R.*, 96 (1922).
[2] Holmes, 'The Path of the Law', 10 *Harvard L.R.*, 456 at 461 (1896). Probably the most widely misunderstood statement in the whole corpus of jurisprudential writing.

House of Lords in Great Britain has now also adopted a more flexible policy.[3]

The question then arises of how judicial decisions are to be predicted, if the existing rules are not to be considered the sole determinant. There are a number of possibilities. One is to try to establish the attitudes of the judges to social policies, and to try to demonstrate a correlation between those attitudes and their decisions. Another is to try to establish a link between the circumstances which occur in the cases and the decisions of the judges. In both approaches computers have been applied to assist with the complicated calculations often involved. The writers labelled as legal realists between the wars, while interested in predictions as a matter of theory, generally contented themselves with expounding the theories without demonstrating their truth by statistical studies. Since the war, however, these writers who were mainly lawyers have been succeeded by political scientists who have been prepared to apply statistical techniques to the measurement of behaviour. These scientists have found in the law, and more especially in the decisions of the Supreme Court of the United States, a fertile and well-documented field for their application.

2 METHODS

As indicated above a rough distinction is made here between those who seek to predict judicial decisions on the basis of the policies adopted by the judges, whether gathered from extra-curial sources or from voting patterns on particular issues, or from voting alliances between different groups of judges; and those who seek to predict decisions on the basis of the reaction of the judges to particular sets of circumstances with which they are confronted. For the former, the horizon is limited to the prediction of decisions in terms of the probability of a particular outcome. For the latter, at least in theory, there might be further possibilities. If it is indeed possible to analyze cases into finite groups of facts and to establish accurate values for these facts, it might be a short step to the replacement of some of the functions of judges by the use of computers. The judges would still be needed to determine the facts, or at least to guide juries in their determination of the facts, but the application of the rules to the facts could be handed over to the computer so as to avoid any possibility of inconsistency induced by human error. If the

[3] Note [1966] 3 All England Reports, 77 (House of Lords).

236 COMPUTERS AND THE LAW

rules required changing this could equally well be handed over to
the legislature which is at least as democratic as the judiciary. It is
ironical that techniques nurtured by a distrust of mechanical jurisprudence and the tyranny of precedent should lead to such a possibility. In the sections which follow a distinction is made between
those who are primarily concerned with broad attitudes, and those
who are more concerned with reactions to particular concatenations
of facts.

Attitude studies
In a way this is the most sceptical approach. It assumes that judicial
decisions are swayed by unavowed, and perhaps unavowable, factors
separate both from the legal rules as the conventional view of *stare
decisis* is thought to assume, and from the factual content of cases
as the studies in the following section assume. One difficulty is to
determine the attitudes to be investigated, and to secure data in a
sufficiently reliable form for it to be correlated with the decisions
that the judges are assumed to make on its basis. Three particular
studies will be mentioned as examples of the research which has
been conducted into the wider attitudes of the judges, and the way
in which their decisions are influenced. Sometimes the attitudes
of the judges are regarded as linked to their attributes, sometimes
they are deduced from their behaviour on the bench, and sometimes
they are directly investigated. Professor Nagel links the first and third
of these approaches in his study of criminal cases.[4] He took as his
sample 313 state and federal Supreme Court judges as listed in the
1955 directory of American judges. He established such attributes as
age, education, religion, ancestry, previous occupations, pressure
group affiliation and politics from published sources, and attributes
by a special questionnaire. The results were then tabulated, and
compared with a tabulation of the decisions arrived at by these
judges. Only full Court criminal case decisions were considered in
this study. A case was regarded as a full Court decision if all the
judges from that Court included in the sample participated, and a
criminal case was defined so as to exclude tax and business regulation cases. This still, of course, leaves a very wide variety of issues,
especially as criminal appeals tend to vary in content depending
upon the particular rules for appealing which apply in the juris-

[4] Nagel, 'Judicial Backgrounds and Criminal Cases', 53 *Journal of Criminal Law,
Criminology and Police Science*, 333 (1962).

diction. Thus in some jurisdictions most appeals will turn on pro-
cedural questions, while in others with a more liberal system more
will turn on the provisions of the substantive law. It is not clear that
sufficient allowance was made for this.

The judges were scored simply in terms of the proportion of votes
which the judge cast for the defence out of his total number of
votes. Thus a judge voting twice for the defence in ten decisions
would be given a score of 0·20. The scores for all the judges on a
particular Court were then averaged, and the results presented in
terms of the relation of the scores of judges having the particular
attribute under investigation to the average of the scores of all the
other judges on their particular Court. Thus two judges of the
same degree of defence-mindedness would score differently depending upon the defence-mindedness of their colleagues. It should also
be noted that only non-unanimous decisions of the Courts were considered, and then only if both the presence and the absence of the
attribute in question was represented on the Court. It is argued
that it is reasonable to exclude unanimous decisions since their
inclusion could make no difference to a judge's being above or below
the average for his particular Court. This is true, but the exclusion
of unanimous decisions exaggerates the degree of deviance from the
mean, and this must be borne in mind in interpreting the results.
A result was considered statistically significant if the distribution of
votes according to the relevant characteristics could only be explained on the basis of chance at the 0·05 level, that is to say that
there are less than five chances in a hundred of this being the
explanation.

As might be expected the attributes correlated less well with the
decisions than the attitudes. It is reasonable to expect judges with
a low score on a test designed to reveal liberalism on criminal law
issues will give a below-average number of votes for the defence on
criminal charges, and lower than a group composed of, say, judges
who originally practised in small towns. In fact, of the twelve attributes isolated it was found that in only four was there a statistically
significant correlation with the casting of votes in criminal cases.
These were religion and politics where the Catholics and Democrats
were found to be more defence-minded than Protestants and Repub-
licans, and pressure group affiliation and previous occupation where
it was found that those indicating membership of the American
Bar Association and former public prosecutors were less defence-

minded than those who gave no such indication.

The attitudinal survey used in this work was a modified and cur-
tailed version of one devised by Professor Eysenck. It was part of a
much wider study described elsewhere.[5] The questions were reworded
for an American sample, and regrouped into eight sets of three
questions each purporting to relate to a different facet of liberalism.
Only 118 of the 313 original judges returned usable answers, thus
introducing an additional element of unreliability into the results
as the result of this degree of self-selection. The full test had previously been tested on the members of the British parliamentary political parties, and it is perhaps interesting to note that the scores of
the American judges correlated very closely with those of the British
Conservative Party members. The consistently highly conservative
scores recorded by the judges, and it should be remembered that
these were those who were interested enough in this somewhat unconventional research to return their questionnaires, made the techniques very hard to apply. They depend upon finding decisions in
which both attitudes are represented in the same Court, and in this
respect examples of such situations were relatively rare. Nevertheless
it was found, again as might have been expected, that the more
conservative judges on the test tended to score above the average in
favour of business concerns in government regulation cases, for the
defence (usually an insurance company) in running down cases, for
the prosecution in criminal cases and for the employer in workmen's compensation cases. The study also attempted to test various
proposed methods of eliminating the influence exerted by personal
attitudes on decisions, such as a requirement of prior judicial experience before appointment, the abandonment of wearing robes and the
limitation of appointment to those with a record of academic excellence. On the basis of Nagel's tests, none of these seemed likely to
make much difference.

Statistical studies of this sort can be supported by more detailed
examination of specific Courts, and two examples among many are
given. The first is a simple study of the effect of the political affiliation of judges of the Supreme Court of Michigan on their decisions
in workmen's compensation and unemployment compensation

[5] Nagel, 'Off the Bench Judicial Attitudes', in Schubert (ed.), *Judicial Decision
Making* (1963).

cases.[6] In Michigan the political affiliation of judges is well known
and more narrowly ideological in character than in many American
states, and the balance altered in the middle of the period reviewed.
It is thus a convenient vehicle for the study of the thesis that decisions in these areas are governed more by political allegiance than
by a political legal technique. Unfortunately, the sample of workmen's compensation cases is a small one, with on average only ten
cases decided by the Michigan Supreme Court each year, but even
so the strength of the influence apparently exerted by political
allegiance is quite remarkable. In the twenty-nine workmen's compensation cases decided between 1957 and 1960, out of a total of
approximately 230 votes which were cast, only twice did judges vote
inconsistently with a pattern based upon their party allegiance, and
every split decision was split along strict party lines. This is supported by the other area studied. In the twelve unemployment compensation cases studied during the same period, ninety-four votes
were cast by the members of the Court, and again only twice was a
vote recorded inconsistent with an allegiance-based voting pattern.
Once a democrat voted for the employer when he would have been
expected to vote for the workman, and once another democrat voted
for the workman when he would have been expected to vote for the
employer, so in his case the inconsistency was of stronger allegiance
than might have been expected.

The second example is taken from among the multitude of similar
studies of the United States Supreme Court carried out by Professor
Schubert.[7] The technique is basically similar to those indicated
earlier, but on account of its greater complexity necessitated by the
use of a greater range of mutually inter-acting variable factors, it
does indeed demand the application of computerized calculation.
In this particular piece of work Schubert examines the decisions of
the Supreme Court of the United States during the 1961 term, excluding only unanimous and jurisdictional decisions. This leaves a
total of eighty-three cases in which the Court was divided. These
eighty-three were then analyzed and divided according to their subject matter into two large, and a number of smaller, categories. The
two large categories, which became the basis for cumulative scaling
techniques, are civil liberties (c scale) and economic liberalism (E

[6] Ulmer, 'The Political Party Variable in the Michigan Supreme Court', 11
Journal of Public Law, 352 (1962).
[7] Schubert, 'Prediction from a Psychometric Model', in *Judicial Behaviour* (1964).

scale). The former is defined as including cases on political equality such as school integration or electoral reapportionment, political freedom such as the freedoms of speech or the press, religious freedom, fair procedure and the right to privacy. The latter includes workmen's compensation, business regulation, labour law, anti-trust and the constitutionality of various forms of state taxation.[8] In the 1961 term thirty-nine cases related to issues included in the c scale and thirty-four to issues on the e scale. Schubert recognizes four other variables, but too few cases fell into them in the 1961 term for his statistical techniques to be applicable.

The technique, oversimplifying to some extent, is to arrange the cases constituting each scale in a matrix which plots case references against the individual members of the Court so as to indicate the vote of each judge in that case in terms of the relevant scale variable. The technique for arranging the judges and cases is known as Guttman scaling. The judges are arranged in order of their propensity to cast votes in favour of the scale variable. Thus Justice Black who voted most consistently in favour of civil rights appears in the first column, while Justice Clark who voted least consistently in favour of civil rights appears in the last column. In fact his positioning indicates a drawback in including such a wide range of issues in the scale, since in one of the areas, legislative reapportionment, he was clearly inclined to vote more often in favour of the scale variable than on any of the other issues. The cases are arranged in descending order of the pro-civil rights votes cast, thus the case in the first row is one in which the only pro-civil rights vote cast was that of Justice Black, and the case on the bottom row attracted most consistent pro-civil rights votes, including the only one cast by Justice Clark. Each judge is allocated a scale position corresponding to the number of the row on which his last consistent pro-civil rights vote was cast. Justice Black is thus placed in scale position 39 since his last consistent such vote was last in the case on the topmost row which is thus case 39, and Justice Clark is placed in scale position 1 since his only consistent pro-civil rights vote was cast in the case on the bottom row, and hence case number 1. A similar scale was also prepared for the e variable. These scales are then compared by statistical techniques with positions plotted for

[8] Other writers subdivide the e scale into anti-business and pro-labour scales, e.g. Spaeth, 'Warren Court Attitudes towards Business: the B scale', in Schubert (ed.), *Judicial Decision Making* (1963).

the judges in a three-dimensional space on the basis of the correlation of voting patterns for all the different pairs of individual judges. It is important to notice that these are established indepently of the issues raised in the cases, and no attempt is made to decide whether the vote is pro- or anti- civil rights, but simply whether it agrees or disagrees with that of another judge, and whether that agreement is in majority or minority, or in the case of disagreement which was a majority and which was a minority vote.

The complicated statistical and mathematical techniques of comparison employed appear to reveal that the correspondence between the decisions made by the judges and their positions on the scale variable is so great that they must be causally related.[9] Schubert goes on to quantify the distance of separation of the judges in five-dimensional space, and shows that in 1961 at least Justice Black was closer in his pattern of voting to Chief Justice Warren than he was to Justice Douglas, contrary to popular belief. On the basis of these calculations Schubert went on to make a set of predictions of the outcome of cases to be decided during the 1962 term of the Supreme Court. These predictions related to the number and type of cases constituting the work of the Court, the ranking of the judges on the two scales, the proportion of liberal decisions, the scale axes in factor space, and the outcome and likely voting splits on the docketed reapportionment cases. In an Appendix to his article the results of the predictions are analyzed. The most striking failures were in the predictions relating to the universe of raw data since this was based on trends up to 1961, and 1962 broke all records. The ranking predictions also failed, though in the case of c and e scales this was due to misplacing one of the new judges, Justice Goldberg, for predicting whose pattern only different and less reliable data was available. It might also be true that his pattern was distorted on account of its being his first term in a new environment and with new colleagues. The predictions relating to the reapportionment cases were strikingly successful, though a number were not in fact decided until 1963.

A rather different approach to prediction, though still within the area of general attitudes, is shown by the application of game theory. This is a technique whereby in situations where there is a winning and losing position, and a number of participants, it is possible to

[9] The chance of such correspondence occurring by chance was 1 in 66,666 for the c scale and 1 in 20,000 for the e scale.

I

calculate the optimum strategy for each player given the rules of the game. Here too the Supreme Court of the United States has been a fertile field for examination. It is composed of a small number of men, it makes a large number of well-documented decisions, and they can easily be expressed in terms of winning or losing. Ulmer has applied[10] the Shapley-Shubik power index to the Court in which the strategy of the players is assumed to be aimed at maximizing power by casting the decisive vote. In this study the power ranking of the members of the Court is established for each term, and these terms are grouped together according to the identity of the Chief Justice. It is interesting to discover how the various Courts differ, and how the power ranks change over a period of time, and with changes in personnel. The Court is regarded as unstable when there are frequent changes of rank, and stable when there are few. It is then possible to measure mathematically the degree of stability in the Court prior to Roosevelt's packing proposals in 1937, and the precise measure of disturbance which that generated.

While this technique might indirectly serve to predict particular decisions, a more direct relationship is established by Schubert in another study, employing a basically similar technique.[11] This uses as its data-base the *certiorari* decisions made by the Supreme Court in workmen's compensation cases since the war. It hinges on Justice Frankfurter's policy difference from some other members of the Court on the jurisdictional question of whether such cases should be accepted for decision on the merits. The decision to accept a case depends upon there being four concurrent votes, though of course once the case has been accepted a majority vote, usually of five concurrent votes, is necessary to achieve a decision on the merits. It can be shown that over the period under reveiw the size and composition of the block opposed to Frankfurter's policy varied in size and degree of adhesion as the membership of the Court changed. Schubert employs the theory of games to establish optimum strategies for both Frankfurter and the opposing block. These take into account factors such as whether the application comes from workman or employer, and whether the vote is on the question of jurisdiction or on the merits. It is even possible to take into account such factors as the need not to alienate the uncommitted members of the Court

[10] Ulmer, 'Homeostasis in the Supreme Court', in Schubert (ed.), *Judicial Behaviour* (1964).
[11] Schubert, 'The Certiorari Game', 14 *Stanford L.R.*, 284 (1962).

by too blatant a use of power. By postulating that a decision on the merits is as likely as not to be decided either way by a member of the Court who is not committed to either block, it is possible to employ the probabilities of different decisions on the merits as a motivating factor also.

The usefulness of such an analysis as a predictive technique is limited by the adherence of the members of the Court to their policies, and hence to their blocks. As Schubert himself points out, the nature of the game changed suddenly in 1960, and the strategies and blocks which had been found to work up to that time could no longer be used. While most such studies have so far been made of the Supreme Court, their application to other Courts has been canvassed.[12] These provide an interesting contrast to the studies of the Supreme Court, particularly for British readers since they deal with the phenomenon, which obtains in British appellate Courts, of the judges constituting any particular division of the Court being selected from among a panel. This changes the situation completely from the point of view of the theory of games. For example, if a Court consists of five judges, three of whom are in favour of civil liberties and two of whom are opposed, then if the Court always functions as a full Court, and if the judges always vote according to their predilections, all the decisions will favour civil liberties. But if it functions as a series of randomly selected Courts of three, then in 30 per cent of the cases there will be an anti-civil liberties majority. In situations where there are other more complicated rules, say selection by a chief justice, or many divisions sitting simultaneously, there will be still further combinations of possibilities to be explored.

Yet another line of enquiry, briefly mentioned earlier in connection with Schubert's work, is known as block analysis, in which the decisions of the Courts are examined to detect the patterns of agreement between judges, usually in non-unanimous decisions. This technique has been applied to both Supreme Courts[13] and lower Courts.[14] The study of the Supreme Court took in non-unanimous cases decided between 1946 and 1963, amounting to some 1,659 decisions. During this period eighteen different judges participated at different

[12] Atkins, 'Some Theoretical Effects of the Decision Making Rules on the United States Courts of Appeals', *Jurimetrics Journal*, September 1970, p. 13.
[13] e.g. Schubert, *The Judicial Mind* (1965).
[14] e.g. Goldman, 'Conflict and Consensus in the United States Courts of Appeals', 1968 *Wisconsin L.R.*, 461.

244 COMPUTERS AND THE LAW

times in the Court's decisions. The decisions of the judges were considered in pairs for each term, and the number of times they agreed in the majority, the number of times they agreed in the minority, the number of times they disagreed with the first voting with the majority and the second voting with the minority, and the number of times they disagreed with the second voting with the majority and the first voting with the minority were tabulated. From these totals it was possible to tabulate a coefficient of agreement ranging from $+1$ indicating total agreement to -1 indicating total disagreement, while o indicates an equal amount of agreement and disagreement. Tables setting out the results of such calculations are included for every term of the Supreme Court in the period under review. They were carried out by a simple and standard computer programme. This sort of information can then be used to establish in mathematical terms the varying strengths of different voting blocks. Such block tables have been published for the Supreme Court of the United States[15] and for all the Circuit Courts of Appeals.[16] Quite apart from their intrinsic interest, such tables can then be elaborated by reference to particular factors present in the cases, and after being subjected to further statistical programmes can be used for other purposes, as in the case of Schubert's work where they are used to constitute a test of the results arrived at by Guttman scaling techniques.

Fact studies

The main difference here is one of emphasis. The attitudes of the sort usually considered above are of great generality, and embrace huge ranges of fact patterns. Thus Schubert has as one of his two main attitudes, the support of civil liberties. Those theorists to be considered here have split fact situations down into much more minute categories. Thus one type of civil liberties case included by Schubert in one of his scales among many others involves the question of the admissibility of confessions in evidence. This small fraction of Schubert's scale has been analyzed by Kort into twenty-two independent variables,[17] while Lawlor has found no fewer than sixty-eight in an analysis of only fifteen Supreme Court decisions

[15] Ulmer, 'Toward a Theory of Sub-Group Formation in the United States Supreme Court', 27 *Journal of Politics*, 146 (1965).
[16] Goldman, *op. cit.*
[17] Kort, 'Content Analysis of Judicial Opinions and Rules of Law', in Schubert (ed.), *Judicial Decision Making* (1963).

on the subject.[18] Thus on Lawlor's analysis part of one element on one scale might comprise as many as 1,268 different situations, or a number with over twenty zeros behind the first digit. If this sort of analysis can be conducted consistently and successfully it has more immediate implications for lawyers than the studies described in the previous section. Lawyers will be able not only to predict how the judges will react to their cause of action, but also how that reaction may differ according to which facts are proved, and which are not. They will also be able to determine after the trial, in considering a possible appeal, not only whether the decision was consistent with previous ones, but also with regard to which particular facts the Court was inconsistent. Similarly, academic lawyers will be able to test doctrinal views as, for example, whether the inadmissibility of involuntary confessions is to be explained by their untrustworthiness, or by the need to restrain police malpractices. In Kort's study one of the variables in the confession cases is the presence or absence of other evidence sufficient to show guilt apart from the confession. It was found that the Court reversed some convictions where confessions had been admitted notwithstanding that there was other evidence sufficient to show guilt, thus indicating that, at least in those cases, the deterrence principle was operative. This variable was then omitted from the analysis since it could be assumed that if the analysis gave equally good results whether it was included or not, the Court was attaching no weight to it. In fact its omission did make a difference, and it could therefore be assumed that both rationales play some part in the application of the doctrine.

Kort and Lawlor have developed slightly different methods, and they will be briefly discussed in turn. Each of them has indicated slight differences in methodology from one experiment to the next, but it is hoped that these necessarily summary accounts will give some general indication of their line of approach.

One of Kort's approaches is by way of simultaneous equations.[19] He first of all regards the decisions in the cases as dependent upon the combination of facts before the Court. The facts are taken from the majority opinion, and others stated in concurring or dissenting

---

[18] Lawlor, 'Fact Content Analysis of Judicial Opinions', *Jurimetrics Journal*, 1968, p. 107.
[19] Kort, *op. cit* and 'Simultaneous Equations and Boolean Algebra in the Analysis of Judicial Decisions', 28 *Law and Contemporary Problems*, 143 (1963).

opinions are ignored. So far as possible they are stated in the same terms as those used by the Court, and a list of different facts is drawn up for each case. At the same time a cumulative list of facts for all the cases in the sample is chosen. Thus as previously noted Kort found twenty-two such facts, or variables, in the twenty-six cases constituting his sample. This is, however, rather unwieldy both from the point of view of solving the equations and from that of gathering sufficient data to permit a solution. It is thus necessary for him to reduce the number of variables. This is accomplished by the use of factor analysis. These factors correspond to groups of facts, and may indeed be the counterpart of legal concepts in traditional analysis. Thus in Kort's scheme 'no advice of right to remain silent' is one fact, and another is 'no advice of right to counsel', and these might be grouped together by factor analysis to constitute a concept capable of being characterized as 'failing to inform the accused of his constitutional rights'. However, Kort identifies such grouping of facts not qualitatively but quantitatively. He first performs a correlation analysis of each pair of facts in the case, like the technique applied to the judges in block analysis. By further statistical processes the twenty-two original facts in the confession cases are reduced to nine factors, and a numerical loading is also calculated and translated by regression analysis into a value for each factor in the case. The weightings so arrived at are calculated at a level such that they indicate the likely number of judges voting in a given direction. These can be compared with the actual number of judges voting in that direction in the cases constituting the sample. The method succeeded in predicting the correct result in twenty-three out of the twenty-six confession cases in the sample, and such a result could have been achieved by chance only once in a hundred attempts, and is thus statistically significant. If, however, the more stringent test of predicting the exact number of judges voting on each side is considered, the method succeeded on only seven of the twenty-six, which is not statistically significant. The results were also tested by using the first half of the data to predict the results in the second half, and vice versa. The distribution of factors between the two halves of the data turned out to be such that no statistically significant results were achieved. When the sample was larger, as with the workmen's compensation cases, this difficulty was averted. As a result of such analysis, it should be possible to compute the number of judges who will vote for any given combination of facts, providing only that those facts have occurred in the sample.

Lawlor's technique is not subject to this limitation. As stated, like Kort's, his first step is to determine the presence or absence of particular facts as seen by a particular judge. Lawlor differs from Kort in analyzing the decisions of judges, rather than of Courts, on the basis of an assumption that judges are more likely to be consistent in their reactions over a period of time than are Courts with their changing personnel. This approach has the incidental advantage of greatly expanding the fund of available data. Lawlor recognizes that the ascertainment of the presence or absence of facts in the opinion studied is absolutely crucial to his technique, and he has therefore conducted tests upon his evaluators to ensure that they agree as to the presence or absence of facts.[20] He found that for experienced analysts the level of reliability in determining the presence or absence of particular facts in the light of the statements made in the judgement was around 95 per cent, and that performance is improved if the analysts are allowed to discuss their work with each other. Clearly a great deal depends upon the exact phraseology of the facts, and the research showed that once settled it was best left alone. He also found, as might have been expected, that precise phraseology was more popular than vague, but also that there was little consensus in the application of such nebulous concepts.

Lawlor employs the further notion of fact polarization. This refers to the way in which the fact is stated in relation to its likely impact upon the decision of a given issue. Thus in an involuntary confession case, the fact stated as 'the accused took a requested lie detector test' would have positive polarization since its presence would tell in the accused's favour, whereas if it were stated in a negative form as 'the accused refused to take a requested lie detector test' then it is negatively polarized in the sense that its presence is likely to tell against a decision in the accused's favour on that issue. The direction of polarization can be determined in a number of ways distinguished by Lawlor, but the preferred method is the juxtaposition of facts stated positively and negatively like those in the example given above, and then asking experienced lawyers which they would regard as more likely to conduce towards a decision in

[20] Lawlor, 'Fact Content Analysis of Judicial Opinions' *Jurimetrics Journal*, June 1968, p. 107.

favour of the accused.[21] It is then possible to characterize pairs of opinions by reference to the presence or absence of enumerated positively polarized facts. If case A has three positively polarized facts, 1, 2, and 3, and case B has only facts 2 and 3 but no negatively polarized facts then it is possible to argue that although the facts of case B are different from those of case A, it ought, if the judge is to be consistent, to be decided the same way. Lawlor further argues that facts can sometimes be ranked in order of importance. Applying these concepts he is able to distinguish four different possible types of consistency between pairs of opinions, identic consistency where the same facts are present in both cases, convex consistency where the facts of the second case are a subset of those of the first, as in the example of A and B above, ranked consistency where each of the facts present only in the second case has a lower rank than one corresponding fact present only in the first, and random consistency where each case includes at least one positively polarized fact not present in the other, and no relationship of ranking exists between them. Inconsistency can also be established in the first three of these ways. The validity of comparisons of this type was tested in a series of expectancy experiments in which the ranking between the cases on the basis of the polarization of their facts was compared with the results to be expected in terms of inconsistencies if they were in fact decided upon the basis of some completely independent variable. These tests showed conclusively that the ranking procedures were related to the decisions, and indeed in the sample chosen for the experiment the technique yielded no inconsistencies at all, as against nineteen to be expected on the random basis. The same process was applied to individual judges, and in only one vote out of a total of 68 was there an inconsistency, and that was explained on the basis that an additional fact had been found important by the judge concerned. Similar tests were also conducted by reversing the polarity ascribed to the facts in a group of cases, and observing the results on the rankings, but these did not produce such good results for completely extraneous reasons.

Lawlor uses the Guttman scaling technique, described in connection with Schubert's scaling of the judges, to rank cases according to their fact patterns. He shows how from only five decisions involving combinations of four facts, it is possible to establish the con-

[21] Lawlor, 'Axioms of Fact Polarization and Fact Ranking – Their Role in Stare Decisis', 14 *Vill. L.R.*, 703 (1969).

sistent decisions in relation to all the eleven other possible ways of combining these facts.[22] In another study[23] he analyzes an attempt to apply similar techniques to forecasting the result the Supreme Court would arrive at it in the celebrated case of *Gideon* v. *Wainwright*.[24] There was no satisfactory data for Justices White and Goldberg, who had only recently been appointed to the Court, so he contented himself with forecasting the decisions of the other seven judges. He predicted that the facts in *Gideon* would be regarded as more favourable to the accused than those in *Betts* v. *Brady*,[25] an earlier Supreme Court decision which went against the accused. In fact, the Court held that the cases were indistinguishable. He predicted that the odds were 20 to 1 that *Gideon* would be decided different from *Betts*, and that *Betts* would be overruled. Both of these predictions succeeded. He predicted that the vote would be 5 to 2, and that Justice Clark would vote against the accused. In fact it was 7 to 0, and Justice Clark voted with the majority.

In his most recent work Lawlor has sought to introduce fact weighting as a method of improving predictive power. Thus in each case the facts are given a total weighting of one, and each individual fact is ascribed the appropriate fraction, $\frac{1}{2}$ if there are two, $\frac{1}{3}$ if there are three, and so on. He plans eventually to combine fact weighting, judge ranking, and case ranking into a composite technique for the prediction of judicial decisions.

3 EVALUATION

Although the statistical techniques employed by some of these workers have been criticized,[26] there can be no real doubt that this work provides a successful approach to the analysis of the decisions which have been reached in the past, and at least as satisfactory a method of predicting future decisions as can be arrived at by native wit and unaided intuition. In so far as attitudes are the object of study, the broad conclusions drawn can hardly be disputed given the level of generality. There is, however, room for argument as to the value of using such elaborate statistical techniques to draw such broad conclusions. It might be more interesting to examine the com-

[22] Lawlor, 'The Chancellor's Foot: A Modern View', 6 *Houston L.R.*, 630 (1969).
[23] Lawlor, 'Personal Stare Decisis', 41 *S. California L.R.*, 73 (1968).
[24] 372 US 355 (1963).
[25] 316 US 455 (1942).
[26] Tanenhaus, 'The Cumulative Scaling of Judicial Decisions', 79 *H.L.R.*, 1583 (1966).

I*

ponents of those broad attitudes, yet at that point the interpretation of the data would become more controversial. It is not always clear why a judge comes to one conclusion rather than another, and which of the many policies which entail a decision in a particular direction is to be selected as characterizing the decision, or if more than one are selected then in what proportions they should be combined, especially if the only criterion is what the judge does, and not the reasons he gives for doing it. The fundamental difficulty with this approach is that actions, and here the action is a decision one way rather than another, are inherently ambiguous. Either the behaviourist is to content himself with observing the objective phenomena, in which case he can conclude nothing as to motivation, or he is to ascribe motivation to the phenomena, in which case he ceases to be objective. It is precisely at the point at which decisions of the Supreme Court, for example, are characterized as pro-civil liberties or anti-labour that doubts arise as to the real objectivity of the studies.

The same general line of argument may be advanced against the fact-orientated approach, though in perhaps a less obvious way. Here the point at which the study loses its objectivity is in the characterization of the facts present in the case. Lawlor is clearly aware that this is the weakest link in his armour, and characteristically chooses to challenge the traditional lawyer at this very point. The traditional lawyer, as conceived by Lawlor, argues that a case is authority for the decision of another only when the facts are the same. Lawlor rightly points out that everything depends upon the concept of similarity, which deserves close consideration. He argues that at the very least a subsequent Court is bound when its facts are not the same as a previous one, but differ only in being more favourable to the same decision. This is obviously true, but it has not, as Lawlor appears to imagine, been ignored by the traditional lawyer. Indeed the notion is so old and so well established that it is characterized by a Latin phrase; the later case is said to be 'a fortiori'.[27] Lawlor also recognizes that facts are not something which occur in nature, but are a characterization of what occurs according to a schema which differs according to the purpose which the particular expositor has in mind. A physicist, a doctor and a lawyer would characterize

[27] See Tapper, 'Legal Analogy', *The Listener*, 30 November 1961, for a fuller account of the meanings of the concept of similarity in the context of the doctrine of precedent in law.

the circumstances of a road accident in completely different ways corresponding to their different purposes. Thus 'the facts' for a lawyer correspond to the schema imposed by the structure of legal rules. It is quite fruitless to imagine that any characteristics can be independent of the categories established by the rules. But these categories are necessarily expressed in general terms in order to achieve economy in the number of rules, and more importantly to allow for flexibility in their development. This is why legal rules are so often cast in terms of such vague generalities as what is 'reasonable' or 'unnecessary'. Nevertheless legal concepts are not completely uncertain, but have an inner and an outer shell; some things fall clearly within their bounds and others fall just as clearly outside. In between there is uncertainty, and decisions can be made one way or the other depending upon the policy, in its widest sense, of the judge. These policies are partly expressed in the way in which the judge chooses to characterize the situation with which he is faced. Such characterization is not determined by the events which have occurred and is not even necessarily inherent in them, but is determined by the judge, and is used to express his determination.

The general point is that the law must respond to changes in society. Legislation supplies strategic change, case law tactical change. Both in their different ways are subject to restraint, but both necessarily have a measure of freedom. It is the judge's view of the past and the needs of the present which determines his decision, and neither a study of broad attitudes derived from his decision pattern by external observers, nor a characterization of 'facts' projected into the decision by observers can hope to correspond closely enough either with his view of the past, or still less with his view of the needs of the future. The attitudes of the Courts will appear to change in an unpredictable way because they have been too widely generalized, and new 'facts' will be ascribed importance because the old ones are no longer sufficient to achieve the desired results.

This is not to decry the value of such studies as those described here as a matter of analysis, where they certainly can contribute to a sharpening of perception of what is really happening. It is merely to point out that they should not expect to do more.

10

Computers and international law

International law shares some of the characteristics of legislation in that its most important category of document, the treaty, is akin to a statute in municipal law. It also shares some of the characteristics of litigation in that its data is drawn from a diverse range of sources, is found in a vast number of different places, and is generally not quite so necessarily accessible to the general public as is legislation. Of course it comprehends some parts, resolutions of the United Nations for example, which are virtual counterparts of municipal legislation, and others, decisions of the International Court of Justice for example, which bear the same relationship to municipal case law. But it presents its own range of special problems so far as information retrieval is concerned, and they are special enough to justify separate attention here. The computerized techniques themselves are basically the same as those described in the previous chapters, and it will only be necessary to describe here features especially orientated toward the problems of international law.

The greater part of this chapter will deal with information retrieval problems in relation to the different types of international law and the contribution which computers might make to their resolution. A short section at the end will also mention an application to the prediction of judicial decisions in the field of international law of those techniques described in the previous chapter in relation to municipal case law. There will be here no sections comparable to those on drafting in the chapter on legislation, or Court administration in the chapter on litigation, since such problems, in so far as they exist at all in the international law context, differ hardly at all from those in municipal law, and have attracted no substantial attention in the international area.

1. INFORMATION RETRIEVAL

This section will first of all set out the special problems for retrieval posed by international law, and will then describe a number of attempts to apply computerized techniques to their solution.

Special problems

These problems relate first to the nature of international law and its pattern of use, secondly to the need for, and difficulty of, obtaining international cooperation, thirdly to the difficulty of gaining access to international legal materials, fourthly to language problems, and finally to the problem of supplementary materials. Each of these will be discussed separately. It should be mentioned that much of the documentation in this area is concerned with the special problems of treaty law, and the bias of illustration is accordingly orientated in that direction.[1]

USAGE : In this chapter the concept of international law is used in a wide sense to include three main areas : private international law, public international law, and the law of international institutions. Private international law is largely concerned with the effects upon the legal relations of two parties of the presence of relevant elements of different legal systems. Such relations will usually be resolved by a municipal Court, and it may even apply quite simply its own municipal law, but this will not always be true, and often some reference will need to be made to the rules of the relevant foreign system. Thus if a question arises as to the recognition of a divorce granted in a foreign country, it is quite likely that one of the questions to be decided will relate to the validity of that divorce under the municipal law of the foreign country. Thus in this area the typical problem is concerned with securing access to the municipal law of a foreign country. This may be needed, as in the example given above, to allow a dispute to be resolved, but it may be needed for many other legal purposes, such as a decision as to which legal system should be chosen to govern a contract, or where an international company should establish its factories or registered office.

The second main area included here is public international law, and this corresponds most closely with the common usage of the term international law without a qualifying adjective. It compre-

---

[1] For an excellent survey of this field see Sprudzs, *Information on Recent Treaties – Some Observations on Tools, Techniques and Problems: The Conventional and The New* (1970).

hends the law relating to the relations between states, though exceptionally individuals may also be subjects. There are many disputes as to the theoretical basis of this branch,[2] but this is a somewhat barren controversy since there can be no doubt that it is continually treated in very much the same way as any other branch of law; it is formally laid down, claims are made upon its basis, actions are justified by reference to it, and Courts, especially the International Court of Justice at the Hague, decide disputes by reference to it. A special difficulty is that at the level at which it is applied it is not a universal system binding all states to the same behaviour. A much greater proportion of its rules and obligations stem from agreements between its subjects than is true for municipal law. These agreements are made in many different ways, and with different degrees of formality. Sometimes they are bilateral, and sometimes they are multilateral. The difficulty that this creates in relation to finding the relevant law to apply to any given relation will be considered later. Here it is sufficient to note that a retrieval problem exists, and indeed occupies a great deal of the time of legal departments in most Ministries of Foreign Affairs.

The third main area covered by this chapter is the law of international institutions. This is a relatively modern phenomenon. Before the last century it was unusual for any international body to be set up otherwise than on a completely *ad hoc* basis so that on the completion of its business it would become *functus officio*. This is increasingly ceasing to be the case, and there are a number of examples of international bodies operating on a permanent basis. Some of these are very broad in composition and jurisdiction, like the League of Nations and its modern successor, the United Nations. Others have a more limited jurisdiction but a similarly wide geographical base, like the International Labour Office or the International Postal Union. Still others have a wide jurisdiction but a limited geographical base, like the Organization of American States or the Council of Europe. As such institutions grow in stature, it is becoming increasingly more convenient to allocate new problems to them, rather than to set up further *ad hoc* bodies. Such permanent organizations have the advantage of being able to provide the necessary facilities in terms of accommodation and staff. They are also accumulating experience and contacts both with other international

---

[2] e.g. Austin, *Province of Jurisprudence Determined* (1832).

organizations and with the member states of the international community. It is natural that they should also develop their own rules and procedures for resolving disputes within their various areas of competence, and in so doing set up their own case law. Such institutions vary greatly in their patterns of activity, and it is not possible to generalize about the most suitable approaches to finding their rules. In some cases, however, such as that of the European Economic Community, there can be no doubt but that the volume of legislative activity in the wide sense, and case law through its judicial organ the European Court, is such that computerized methods are appropriate to deal with them.

Thus in these three areas, three different sorts of information need can be identified. In private international law it is predominantly information about foreign municipal law, in public international law it is information about agreements subscribed to by states, and in the law of international institutions it is the rules generated by the particular institutions. There may indeed be considerable overlapping between these areas. Thus an individual may come into dispute with his government in relation to his liability to tax upon earnings in a foreign country, where the position is governed by the interpretation of a double tax treaty made between the two states, which itself has, or counterparts of which have, been the subject of litigation in the Courts of an international institution, such as the International Court of Justice. In general, private individuals are more likely to be interested in private international law, and governments in public international law, while both may be equally interested in the law of international institutions. The first problem posed by international law is thus that the wide variety of use and users makes the necessary data-base very much larger than in any municipal system since if all private international legal questions are to be catered for, all of the law of every municipal legal system should be included. For the same reasons the variety of user is likely to be extremely great, including all the possible users of legal information within a municipal system, and further governmental and international institutional users in addition.

COOPERATION : The problem here is not, of course, in cooperation once achieved, but rather in achieving it at all. One difficulty lies in the conflicting interests of different states. These can hamper the development of legal information retrieval systems in various ways. To start with, each state has a slightly different legal history, and the influence of history in law tends to be especially strong, for very good reasons. It means, however, that the legal structure in different countries is by no means the same, and cannot easily be understood in the light of the structure of others. The dangers are often greatest when similarity seems closest. If two systems permit an appeal against conviction in a criminal case, for example, it may be natural to imagine that in this respect they are comparable, and that the sort of search which will be effective in one will be as effective in the other. But the rules for appealing may be quite different, and the search might turn out to be quite inappropriately drafted. Each system will also have developed partly in response to accidental events such as conquest or the dominance of a particular faction at a particular time, and partly by a sort of natural selection in which the rules most appropriate for the particular community are retained and refined. There will also be likely to be a certain chauvinism in relation to the legal system of a state, and even if that is absent there will certainly be familiarity with it among the lawyers in the state, and hence a vested interest against changing it. The task of harmonizing such systems so as to permit the easier interchange of information to assist in the resolution of problems of private international law is therefore great. It is beginning to be approached by such supra-national bodies as the Commission of the European Economic Communities, but even there this will remain a problem for some time to come. It is significant that one of the pledges made to the United Kingdom during negotiations leading up to its application to join was that it would not have to abandon its own legal system. The example of the United Kingdom also indicates the resilience of national legal systems since Scotland has retained its own very largely independent system more than 250 years since the Act of Union, and more than 350 years since the union of the Crowns. These divergencies apply not only to the substance of the law in different countries, but also to the institutional procedures set up to develop and interpret it. There is little correspondence between the passage of legislation in say West Germany, and in the United Kingdom, and the different effects of case law in common and civil law systems is notorious. This type of institutional difference makes it very difficult for a lawyer even to know how he should set about extracting legal information from a foreign legal system. In fact the most successful practices in private international law are often those of expatriates who have qualifications and experience of the legal systems of the different countries in question. The advantage of such experience is so deeply recognized in England that foreign law always had to be proved as a fact, thus not accepting that either barristers or judges can find it out for themselves, and then only by an expert witness whose expertise must normally have been acquired by practice in the Courts of the foreign legal system.[3]

In public international law the problems are slightly different. One of the troubles is that disputes between states, even technical legal disputes, are prone to take on political overtones, and to become involved with questions of national prestige. The result is that the very content of public international law is frequently controversial. It is highly unlikely that the leading authority in the Soviet Union will state the subject in the same way as the leading authority in the United States. A legal curriculum including comparative public international law as a subject is more than a weak joke. It is for this sort of reason that compulsory jurisdiction for international Courts is still the exception rather then the rule, and that in such cases the competing states are often allowed to nominate a national judge who usually decides in favour of his own state. With so small a feeling of international solidarity, and so strong an adherence to national sovereignty, it is unrealistic to expect states to devote many of their resources to improving the efficiency of the international legal order. They are much more likely to concentrate upon building up their own national view of that order. Despite the efforts of the United Nations and other international legal institutions it is still the case that the latest, fullest and best information about the existing rules of international law cannot be gathered without access to the individual stores of information held in their own archives by the separate states. These will themselves have been built up in accordance with the legal traditions of that particular legal system, and access to such materials will then present similar problems to those presented in securing access to the municipal law of another state. There is, however, the difference that the sources of international law to be tapped within each state are likely to be fewer, and more easily discovered. In addition the inevitably greater contact between individuals from different countries who are concerned with international materials contributes to a better appreciation of each other's methods, and the situation is likely in that respect to be slightly better than for municipal law. The arguments advanced

[3] This has now been changed by the Civil Evidence Act 1972.

generally above also apply specifically to the use of a computerized system. In general, international institutions are short of the funds necessary to finance such expensive luxuries, except in cases where they command independent budgets, as the Commission of the European Communities. In most cases it is likely that computerization will start within the individual states, and only in that way furnish a basis for truly international systems. This imposes further strains upon cooperation since it is highly desirable that the different national systems for computerizing international material should be compatible with each other. This is a most important difference between the needs in private international law and in public international law. It is not necessary for the system for holding English and French municipal law to be the same in order for an Englishman to be able to interrogate it about French law, or a Frenchman to be able to interrogate it about English law, though the greater the similarity the more convenient it will be. It is, however, necessary for the systems for holding public international law to be compatible since the user of such information is much less likely to require access to only one or two such collections. He will most likely require access to all available collections, and it then becomes highly desirable that they should be not only compatible but merged together into one large store. This will mean as a minimum that each country should adopt similar conventions for dividing up its data-base, and so far as possible make their information capable of being entered into each other's systems, without the necessity for complicated conversion programmes. Here too there are difficulties. Each country will tend to want to divide its data to fit in best with the divisions of its own legal process, and it will frequently want to use its own particular computers and programming systems, either for reasons of national prestige or of national economy. There is thus every temptation for the State Department of the United States to use International Business Machines equipment with standard United States government software packages to process treaties by reference to their status within the United States legal system, while similar considerations will tempt other advanced nations to do the same. Since many strong computer firms find it in their interest to make their own equipment incompatible with that of their competitors, this is quite likely to pose problems for those working towards international collaboration. It is also true that disparities of wealth and technological advance between different states constituting the

international community are so great that it is quite unreasonable
to suppose that all could be expected to set up identical systems.
They cannot afford to, do not have the expertise to do so, and have
no needs which would justify them in doing so.

In this respect the international institution, if it has the money
to introduce its own system, has an advantage. It is not subject to
such constraints of national self-interest, though regrettably rivalry
between different international institutions is not unknown, and this
could also be reflected in a parochial attitude towards the development of a particular computer system. A further problem for many
international institutions is that their range of work is so limited
that if they are to introduce a computerized system at all its costs
may not be capable of being spread over a sufficiently wide range
of uses for the most effective systems to be contemplated, and
cheaper alternatives may have to be developed instead.

ACCESSIBILITY : The difficulties of finding municipal law, both
statutory and case law, have been described in the previous chapters.
If those difficulties exist for lawyers familiar with the legal systems
in question, familiar with the social context in which they operate,
using a native language, and having access to the largest collections
of primary materials and research aids, it will be clear that the
difficulties for those who do not share all, or perhaps any, of these
advantages will be considerably greater.

So far as public international law is concerned the difficulties are
different but no less formidable. Some conception of the magnitude
of the tasks here may be gleaned from consideration of one major
source of international law, that derived from agreements between
states which will be comprehensively categorized as treaties. The
first difficulty is that there is no single source containing all treaties
in force everywhere in the world. This is partly for historical reasons.
Once made, a treaty continues in force until some event occurs to
terminate it. Consequently some treaties made centuries ago, long
before universal collections were even considered as a possibility,
have some provisions which continue in force. What were intended
to be comprehensive collections of modern treaties have been set
up by the principal international institutions, first the League of
Nations, and since 1945 the United Nations. These series are enormous. There are 205 volumes in the League of Nations Treaty
Series for the years 1921 to 1946, and 665 volumes in the United
Nations Treaty Series for the years from 1946 to 1969. Those figures

also give some indication of the increasing rate at which treaty-making is increasing. Unfortunately it is still not the whole story. Despite an explicit article in the Charter enjoining registration and recording of treaties with the United Nations it seems that these collections are by no means complete, and may underestimate the total volume of modern treaties by as much as 25 per cent.[4] This means that it is necessary to check through all the published collections of treaties to achieve a comprehensive coverage. This is a formidable task. The leading authority on collections of treaties, Myers's 'Manual of Collections of Treaties', listed 3,468 different collections as long ago as 1922. An abbreviated list published by the United Nations contains 698. The research team of Queen's University, Kingston, Ontario has referred to 1,184 different collections in attempting to establish a complete list for Great Britain, and after ten years continuous work has still not succeeded.[5] Even after such monumental coverage of these sources, research is not complete. Many treaties are not published, but retained in manuscript sources, and the Queen's University team has had to examine over three thousand volumes of archival material in its attempt to establish a complete list of British treaties. Then finally there is the problem of new treaties not yet included in the main collections and, if published at all, tucked away in an esoteric selection of official government gazettes.

It is clear that if the primary sources are so difficult to identify and track down, the secondary sources such as indexes and specialized lists are likely to be correspondingly defective, since they will have been compiled from an incomplete base. The only other possible hope is that while the public collections may be defective, the private collections maintained for their own purposes by Ministries of Foreign Affairs may be more satisfactory. This seems not to be the case. The Queen's University team has had access to the official list maintained by the British government, and estimates that it understates by about 40 per cent the treaties which in fact relate to Great Britain. The situation seems to be no better in other countries, and it is somewhat sobering to reflect that no country in the world seems to know exactly what its treaty obligations are.

[4] Rohn, 'Canada in the United Nations Treaty Series: A Global Perspective', 4 *Canada Yearbook of International Law*, 102 (1966).
[5] Queen's University Treaty Project: Cumulative Working Paper No. 8, reprinted in *Law and Computer Technology*, November 1970, p. 246.

A further difficulty with international legal documents like treaties is that they frequently deal with extremely sensitive political questions, and by agreement between the parties may be kept completely secret, or may contain secret clauses. There is clearly no way in which an entirely comprehensive record can be established in any one place given this state of affairs. It also follows that research workers cannot expect to be given a completely free hand to rummage through official archives to discover unrecorded treaties. Since so much of the data is held in sensitive archives, or in proximity to them, it is necessary for examination to be undertaken by persons who have the required security clearances or status, and this can impede the smooth flow of work in collecting information.

Since the primary sources cannot all even be identified, it is impossible to make any reliable estimate of the total volume of information contained in them. It is, however, clear that it is extremely large, and increasing at a tremendous rate. As noted above there are over 650 volumes in the United Nations Treaty Series from 1945 to 1969. It has been estimated that the total volume of information in this one source is something of the order of $32\frac{1}{2}$ million words calculated on the basis of thirteen words to the line, thirty lines to the page, and 150 pages of English text to the volume. If there is indeed a 25 per cent gap in the coverage of this series, the figure rises above 40 million words. If all the languages printed in the series are to be included the total increases by a factor of four.

It is now necessary to consider the effectiveness of current methods of finding information from the published part of international data. So far as the treaty is included in the United Nations Treaty Series, it will eventually be indexed as part of a cumulative index. Multilateral treaties are covered by the 'Index to Multilateral Treaties' published by the Library of the Harvard Law School. Otherwise a variety of national indexes have to be consulted.[6] Unfortunately these subject indexes are at a very high level of generality, and are totally unsuitable for research in depth. It must be remembered that treaties are subject to similar pressures for compression to those operating upon domestic legislation. In consequence they are no easier to index, and certainly no existing index seems to have excited widespread approval among international lawyers. Nor has any scheme for the classification of treaties achieved universal

[6] See Roberts, 'Searching for the Texts of Treaties', 5 *Journal of Documentation*, 136 (1949).

adoption. In 1968 the Council of Europe proposed that its members should adopt the system used by the ASSER Institute.[7] However, a survey of the practices of members in 1970 revealed not only that none of the governments of member states had adopted this scheme, but that a number of them were actively working on their own individual systems which they proposed to introduce independently. Here too the fundamental objection is that the level of generality is too high for the system to be able to meet the practical problems facing the users.

A special problem of accessibility raised by international law concerns the nature of the subjects. The subjects of public international law are primarily states and international institutions. Both entities are artificial, and tend to be more unstable than the subjects of a municipal system. Their identity is also more important because of the larger proportion of public international law which is constituted by agreements between them. So far as states are concerned, the main problem is with state succession. Throughout history national boundaries have been subject to change, old states have continually been replaced by new. This raises an extremely difficult set of problems relating to the precise status of treaty relations for a new state constructed perhaps from parts of three or four old ones, each with its own different set of treaty relations. Similar problems arise when a former colony is granted independence by the old colonial power. Some of the treaties entered by the old power will bind the new nation, and others will not. In either event the new state will probably not be mentioned by name, since the new name may well not have been chosen until shortly before independence. These problems are attaining epidemic proportions as the old colonial empires crumble in the modern world. Thus membership of the United Nations has more than doubled since its inception of 1945 with only fifty-nine members, largely on account of the accession of newly independent states. This increase in the number of states has been matched by a corresponding, and in part consequential, increase in the number of international bodies. Thus the Yearbook of International Organizations showed an increase in their numbers from 132 in 1957 to 229 in 1969. This expansion means not only that the number of different places in which to look for the law has increased, but that the amount of law has also increased more than proportionately since there is a geometrical increase in

[7] Resolution 68 (17).

the different combinations of states and institutions which can be linked by treaty relations.

The most common enquiry in the field of public international law is probably one relating to the obligations existing between states in relation to a particular subject matter. This may well be divided between a number of treaties to be found in different places, often without any adequate system of cross-reference between them. Even if this is not a problem, and the subject is completely comprehended within the boundaries of one treaty, it cannot be assumed that merely because the treaty exists, the obligations which it imposes are in force between the parties to it. As with legislation, so with treaties, the temporal limits of obligation are often extremely difficult to discover in any way at all, and impossible from mere scrutiny of the text. Both the inception of obligation and its termination may depend upon elaborate procedures varying from state to state. The problem of keeping up to date with the status of treaties compounds all the difficulties of municipal legislation described previously, by dint of the multiplication of parties to them. This is most acute in the case of multilateral treaties where accession and denunciation may be taking place all the time, and in the case of long-established treaties the identity of the parties may be constantly changing.

It is hardly surprising that in these circumstances there is a demand for the consideration of any measures, including computer application, which might reduce the chaos in such a vitally important area.

LANGUAGE : There is, of course, no universally recognized international language, nor even a universally recognized notation. The United Nations has four official languages, English, French, Russian and Spanish, but still excludes the languages of the two most populous countries in the world, China and India, neither of which uses alphabetic script. It is clear that international law may be expressed in any of the languages used by any of the members of the international community. So far as international institutions are concerned official languages are normally designated, and the law of the institution appears in all of them. Problems of language can arise within a purely municipal system, either because the language has at some stage changed, as in England legal language changed from Latin to Law French and finally to English, or because the national system includes different language groups, as in Belgium or Canada. A distinction must be made between a situation in which there is only one system of law in question but expressed in two different languages, and one in which two different systems of law are involved, each expressed in a different language. The former situation is the more common in public international law, which is theoretically one system. The latter situation occurs in private international law where the user may require access to several different municipal systems, each expressed in its own language.

In the former situation the problem should in theory be capable of solution by the creation of a dictionary permitting the automatic substitution of a word of one language for a word of another. This is indeed the approach which has been adopted by CREDOC in Belgium in its keyword system. A table of Flemish and French equivalents has been prepared. The information is held in the computer in coded form, and the computer also contains tables which substitute the code for the search terms in whichever language they have been presented, and which automatically enable the output to be made in the language of the original enquiry. An exactly comparable approach has been adopted by the United Nations in relation to the indexing of legal documents, where a glossary of index terms has been prepared giving equivalents in the four official languages, and thus permitting automatic translation from any one into all of the others.[8] The technique is clearly feasible where the vocabulary can be closely controlled. In effect, the system does not translate between words with existing meanings, but prescribes new meanings for the words which, while they may largely correspond with the existing meanings, will not correspond exactly with them for the simple reason that the substructure of conceptualization in the different languages will not be identical. This is especially true of legal conceptualization, since law is an artefact, and has been created by different people for different purposes in different legal systems. It raises serious problems for computerized retrieval systems which do not depend upon the use of keywords, since they are unable to prescribe meanings, and must depend upon the original meanings in the original systems and languages. Such systems should, however, benefit from fundamental work which is being undertaken in Canada by a number of research teams. In most of the keyword systems the equivalents are chosen by lawyers with knowledge of both languages. This is the starting point for one of the Canadian projects which is under the direction of Professor Pharand at the University of

[8] For a convenient summary see Sprudzs, *op. cit.*, p. 63.

Ottawa. Here the intuitively selected equivalents are tested by the production of keyword in context (KWIC) indexes for them. The context which is thus recorded is intended to show whether the words are always equivalent, and to suggest other possibilities. It is also possible that work on the automatic type-setting of the Canadian statutes which are drafted in both English and French original versions may assist with the discovery of equivalent legal expressions in the two languages. The University of Montreal which has a full-text system operative in English and French also employs a bilingual thesaurus which is used for the automatic amplification of questions.[9]

Where more than one legal system is involved the problem is most acute since it is unlikely that the concepts will be precisely equivalent. On the analogy of the Canadian work it might be possible to experiment with possible equivalents using as a data-base the texts of treaties prepared in different languages, where the signatories have different legal systems. Thus the French and English texts of treaties made between Great Britain and France could be subjected to the same KWIC techniques used at Ottawa. If these were found to yield results comparable to those obtained within the one legal system of Canada, it might be possible to go ahead and apply similar techniques to treaties prepared in other languages. It might also be interesting to examine the French and English translations of the treaties in the United Nations Treaty Series, both against each other and against the original languages.

Technical problems are also likely to arise in connection with the use of non-alphabetic script, though if they can be overcome for the purpose of designing keyboards for typewriters, they should in principle be capable of being overcome for the purposes of designing keyboards for computer input. A more serious problem might arise in connection with non-verbal information. This can arise in a number of areas of law, and is by no means confined to international legal documents, but it is acute there on account of the frequent annexation of maps to such documents. While there are systems which can register maps, or indeed any other patterns, within a computer system, they are prodigal of storage space, and difficult to use. One method is to digitize the information, allowing reconstruction of the original in much the same sort of way as a television picture is reproduced, but this is very expensive. Another which seems more feasible in this context is to maintain the maps on

[9] See 'Themis', no. 1 (1971).

microfilm in an auxiliary store. There are a number of systems, though none are as yet used for legal purposes, which permit the automatic retrieval of the microfilm from the auxiliary store, and its subsequent display on the same terminal device used for the manipulation of digital information. Such a system might be useful if the user has no ready access to the original map. It is, however, of no use to anyone who wishes to use the information contained on the map for the purposes of retrieval, since such systems are capable only of displaying the microfilmed data, not of searching it. It is, however, relatively rare that in the cartographic information will be needed for such purposes. A further category of non-verbal information contained in treaties is that conveyed in the tabular formulation of some types of information. This is very common in economic agreements for example. Here the relationship between the concepts is vital, and expressed by position in terms of row and column in the table. At present the only method of solving it, if the information conveyed by the tables is to constitute search criteria, is the somewhat laborious and cumbersome method of translating the table into consecutive sentences. This is unsatisfactory, since the original decision to use a table will normally have been taken to avoid this very practice. It would be possible to simulate the table in the computer directly, but to do so would involve the use of completely different search techniques from those so far considered, and while such techniques would be undoubtedly efficient in operation, they would be difficult to learn, and could not very easily be combined with the usual form of computer search.

AMPLIFICATION: The last of the special problems arising in connection with international law materials is also shared by municipal legislation, but not to the same extent. It is concerned with the amount of information extraneous to the text of a document, which must be stored together with it in order to make it useful. In case law this is not so much of a problem, since the effect of the decision is usually set out in the decision itself. Legislation is less self-contained, and some indication of extent and time of application is needed. Amendment also presents problems. For treaties and agreements the problems are vast. The most typical query about the obligations in existence between two states cannot, as previously noted, be answered by reference to the text of the relevant primary documents alone, but only if this has been amplified by further pieces of information. Here, as elsewhere, the decision as to which particular pieces of further information should be provided will be partly determined by the purposes of the users of the system. Details which are unnecessary for some purposes may be vital for others. In the field of international legal documents, where political questions are often involved, the additional information required may sometimes be more political than legal in content. Thus it may have nothing to do with the legal quality of the document in question, but may be needed to allow the Ministry of Foreign Affairs to provide information to answer a political enquiry. Thus the status of the signatory may be unimportant in itself, provided he had been granted the necessary power, but will be necessary if, say, a question has to be answered as to how often treaties have been signed by a British prime minister outside the United Kingdom. This problem of amplification has been considered by a number of different organizations in contemplation of the introduction of a computerized retrieval system for international legal documents. One such study was recently undertaken on behalf of the Council of Europe by the International Law Data Subcommittee of its Committee of Experts on the Harmonization of the Means of Programming Legal Data into Computers. This subcommittee first examined a number of existing amplification systems. The most economical of these was found to be that of the British Foreign Office, used in the compilation of its treaty register, according to which twelve items of further information are listed for bilateral treaties, and eighteen for multilateral treaties. The situation is less complicated in the United Kingdom than in many other countries since parliamentary approval is not specifically required before a treaty becomes binding, which means that references to the parliamentary process which appear prominently in other systems of amplification do not appear. One of the more expansive systems turned out to be that used by the Swiss Département Politique which has twenty-three separate categories for bilateral treaties, three of which contain four subcategories, and thirty-two separate categories for multilateral treaties, two of which contain three subcategories. Neither of these systems was designed with a view to computer operation, but the State Department of the United States in the course of a tentative and preliminary study divided necessary amplifying information into five separate sections, which between them contained thirty-one separate categories of which one was subdivided into a further eight subcategories and another into two. It is worth examining this system in a little more detail since it is systematically organized and was intended for computer application. The first section, comprising eight categories, relates to initial information such as the subject of the treaty, the signatories, the place and date of signature by all signatories together with any reservations, the date of entry into force for each signatory together again with any reservations, references to the place where the text has been published, modifications by supplementary agreement, and finally the full-text of the treaty. Thus the full-text is only one category among many, none of which could be compiled from it since they depend upon completely independent events such as subsequent modifications. The second section of this scheme deals with the background regarding approval, and contains nine categories relating to submission to and passage through the Senate as required in the United States legal system, and subsequent ratifications by the president. The third section deals with the negotiating history, and comprises six categories relating to the sort of papers which one would expect to find accumulating in a file while a treaty was being negotiated, such as preliminary drafts and commentaries. The fourth section deals with implementation, contains three heavily subdivided categories, and relates to the passage of legislation and executive action thereon as also required by law in the United States. The final section deals with application, and contains five categories which list different bodies such as United States Courts, foreign municipal Courts and international tribunals whose interpretation of the treaty is of interest to the government of the United States. Such treatment clearly requires considerable organization and effort. It will entail that preliminary procedures are consistently applied, and well documented, that the surrounding circumstances are thoroughly scrutinized and noted, that all legislative stages are recorded as they occur, and that follow-up studies are conscientiously carried through. This will all be extremely time-consuming, but is necessary if an adequate record is to be kept of all the information which may be needed in relation to any treaty. Unfortunately the demands such a system will make upon the resources available in most states are likely to preclude its universal adoption. The danger in the recommendation of an over-elaborate scheme which is impractical is that it will be only partially applied. Such partial application, being unauthorized, is also likely to be inconsistent in its partiality, and the result is likely to be more unsatisfactory than the recommendation of a less ambitious scheme which does at least stand more chance of being put into full operation given the resources likely to be available. The Council of Europe's subcommittee has gone even further than the Department of State in the United States in the elaboration of its recommendations. This system divides the amplifying information into eight major parts. Seven of these are in conventional form, and comprise thirty-five categories comprehending in all 135 subcategories, while part seven is in the form of a chart depicting the history and present status of the treaty, and containing twenty columns to be filled in for each signatory. As an experiment the Council's own staff is applying the system to those treaties for which the Council is itself the depositary. So far, no analysis of the results of this experiment has been published. It is certainly a daunting prospect to have to compile so much information in addition to the text of the treaty itself. Indeed, in an attempt to reduce the burden it was decided to make the compilation of some of the information contained in the Council's analysis optional, but even allowing for the deletion of such items, no fewer than 111 essential items remained. It is interesting to compare the volume of this amplifying information with the much smaller amount recommended by the Council of Europe's other subcommittee which dealt with municipal legal information. The volume of such amplifying material is indeed a peculiarly exacerbating factor in relation to international legal documents.

It seems then that the retrieval problems are here almost intractable. The information is difficult to find, impossible to exhaust, resistant to classification and indexing, and requires a huge amount of amplification. The resources devoted to its retrieval are meagre and subject to conflicts of national interest. It raises unique linguistic problems, and is increasing in amount and complexity at an increasing rate. Yet at the same time it is of more importance to the well-being of the human race than ever before that it should be handled adequately. This Herculean problem has not so far been solved by conventional methods, and is clearly unlikely to be resolved. Little has been attempted to date in the way of computerization, but that little may indicate ways of dealing with at least some parts of the problem, and it will be discussed in the next part of this section.

Computerized Systems

Some of the various, and for the greater part tentative, advances which have been made in this area will be described briefly in this part. As in the previous chapter considerations of space prevent more than an outline of the various systems, but where appropriate an indication is given of a source from which further information may be obtained. The systems will be divided according to the tripartite classification of international law advanced earlier, namely into private international law where the aim is to provide access to foreign municipal law, general public international law where the aim is to provide access to a theoretically unitary system though once again the main emphasis will be on treaties, and finally international institutional law where the aim is to provide access to the rules made by international institutions.

PRIVATE INTERNATIONAL LAW : So far, relatively few computerized projects have attempted to provide access to foreign municipal systems of law. As indicated earlier there are extremely sound reasons for this reluctance. It is very difficult for lawyers to interrogate successfully a data-base containing their own municipal law, as the results obtained in the experiments discussed in the last chapter show. When the further disadvantages of unfamiliarity with the foreign legal structure, the foreign context and the foreign language are added, the results are likely to be even worse. Perhaps more important even than any of these factors is unfamiliarity with the detail of the foreign system of law. There will not be the same fixed and well-known points of reference by which to orientate the search. In a municipal system the user may formulate his initial search on the basis of a case which he knows to be relevant to his problem, rather than on the basis of the facts of the problem itself. It is also useful to be able to check the output of the computer by looking for authorities or provisions known to be relevant, and which will be expected to appear. If they do not, the user is immediately put upon his guard, and may wish to go on reformulating the enquiry until they are found.

Nevertheless some systems do seek to provide access to foreign municipal law. In some cases the factors mentioned above may be reduced in force on account of some connection between the systems in question. Thus there is very little difficulty in the United States in providing access in one state to the law of another, providing the other is not that of Louisiana. At another level the systems of the newer Commonwealth, those of the old dominions and those of the United States are all based to a greater or lesser extent upon the British system as a result of the original British connection. It is thus not surprising to find that lawyers practising in these systems are already familiar with each other's materials, and that a good deal of cross-reference takes place between them. In other cases also similarities of structure may exist for historical reasons, for example between those systems derived from the Napoleonic codes, or between countries which have for many years been closely associated, such as the Scandinavian or Latin American countries. It is for these reasons that the CREDOC system provides access to some parts of French law as well as Belgian. A more ambitious project has however been mooted in Italy, and desrves more detailed scrutiny.

M.I.D.A. :[10] This work, which under the direction of Professor Lupoi of the University of Perugia, was started in June 1970. Its aim is to conduct an experiment to test a computerized retrieval system which will give access to British, French and Italian municipal law, either internally to national users, or externally to foreign users. It is intended that it should be capable of providing both broad general information about a large topic, or an answer to a specific enquiry. For the purposes of the experiment the data is taken from English, French and Italian company law, but it is envisaged that the method, if successful, should be capable of being applied to other areas equally well. The experiment proceeds upon the basis of a number of assumptions. The first is that there is indeed no exact conceptual equivalence between different systems of law, at least those as different as those chosen for the experiment. Secondly that full-text is unsuitable for these purposes because it contains many components which are uninformative, and much that is informative is not contained in it. It is, however, assumed that the language used by the framer of the document should not normally be suppressed by the system solely on account of ambiguity. Finally it is asserted that for these purposes the free association of keywords is unlikely to be successful. Instead the system plans to incorporate role indicators, broad subject matter descriptors, and lists of synonyms, related, generic and specific terms.

Each document is classified from a particuliar point of view operating in a particular area of law. This meets one of the arguments against traditional indexing, that it is too general, but at the cost of

---

[10] Lupoi, 'M.I.D.A.: A Project for Comparative Legal Information and Retrieval', XLIV *Annuario di Diritta Comparato e di Studi Legislativi*, 39 (1970). Further information may be obtained from Professor Lupoi, Via Bertolini 119, 0097 Roma.

multiplying the effort which has to be applied to each individual document. In this experiment six points of view are included. Then each document is analyzed by reference to the type of corporate entity with which it is concerned from a list of twenty, and this and the subject area concerned are both expressed by a numerical code. There is finally a dynamic aspect where the codings are said to change with each subsequent point of view, but the precise operation of this facility is not made very explicit.

At the end of this process each document is represented by on average twenty keywords, each expressed by a six-digit numerical code. The retrieval system can be based either on pre-set codings, or on freely chosen keywords according to whether a broad or more specific search is required. An important feature of the system is the provision of an automatic thesaurus which incorporates references to related terms in all three languages, and to more specific and more generic terms, also in the three languages. If a generic term is used, then the system will, if the user wishes, also search on the basis of all the more specific terms linked to it. These features should assist the foreign lawyer. He can by using them discover not only the appropriate foreign equivalents to the term in his own language, but also search under more specific terms, even though they may not be known to him. The system is designed to operate conversationally, and the output may be the number of documents satisfying the search criteria, references to those documents, a print of the pre-set codes and keywords characterizing those documents, or a microfilmed copy of the complete original text.

So far only a few statutory materials have been included in the system, and the short-term plans envisage only a modest increase in the data-base in the immediate future.[11] While the system remains in so early a stage of development, final judgement must be suspended. It is, however, hard to believe that the quality of the thesaurus is likely to be so far in excess of anything hitherto achieved as to make the project really workable. It should nevertheless provide a store of much needed empirical data upon which further work may then be based.

PUBLIC INTERNATIONAL LAW : There has been more work here, largely centred on the law of treaties, where as noted above the situation is particularly serious. The predominance of treaty law as consti-

---

[11] Only a hundred cases were to be included by July 1971, ten English, forty French and fifty Italian.

tuting a retrieval problem is largely explained by the fact that public international law is relatively defective in law-making authorities. Much of it depends upon the custom of states, which is necessarily slow to change. The main avenue for innovation is therefore by way of treaty provision, and it is in the identification of new rules and the detection of change in the old that the retrieval problem lies. In so far as the rules are well settled, there are plenty of conventional sources to rely upon. Thus this part of the chapter will concentrate upon retrieval systems for treaty law. The only other major sources of innovatory rules are the international institutions, and they will be dealt with in the concluding part. So far as treaties are concerned four projects will be mentioned, all of them situated in North America, two employing an indexed or keyword approach, and two making use of the full original text.

International Treaty Data Bank: This project was conceived by Professor Triska of Stanford University, and although pilot work was done, it seems not to have developed into a working system. A most unusual feature of the system is the idea of preparing the data at three different levels. Although access was to be by the use of keywords, and for that reason it is included here as an indexed system, the full-text of the treaties was also to be stored. It seems that this was primarily to be for the purpose of presentation. If the full-text was available, then of course it could be printed out in satisfaction of a search request. This is a reasonable procedure where the original material is inaccessible to the enquirer. In fact, in this project the data-base was to be the treaties contained in the United Nations Treaty Series, and would thus be relatively accessible to most likely users, and it is slightly surprising that such access should have been thought necessary. It is, however, possible that the full-text was put into machine-readable form for another reason. This is related to the provision of the lower of the two levels at which interrogation of the data-base was to be permitted. The data-base was first divided into thirty-six different functional areas, each with a different numeric code. These included topics of such generality as 'aliens', 'the high seas' and 'economic transactions between states'. These were to be further subdivided into smaller areas, again with numerical coding. Thus the category of economic transactions was to be subdivided into trade treaties, trade agreements, payment agreements, credit agreements, agreements on general conditions of delivery, and agreements on separate economic and trade problems.

K

Where possible a further subdivision, again represented by a numerical coding, was also to be made; thus separate economic and trade problems were to be subdivided into such topics as arbitration, protection of trademarks, and most favoured nation clauses. Then for lower level searches a dictionary was to be constructed of words and phrases which were found in the documents within a particular main functional area. There were thus to be thirty-six separate dictionaries. The method of constructing such dictionaries appears to have combined human and machine capabilities. Human beings selected words and phrases which it was thought would be useful for retrieval purposes, and these manually compiled lists constituted the dictionaries to be distributed to users. The computer, however, seems to have been intended to be used to compile a concordance for each of these terms, and it was presumably also for these reasons that the text was originally punched in full. By this means a dictionary of some 250 words and phrases was compiled for the economic area. This system represents an interesting compromise between the usual full-text techniques and conventional indexing. The number of terms is about the same as would be found in a conventional index, but the nature of the terms is as in a full-text technique. Synonyms, grammatical variations and problems of specificity would have to be dealt with in the concordance programme, exactly as in a full-text searching system. It would be interesting to discover how such a dictionary would be received by lawyers, and how satisfactory a level of initial compilation could be achieved, though in view of the methods employed to prepare it, it could be changed much more readily than any conventional index, if and so far as it were found to be unsatisfactory.

A further human operation in this system was to be the amplification of the text of the treaty by the inclusion of certain categories of identifying information. This was to have been by no means as elaborate as the information held by most Ministries of Foreign Affairs at present, and would not have been remotely like the plans of the State Department in the United States or of the Council of Europe as described above. Here the identifying information was to have been limited to the names of the contracting parties, the date of signature and agreement number, the United Nations Treaty Series citation, the United Nations Treaty Series number, the name of the treaty, the subject corresponding with one of the thirty-six subject areas, and finally details relating to ratification and history.

It was envisaged that all of this information could be punched on a standard eighty-column card by the use of numerical coding. While the system seems not to have been put into practical operation, and indeed reveals a number of crudities of conception, it also embodies a technique which is unusual, and which might repay further attention.

United Nations Treaty Series Project :[12] This project was inaugurated by Professor Rohn at the University of Washington, Seattle, in 1963. It is important to note that it has always been intended more as a quantitative political study than as a documentary source for international lawyers, and this orientation has determined a number of crucial decisions. Here again the basic data has so far been limited to published sources, principally the United States Treaty Series and the League of Nations Treaty Series.

The system records certain basic information about the treaties constituting the data-base. This basic information includes the names of bilateral signatories; dates of signature, coming into force and registration; title; one topic to characterize the contents; number of articles; and citations to United Nations Treaty Series volume and page, and series and number. It is planned to enrich the data-base by including also multilateral signatories and post-registration history as documented in the United Nations Treaty Series annexes, and to expand the number of terms which may be used to characterize the contents of the treaty from the single one allowed at present. It is also planned to expand the sources from which the treaties are taken, largely because of the gaps which Professor Rohn has discovered in the coverage of the United Nations Treaty Series in the course of his work.[13] At one stage Professor Rohn contemplated going over to a full-text system, but later abandoned the idea because it was not really appropriate for the purposes of his quantitative studies, and especially at the stage at which it was considered was likely to be too expensive. It is, however, apparent from the nature of the proposed additions to the data-base how unsuitable the original material was for *legal* research. In particular the absence of post-

[12] This is fully documented. No fewer than twenty-three articles were published about this project by Professor Rohn and his associates between 1964 and 1968. See for an example and further references, Rohn, 'United Nations Treaty Series Project', XII *International Studies Quarterly*, 174 (1968).
[13] Rohn, 'Registration and Publication of Treaties', a working paper presented to the Study Group on the Law of Treaties of the American Society of International Law in December 1967. Copies are available from Professor Rohn.

registration history meant that only the original versions of the treaties were included, and thus treaties were included in the database even though they might have long since ceased to be in force. Similarly the coverage was only partial in that all multilateral treaties were excluded. Finally, the limitation of the characterization of the contents of a treaty to one topic leads to inevitable distortion, since as previously noted, treaty-making like statute-making is a process requiring considerable expense and organization, and it is economic to spread such costs over as much content as possible. All of these defects are of course explained and excused by the fact that the system was never intended to be used for legal research.

This orientation of interest is also reflected in the type of retrieval systems which have been set up. There are, in fact, two quite independent systems which operate on a common data-base. One is an interactive system employing teletype terminals which will operate on line to print-out certain items of basic information such as citations to all the air transport agreements between Sweden and Italy contained in the data-base. The current aim is to expand the facilities of this system so as to permit much more sophisticated questions to be answered. This will replace and improve upon facilities which are at present only available on the other retrieval system which operates on a bespoke basis, with each enquiry specially programmed. This means that there are few restrictions on the form of question and the type of response, subject only to those inherent in the form of the data. This system is, however, suitable only for long research projects since the writing and verification of programmes for computers is always a time consuming, and often a frustrating task, though this may be ameliorated to some extent if questions fall into a repetitive mould.

An example of the sort of work to which this project is well suited is a recent investigation into the pattern of treaties made by the Soviet Union.[14] This illustrates the dynamic nature of the work that can be carried out in this way, as the computer opens wider perspectives. The original intention was simply to discover the incidence of references to *ad hoc* commissions in bilateral treaties to which the Soviet Union was a party, as compared with references to the International Court of Justice in the same segment of the data-base, in order to test the hypothesis that the Soviet Union preferred the former to the latter. The initial processing showed that

[14] Rohn, 'A Computer Search of Soviet Treaties', 2 *International Law*, 661 (1968).

there were forty-seven such bilateral treaties containing references to *ad hoc* commissions, and none containing references to the International Court of Justice. It then seemed that some basis for comparison should be made to test the deviation of this pattern from normal, and Poland was selected for a comparative study. But then the horizon was widened and the comparison between the Soviet Union and Poland was itself compared to a comparison between a similar Western pair of states, the United States and Canada, and this in its turn led on to similar consideration of all sorts of different states and groups of states. This further manipulation of the data-base was made easier since it was possible to use the original programming with very little modification. The result was that the original version was progressively broadened in the light of the first results, and many new and interesting questions were suggested which had not at first been considered. Macro-analytical studies, as Professor Rohn calls them, of this type are characteristic of this system, and it is for them that it is primarily valuable, though when the current improvements have been incorporated, the data-base should also be much more useful for practical legal research.

Legal Information Through Electronics (LITE) : This project has already been described in connection with legislative applications which were its original focus, and case law where it has developed extensively. It is not necessary to rehearse again here the techniques employed by this system which, it will be remembered, were essentially those developed by Professor Horty. The work on international law started in 1965 in conjunction with the United States Department of Defense. The Department wished to compile a data-base of international agreements which might be of interest to it, and to be able to secure speedy access to any part of that data-base. The collection of materials for input to the system was somewhat difficult since some of the documents to be included were infomal agreements not requiring registration with the United Nations, while many international agreements to which the United States is a party were of only marginal interest to the Department and for that reason excluded. A source of constant difficulty was the politically sensitive nature of many of the documents, requiring all those working in the system to have security clearance, which entailed that the data-base itself had to be kept in conditions of complete security, as well as strict supervision of the programming to eliminate all danger of the documents being copied. The agreements so compiled amounted in all to some 7 million words, and constituted between 40 and 50 per cent of all treaties to which the United States is a party. The data-base is divided into three parts : unclassified published agreements constituting about 40 per cent of the documents, and unclassified unpublished and classified unpublished agreements constituting about 30 per cent each. One unsatisfactory feature was that in 1970 at least the data-base had not been verified to remove agreements which were no longer in force. This is quite significant. It draws attention to the fact that the system contains no standard up-dating routine, and this in turn illustrates a basic defect in the design of the system. The full-text of the agreements is included, but the amount of amplifying and explanatory material was cut to the bone. Indeed the only additional information stored was the names of the states which were parties, its date, whatever title was to be found in the original, and in the case of published agreements a citation to the place of publication. Thus it is not possible to provide any automatic up-dating system without altering the whole format of the system, and reviewing the whole history of the agreements so far included. This dearth of supplementary information is a general defect in systems derived from the early Pittsburgh work, and reaches its zenith in this particular application, where as demonstrated earlier the need and demand for such supplementary information is greatest. It was for this reason that the United States Department of State rejected a move to employ similar techniques in the computerization of its own internal treaty data bank. As a result of a series of unfortunate administrative and technical difficulties a further problem with the data-base in 1970 was that the classified part had become two years out of date so far as the inclusion of new material was concerned.

Nevertheless, the data-base is available to those prepared to put up with these defects for searching in the normal way, that is by freely chosen and combined natural language words. Such searching is, however, only available on a batch processing basis, and this presents problems since the LITE computer is in Denver, Colorado, and the main departmental user is in Washington DC, and the responses are too sensitive to be entrusted to the ordinary channels of communication. In these circumstances little direct use seems to have been made of the facilities for searching the data-base. Parts of it have, however, been usefully employed in a different way. This is by providing the basis for the compilation of hard copy keyword in context (KWIC) indexes to documents in frequent use. In particular, the texts of the North Atlantic Treaty Organization Status of Forces Agreements and the German Supplemental Status of Forces Agreements have been dealt with in this way. An indication of the scale of such an operation is provided by the text of the negotiating history of the NATO Status of Forces Agreement supplementary agreement which occupies four volumes in its normal form, but is represented by a KWIC index of no fewer than seven volumes. These could not, of course, be compiled until the text of the original had first been put into computer readable form, and this application alone probably justifies the cost of the original transcription. The department thinks that in this context one hundred characters is more useful as a context than the normal sixty-five, and that for specific searches, though not the compilation of a permanent hard copy version, twenty lines of surrounding text would be useful. In many cases of course, such an amount would extend beyond the document, which is in this context usually a paragraph or a clause.

Queen's University, Kingston, Ontario :[15] The work carried on here in international law is also associated with a project which has been described earlier in connection with case law. At its inception in 1961 this was a project for the compilation of treaty information in relation to the British Commonwealth, by conventional means. But in much the same way as in the original work at Pittsburgh, so it was found here that conventional methods were quite inadequate, and that computerized techniques had to be employed. At first each treaty was assigned a page in a loose-leaf notebook, and on it were entered the date and place of signatures, the names of the parties, the dates of ratification by each party, the date and places of exchange of ratifications, the date of entry into force, the language of the text, the citations of treaty collections containing the text of the treaty, references to treaties or other documents subsequently modifying or terminating it, territorial application, and Canadian practice in relation to it such as proceedings in the Canadian Parliament or decisions in the Canadian Courts. As further treaty collections were examined, and as time passed, many of these details required alteration, and there were numerous additions and

[15] 'Cumulative Progress Report to the Canadian International Development Agency', Working Paper No. 8, reprinted in *Law and Computer Technology*, November 1970, p. 246.

amendments often made by different people. Retyping provided further scope for the introduction of errors. It was felt that this difficulty could be best met by the computerization of the treaty records. The preparation of such records has now gone so far that 5,760 treaty records have been prepared in computer readable form, though technical difficulties with the computer system originally held up the work so that only 600 of these have been used as the basis for retrieval experiments. Here, as in their work on case law, the Queen's team has shown great flexibility of approach. It has experimented with free natural language enquiry techniques in which the requests are writen in the form of ordinary English sentences, and the output is presented in putative order of relevance. These programmes work on a basis of word importance derived from sentence position and iteration within the document.

It is envisaged that eventually the full-text of the treaties would constitute a suitable data-base upon which such retrieval techniques could operate, but at present only experimental work has been carried out on treaty law. This project also incorporates a training programme for treaty lawyers in developing Commonwealth countries, and is thus disseminating knowledge of the possibilities of the application of computerized techniques to law in general, and to treaties in particular, much more widely than ever before, though for financial reasons it may be some time before the fruits of this aspect of Canadian work begin to appear.

International institutional law

This section will deal with four different international bodies, each operating in a different way, and with computerized systems differently related to their work. In one case, that of the General Agreement on Tariffs and Trade (GATT), the computerized system is independent of the organization, and simply refers to its documentation. In all of the others the work is under the control of the organization itself; in the United Nations it is a library project, in the Commission of the European Economic Community it is a legal project under the guidance of the legal department, and in the case of the Council of Europe the work involves forward planning for future systems rather than current operation.

United Nations : One of the first computerized projects undertaken by the United Nations in relation to law was the provision of the tapes used for the conventional printing of the United Nations

Treaty Series to a university for conversion into a computer readable form. This was, however, abandoned when no financial support could be obtained to continue the work. Apart from this the only legal application has been part of the general project to apply computerized techniques to the collection of documents held in the Dag Hammarskjold library of the United Nations. With documentation increasing at the rate of 10,000 items each year it was found that conventional indexing systems were increasingly unable to cope, and that the backlog of unindexed documents was growing all the time. The documentation to be included in this scheme excluded that relating to specialized agencies such as the International Court of Justice or the International Labour Office, but included all documentation relating to the legislative work of the General Assembly and Security Council, and associated documentation including treaties registered or recorded pursuant to article 102 of the Charter of the United Nations. The project is primarily concerned with indexing the materials for library purposes, and is not orientated towards giving practical legal access to the more legal materials. Thus international agreements are entered only by parties and main subject matter, and do not contain the supplementary material, for example on post-registration history, necessary to turn the index into a legal working tool. One useful feature of the index is that it includes key extracts from the document as well as references to the microfiche form of the full original text. This can be a most useful browsing device. As noted earlier the subject index is held in the four official languages, and works automatically upon the basis of a table of equivalents so that an entry in any language automatically generates entries in the other three. There are a number of separate but complementary indexes relating to the work of the General Assembly, such as indexes of resolutions and decisions, of speeches arranged alphabetically both by name of state and speaker, of voting records arranged alphabetically by name of subject and country, of membership of committees, of agenda items, and of citations to documents referred to. This project was tested in 1968, and became fully operational only in 1969 so it is far too early to express any concluded judgement about it. It is to be hoped that further details of the performance of the system will be published when experience has accumulated a little further.[16]

[16] In the meantime the most accessible source is Sprudzs, 'Information on Recent Treaties – Some Observations on Tools, Techniques and Problems: The Conventional and the New', op. cit.

General Agreement on Tariffs and Trade (GATT): This is an unusual computer system in a number of ways. As noted above it was
devised not by the organization itself, but by a university teacher,
Professor John Jackson, though it is fair to say that he had previously served on the staff of GATT. Secondly, it was compiled not
for general research but for Professor Jackson's personal use in
writing a book about the law relating to GATT. Thirdly, and perhaps
consequently, it is probably the least expensive computer system ever
developed in relation to law, since its total cost was less than 1,500
dollars.

The first step in this system was to analyze the subject area,
and to prepare a hierarchical coding scheme listing the subject
matter of the various documents. Since the documents all related
to GATT, they could be arranged on the basis of the logic of the
agreement itself. In this respect the example chosen was particularly
favourable for the application of such a method. Professor Jackson
has, however, designed a similar scheme for international law
generally, and believes that it would be possible to design schemes
at any intermediate level, say for all treaties. Once the hierarchical
scheme is prepared, each document in the collection is given a
unique reference number. Then a human being simply reads through
the entire collection, completing an index card for each document bearing the document number, and entering upon it the
hierarchical codes corresponding to the content of the document,
and the document numbers of any documents referred to in it.
When this is completed the computer is simply programmed to
print out an inverted file in which hierarchical codings are used as
headings, and document numbers as entries, together with a list of
documents cited in other documents. This is designed for use as
a basic reference source in hard copy form, so the only operations
are a sort, and subsequent print-out. It would have been possible
to use the data for direct computer searching, and so to permit the
combination of different terms, but Professor Jackson felt that it
was unnecessary to incur the extra expense. Any anticipated combinations of such complexity as to resist simple manual resolution
with the aid of the hard copy inverted file, can be included in the
original programming and printed out as a special part of the file.

The technique is suitable only where a hierarchical code can be
devised and applied consistently and reliably. This means that it will
be most appropriate for limited subject areas and relatively small

collections of documents. Under these conditions the quality of the index is more amenable to control, and the hard copy version should remain of manageable proportions. The great advantage is that the computer is used only once, and to perform an operation which is simple and straightforward for it, but extremely tedious and time-consuming for any human being. Subsequently the search is made manually, and the use of the hard copy version gives all the advantages of the use of books, namely instantaneous response and complete acceptability. It is interesting that two of the most useful schemes in practical use in the United States, this and the LITE system in Washington, employ the computer to produce a conventional tool. This carries heavy implications for the designers of terminals, and other more sophisticated direct access systems.

Commission of the European Communities:[17] This computer system which is installed in the offices of the Commission in Brussels has perhaps the greatest potential of any of the systems described here. It has been developed by the legal department of the Commission to meet a number of pressing problems. The European Communities between them constitute an international organization having nearly all the functions of a municipal state, legislative, administrative and judicial, and at the same time interacting with member states and the legal systems. It is one of very few supra-national institutions with its own assured budget and direct executive power which is both habitually exercised and habitually accepted by the member states. The computer system which was designed in 1967 and came into preliminary operation in 1970, will eventually assist with all phases of the legal work of the Commission. The first objective of the system has been to deal with the Acts and regulations produced by the Commission itself. These present problems because they are produced at an extremely rapid rate, and now number around ten thousand. They are also in many cases quite ephemeral, but cannot be discarded as soon as they are replaced, since in common with most legal applications it is necessary to be able to reconstruct the precise state of the law as it existed at any particular moment in the past. The situation is further complicated, again as in many municipal systems, by the possibility of implicit as well as explicit

[17] See Gaudet, 'Computerized Retrieval of European Community Legal Material', *Law and Computer Technology*, September 1970, p. 203. Further information may be obtained from Mme Bauer-Bernet, Communautés Européennes, Service Juridique de la Commission, 200 rue de la Loi, 1040 Brussels.

repeal. Another problem is that these documents vary enoromously in their complexity and importance, covering the same gamut as that from constitutional amendments to departmental directives establishing subsidy rates for pig-feed in a municipal system. This means that the computer system has to be sufficiently flexible to operate at a number of different levels. There is also the problem of language. At present documents are produced in Dutch, French, German and Italian. English is likely to be added in the near future as the Community expands. These languages present no problem at present while the system is limited to community rules which are drafted as duplicate originals in the different languages, but will become acute as the documentation expands into the law made by the domestic systems of member states in adopting, adapting and interpreting Community law. At present the Commission's system works primarily in French, but tries to substitute numerical codes wherever possible to minimize linguistic dependence. The first problem is that the system must ultimately be capable of handling the complete range of legal documentation, legislation both of the Communities and the member states, case law similarly from both sources, commentaries, and any other miscellaneous documents such as treaties, collective agreements and all other legal documents to which reference might be advantageous.

The current computer system uses as its basis the technology of the International Business Machines Document Processing System (DPS). This permits both the richness of full-text processing where that is required, and the economy of indexed searching when that is preferable. A feature of the Commission's system, called CELEX, is the generous use of bibliographic headings or rubrics to provide supplementary information about the documents within the system, and to serve to delimit the ambit of particular searches. Twenty-eight different items are included in the system apart from the text of the document itself. These headings are used to number and identify each document, to give relevant dates (there are no fewer than six of these), references to secondary sources, language references, associated documentation and general and specific descriptors. The relationships between the different documents are regarded as being particularly important, and as many as twenty different types of relationship are provided for.

In December 1970 the system was operating with a data-base of 1,000 Acts and regulations, which are expected to build up to 4,000 by the end of 1972, by which time it is also expected to have 500 decisions of international judicial organs, 100 decisions of national courts, 500 secondary commentaries, and 500 further miscellaneous documents also included.

At present the system operates on a batch processing basis, with two batches of up to about eight enquiries each day. In November 1970 the rate of enquiry was running at about three hundred per month. The enquiries are framed by lawyers at the computer centre in free natural language text by reference to all the usual operators offered by Boolean systems and by the DPS programmes. Word position and special groupings can also be provided for. Response can be in any of the usual forms, that is statistical information, lists of references, or the full-text of the documents. In addition the various bibliographic headings can be used to control and restrict the searches.

The main significance of this system lies in its wide scope, and the power and importance of the body it is designed to serve. There can be no doubt that the combination of these factors will eventually make this one of the most important legal information retrieval systems operating anywhere in the world. It is perhaps surprising to find it so dependent upon a commercial package for its programming, but this has enabled it to establish itself quickly, and will no doubt undergo such progressive modification as the system develops and spreads into other fields, as to become unrecognizable. Even now political difficulties over the use of an American computer by the primary European institution are beginning to foreshadow possible changes in approach. So too the enlargement of the Communities, and especially the accession of members with fundamentally different legal systems, will increase the pressure for adaptation.

Council of Europe : The Council of Europe is older than the European Communities, and has more members. It too has a legislative body, the European Parliament, but this body has no direct executive power, and has no comparable budget of its own. It is accordingly less powerful and less wealthy than the Commission of the European Communities. Nevertheless it is backed by a strong administrative staff, and has its own legal directorate. It is clearly inappropriate for it to set up its own computerized retrieval system, but it has nevertheless shown considerable foresight and interest in relation to such developments. The work of the Council has chiefly lain in the coordination of work being carried on in member countries. It realized that without such coordination there was a grave danger of the duplication of research effort, and of the waste of scarce resources. One of the features of computerized techniques in law is that a very high proportion of the expense is incurred in the preparation of the data-base. It seemed important to the Council to try to prevent the development of incompatible data formats by different states. Although format is to some extent dictated by the purposes of the project and the configuration of the machines used, many decisions which have to be made are free in the sense that they could equally be made in any one of a number of ways with equally successful results, but one must be chosen. But once they have been made, and large quantities of legal documents have been prepared in accordance with them, it can be very difficult to go back, and to adapt the system to a different specification.

As a preliminary step the Council set up a Committee of Experts on the Harmonization of the Means of Programming Legal Data into Computers. This Committee held its first meeting in 1969, and quickly decided that it should first learn more about the work already under way in Europe and elsewhere, and about the demands which it was envisaged would be made for legal information in the future. To this end it appointed three subcommittees, charged with international legal data, national legal data and legal statistics. It was eventually decided that the question of legal statistics could not be divorced from that of the computerization of other forms of statistics. In the case of international legal data, as previously noted, an elaborate analytical system was established with a view to computerization, and this is being tried out on treaties for which the Council is the official depository.

So far as national legal data is concerned, the relevant subcommittee has conducted elaborate surveys into current projects in Europe, has organized a symposium for their discussion, and has recommended the use of standardized bibliographic headings for national computerized systems for legislation, case law and commentaries. It is too early to know whether the full committee will adopt these recommendations, and if so what action will follow. The work of gathering information has however itself achieved very useful results in putting research workers all over Europe into contact with each other, and the opportunities for international understanding and eventual collaboration have been established.

2 PREDICTION OF DECISIONS

There has been relatively little application of the techniques for the prediction of judicial decisions, discussed in the previous chapter, to international law. One possible reason is that in international judicial tribunals the personalities of the judges are usually less important than in common law countries, and that many of the scaling and block analysis techniques are thus less eligible. One simple application has been made, however, and since the techniques used to differ slightly from those discussed in the previous chapter, it is perhaps worth mentioning here.

In this study[18] Professor Nagel selected as his basic data 137 cases to which the United States was a party, which involved international relations, and which were included in at least one of the leading American casebooks in the field of international law. These cases were analyzed by reference to seven major variables : the main source of law, the main subject matter and position in relation to it of the United States, the decision-making tribunal, the economic interest involved and the position in relation to it of the United States, the industrial power of the opponent of the United States, and the nature of the plaintiff. Each of these seven variables was then subdivided into a number of smaller categories, four under the first, thirteen under the second, six under the third, five under the fourth, five under the fifth, three under the sixth, and six under the seventh. These subdivisions were taken to exhaust the variables, and one, and only one, was presumed to be present in relation to each variable. This meant that some subcategories of a variable merely recorded the absence of that variable in the particular case. Thus in ninety-nine of the cases there was either no civil liberty interest or the United States took a neutral position in relation to it.

The cases were then simply divided into those where the United States won and those where it lost, and the percentage chance of such success calculated for each subcategory of each major variable. Thus where the main source of law was international law and custom, the United States won in 56 per cent of the sixty-three cases decided in which it appeared as a factor. This gives a simple score of 0·56 where that category is present. It was then possible to add the seven percentages for each case, and thus to arrive at a total score for the case. These cases were then ranked according to their

[18] Nagel, 'Judicial Prediction and Analysis from Empirical Probability Tables' 41 *Indiana Law Journal*, 403 (1966).

total scores, and divided into seven approximately equal groups, and the percentage chance of success calculated for each group. These calculations should then be capable of indicating the probability of any case being won by the United States. It is, however, a somewhat crude method, and in the article a more sophisticated weighting technique, based on discriminant weighting, is also employed.

The sample is a small one, and suffers from the disadvantage of assuming that all the major variables are of approximately equal weight, and operate independently of each other. The crudity of the calculation is revealed by the results of applying the tests derived from the results of the 137 cases back to the facts of those cases. On this basis an incorrect prediction would have been made for 32 of the 137 cases, and this figure would not have been improved by the employment of the more sophisticated weighting system. This should not be taken to show that international materials are peculiarly resistant to such approaches, but rather that more sophisticated analysis of the relevant area of international law, and of the reasons for deciding cases in it, should first be undertaken.

Computers and land registration

Some of the most important and financially significant legal transactions are those concerned in dealings with real estate, with land
and houses. Such transactions also occur at a high, and reasonably
constant, rate. It is natural therefore that the application to them
of computerized techniques should be considered. One aspect of
this, namely land registration, will be considered here. In this short
chapter some attempt will be made to assess in turn general considerations relating to such systems, progress which has been made
or is under way in some parts of the world, and possible future
developments.

I GENERAL CONSIDERATIONS

In this section the problems raised by land registation will be considered in outline. First the aims of land registration will be mentioned, then its nature will be discussed, and finally the implications
of these for the application of computerized systems will be
considered.

Aims of land registration
The aims of land registration are set out in the preamble to the Land
Registry Act 1862 :

Whereas it is expedient to give certainty to the title to real estates and to
facilitate the proof thereof and also to render the dealing with land more
simple and economical. . . .

The British system thus aims at providing simplicity, economy and
certainty. It is apparent that while the first two of these may be
complementary, they could easily come into conflict with the third.

It is generally assumed in the United Kingdom, though to a lesser extent in other parts of the Commonwealth where the Torrens system prevails, that these aims should be made subject to the preservation of the majority of the existing provisions of the substantive law of land, for example that relating to restrictive covenants. Thus dramatic simplification of procedure by an Alexandrian stroke through the substantive law is tacitly excluded. It is also clear that complete certainty is unobtainable, as the history of the first attempts at registration of title in Great Britain make uncomfortably clear, and a balance must thus be struck between certainty and expense, subject to minimum and maximum limits in each case.

Nature of land registration

There are several possible subjects for registration, any of which might broadly be described as a system of land registration. First and most fundamental is a register of the land itself. This lies at the root of many proposed systems which proceed on the basis of registering the land in a geographical sense by, for example, aerial photography, and the subsequent application of computer programmes to describe any part of the land by reference to the geographical coordination of its boundaries. In such a system there would be a guarantee of complete coverage of all the land in a given area, and all references would be completely consistent with each other. It is clear that accurate mapping of the land itself is an indispensable necessity in any system of land registration. Equally clearly it cannot by itself serve all the needs of legal transactions in land, if only because the units of exchange in such transactions do not exhaustively and exclusively correspond to physical units depicted on a map, but instead comprehend notional legal characteristics of such areas, which may overlap in relation to any given piece of land, or which may relate one piece to another. It is also the case that in most parts of the world the units do not remain constant over a given period of time, but may be added to or subtracted from, with the result that in most countries with a long history of transactions in land, the shapes of the plots have become highly irregular, and have ceased to correspond, if they ever did, to physical characteristics which might be seen on a map. Thus in all practical land registration systems for legal purposes, some facility must be provided for the registration of legal title to a particular interest in a particular piece of land.

In many such systems, and certainly in those derived from the common law, certainty of title has been secured by the recording of transactions in land in deeds which operate to create, convey and extinguish legal interests. These deeds are generally both operative and evidential. They operate directly to accomplish the relevant transaction, and they amount to evidence that the transaction has taken place. Thus some early systems of registration in England concentrated on the registration of deeds, and these have been exported to other parts of the Commonwealth where they sometimes exist side by side with the Torrens system of registration of title.

Clearly connected with the registration of title is the registration of incumbrances upon title. This is really no more than a way of elaborating the negative as well as the positive aspects of title. Registration of title gives an indication of the utmost rights of its possessor, while reference to the registration of incumbrances reveals any derogations from it, such as leases, restrictive covenants or easements over it.

It is also possible to register details of the person or body who or which has title to land, and this is clearly a necessary ingredient of any system of land registration concerned with transactions in land since it enables the proper parties to such transactions to be identified.

Of these various elements in land registration, title to a particular plot of land, the nature of any incumbrances, and the name of the proprietor, are clearly essential. It seems likely that systems of registration of deeds will decay, and such systems are less compatible with computerized methods than systems of registration of title.[1] The registration of the physical land can be catered for by the annexation of maps to the verbal description of the plot in the relevant certificate of title.

The main problems raised here for computerization relate to the question of devising a system for the identification and coding of particular plots of land, the incorporation of maps, the definition and coding of different sorts of incumbrance, and the provision of comprehensive facilities for dealing with the addresses of plots and the names of their proprietors.

The identification of particular plots is primarily achieved by

[1] For a detailed comparison of the two systems, see Ontario Law Reform Commission Report on Land Registration, Ch. 3 (1971).

reference to a map, but within the system it is still necessary to represent each plot by some unique code. This code can be completely arbitrary, and consists simply of a running number according to the chronological order of registration. This is certainly a simple system to operate. Its disadvantage is that where a complete geographical area is not registered simultaneously, but plot by plot at random, numerical and geographical relationship will be nonexistent. Similarly, where plots are subdivided or amalgamated the codes representing the new units will bear no relationship to the codes representing the old units from which they are derived. It is true that this difficulty could be met by the adoption of some form of decimal notation, but only at the cost of inconsistency in the length of codes. In any system an essential feature must be a general map capable of being up-dated to show the geographical relationship between different plots. It is worth considering whether it might not be preferable to reduce such dependency on an index map, which it would be difficult to include within a computer system in machine readable form. This could be achieved by the assignment of a plot number not on a chronological, but on a geographical basis. This would have to depend in some way upon the geographical coordinates of the plot, perhaps the coordinates of the centroid of the plot. These would automatically change as amalgamation or subdivision took place, but the numbers would always retain some relationship to those signifying their predecessors or successors, and to the numbers of adjacent plots, which would constitute another useful feature of such a scheme.[2] Another, though less eligible, alternative is the identification of a plot by reference to its conventional address. This would have the effect of relating many adjacent plots to each other, but would be neither sufficiently uniform nor comprehensive to serve as a satisfactory substitute for a system of identification by reference to geographical coordinates. Indeed, the introduction of postal codes suggests that movement is likely to take place in the other direction, and addresses may themselves eventually be replaced by reference numbers.

It is unlikely that maps will be directly searchable by computers for some time. Computer graphics systems are at an early stage of

[2] See Cook, 'A Modern System of Land Records', 38 *Univ. of Cincinnati Law Review*, 385 (1969) for a discussion of some of the technical problems involved.

development, and extremely expensive to use at present. In this connection maps are, apart from the index maps mentioned above, largely used for scrutiny as an end product rather than as an integral part of the searching process, and while it might be convenient for microfilmed versions of existing maps to be stored, and perhaps even introduced into the computer system by way of the use of video terminals which can either display microfilmed or digital data, it seems unlikely that any further use could be justified.

The difficulties of identifying and coding incumbrances seem much less formidable. In England and Wales there is aleady a well established coding system which could easily be supplemented by a short natural language description. Indeed the degree of complexity would seem to depend entirely upon the degree of complexity of the substantive law. There is further advantage here in that the descriptions of the incumbrances are in a set legal form, and all those concerned with those transactions know what they are. They differ in this from, say, addresses of lots, or names of parties, which are much more variable and less widely known. The only further point to be made here is that it may be desirable to order a register of incumbrances by reference to the codes not only of the incumbered titles but also of those benefiting from the incumbrance. This should present no problem in a computerized system.

Addresses of plots and names of proprietors present a number of irritating difficulties. In the United States it has been proposed that the problem of names could be overcome by the use of the Social Security number, though how this would apply to, say, unincorporated bodies or foreign governments which own plots, is not entirely clear. In continental Europe similar methods might be employed, in those countries where each citizen has his own personal identification number. There are however, states, and Great Britain is one, where this is not the case. It is true that there are other numbers such as the National Insurance number which could be used, but there would still be difficulties.

If the ordinary form of name is to be used as a means of identification, it then becomes necessary to cater for variations of form, as a result of abbreviation, carelessness or ignorance. To some extent this problem will diminish as a computer system becomes established, as it will become common to use the form currently held within the system as shown on the most recent print-out. To the extent that this is not used it will be necessary to employ a thesaurus technique so that each possible form can be related to all other possible forms. It will not, of course, be possible to cope in this way with all careless errors of spelling, or ignorance of the correct form. The former might be dealt with by an elaborate checking system at the input stage of any search, the latter only by providing suitable browsing facilities. In that case, however, it should be pointed out that the difficulty need be no greater within a modern computerized system than it is in the current manual system.

Implications

In most countries the primary use of land registration is to assist transactions in land by giving some external assurance of the validity of the offer being made. The purchaser will wish to make sure before parting with the price and thus completing the transaction, that the vendor is competent to sell what he is purporting to sell. In most countries large numbers of such transactions take place every day, but any given private individual is unlikely to engage in more than a few during his lifetime. At the same time such transactions are often time-consuming and difficult to execute for those unpractised in them. This encourages the growth of a professional class to carry out such transactions on behalf of private individuals. This is advantageous since it means that dissemination of knowledge of the system, and of changes in it, is facilitated. A further advantage of the high volume of transactions in relation to land registration is that the demand can be predicted within tolerable limits of accuracy. The Land Registry receives about a million applications a year, of which about five thousand a day relate to the register of land charges, or incumbrances. Similarly with proportions of this order of magnitude it can be predicted with some certainty how many searches are likely to be fruitful; in the case quoted above it is known that 17 per cent of the land charges searches will reveal an entry, and the remainder will not. Clearly, well established statistics of this sort assist the design of a computer system.

The result then is that there is a professional class which conducts most of the enquiries, which themselves fall into well-settled and predictable patterns. They are also conducted on the basis that the enquirer and the registry are *ad idem* as to the questions which will be asked, the terminology in which they will be couched and the responses which will be appropriate. This is an inestimable, and extremely rare, advantage for any information storage and retrieval system.[3]

It would appear therefore that land registration presents a number of features conducive to computerization. There is also the further advantage that such transactions are of great economic importance to the parties who will more often than in many legal situations be able to assess in economic terms the advantages of efficiency, and be prepared to pay for them. These parties will usually also be involved in raising relatively large sums of money to finance the main transactions, thus rendering it easier and more acceptable to finance a computerized system in an acceptable way. One of the difficulties, however, is that because transactions in land are so common, and being conducted at such a high rate, the transition to a computerized system presents certain problems. It has to be introduced by an already fully occupied staff without in any way impinging on current activities which must be allowed to continue exactly as normal throughout the entire transition period.

2 CURRENT DEVELOPMENTS

The computerization of land registration still lies largely in the future, certainly in the larger and more heavily populated countries. Here some indication will be given of three examples of possible lines of future development. Reference will be made in turn to the proposed scheme for land charges registration which is already being implemented in England and Wales, the scheme of land registration proposed by the Ontario Law Reform Commission for that province, and a pilot scheme which has been introduced in Sweden by the Ministry of Justice.

Land charges registration in England and Wales[4]
The registers which are kept under the Land Charges Act 1925 consist of volumes of forms relating to land charges. These are not searched directly, but by reference to an index, consisting currently of about 3 million cards bound up in about 10,000 volumes. It is estimated that by 1980 the index will cater for about 5 million charges. The index is arranged alphabetically by the name of the

[3] See Whalen, 'Electronic Computer Technology and the Torrens System', 40 *A.L.J.*, 413 (1967) for a very thorough examination of this aspect of the topic.
[4] See further Ruoff, 'A Computer for the Land Charges Department', 67 *Law Society's Gazette*, 115, 545 (1970).

estate owner, and in the case of common names is subdivided by reference to the county in which the plot is situated. Each entry also indicates the address of the plot, class of charge, official reference number, date of registration, county and parish where the plot is situated, and a short description of the plot. Searches may be made either officially by the staff of the Registry, in which case the official certificate is conclusive, or personally by an individual enquirer, or more commonly by his agent, in which case the result is not conclusive. The system is slow, labour-intensive and inconvenient. It is also subject to error on account of faulty matching of names,[5] or of descriptions of property.[6]

It is proposed first to microfilm the existing index, a quick process which will take each index out of commission for only a very short time, and then to prepare a paper tape version from these microfilmed records, ensuring of course that the tapes are kept up-dated by reference to subsequent transactions. In essence the computerized system will operate in the same way as the existing manual service, that is to say on the basis of the name of the estate owner and the location of the plot. There will have to be some modifications, however, since about 14 per cent of the existing entries lack a description of the plot charged. By agreement with the Law Society the address of the estate owner will be entered in such cases. It is also possible that other descriptions will now be outdated. Accordingly it is proposed to identify a plot's location by reference only to the county within which it is situated. This would, however, lead to multiple entries for common names in populous counties, and so as a further parameter the dates of ownership of the relevant proprietor will be added. These should normally be available to the enquirer, and it is envisaged that their inclusion will reduce the number of entries to manageable limits, with an estimated maximum of about ten. It is proposed to use disc storage for the first stage of the search against the name of the proprietor which will account for 55 per cent of the searches which will reveal no entry at that level. For the 45 per cent which do reveal a match at that level, further searching will be conducted on a data cell by reference first to the county and then to dates of proprietorship, which will finally disclose a complete match in approximately 17 per cent of the original volume of searches. It is proposed to deal with problems over names by dividing

---

[5] e.g. *Oak Co-Operative Building Society* v. *Blackburn* [1968], Ch. 730.
[6] e.g. *Du Sautoy* v. *Symes* [1967], Ch. 1146.

them into three groups : simple names of private individuals, complex names of private individuals, and names of corporate bodies. In the case of simple names some aggregation will take place by the use of initials. Thus a search for Francis Davis Blackburn will also run against entries for F. D. Blackburn which will include entries registered under Frank David, Francis David, and Frank Davis Blackburn, for example. Thesaurus techniques will be used to cope with multiple alternative names of private individuals, such as those possessed by some peers, and with the names of corporate bodies which may be capable of numerous permutations of form. Similarly in the case of location, thesaurus techniques will be used to cope with situations where the county has, or may have, changed as a result of local government reorganization. These facilities should certainly improve the efficiency of the service provided by the land charges department.

Even more dramatic improvements are planned in relation to the techniques for searching. It is envisaged that most of the work will continue to consist of official searches conducted in response to postal enquiries on official forms. This service will remain substantially unchanged so far as the enquirer is concerned, except that his official certificate will have been printed by the computer. The advent of computerization has, however, made it possible for the department not only to entertain telephone or telex enquiries, but also to guarantee the results of the search. This will be accomplished by the installation of video terminals on-line to the computer. Searches coming in over the telephone will be received by operators sitting at these terminals. The operators will first check the details to be searched carefully with the enquirer, keying them in as they are established, they will then read the result of the search back to the enquirer from the screen in front of them if there are six entries or less. If there are more they will simply report the number over the telephone. In either event a hard copy version will also be prepared, and this will be sent off as an official certificate by post. It is this certificate, not the telephone answer, which will be guaranteed. This service will be tied in with a new system of credit accounting which is being introduced at the same time, and which should achieve further economy in the use of human labour.

The work of converting the records and installing the computer is already well under way, and it is hoped that the system will become fully operational in 1973. Studies are also being made into the

L*

problems involved in extending computerization to the other principal land registries in England and Wales.[7]

Land registration in Ontario[8]
There are about 2¼ million plots of land in Ontario, 85 per cent of which are currently governed by a system of registration of deeds, and 15 per cent of which are currently governed by a system of registration of title. Neither of these was felt to be completely satisfactory so the Ontario Law Reform Commission undertook an enquiry with the assistance of a firm of consultants, who at first independently, and later in cooperation with the Commission, planned for conversion to a computerized system. The view taken was that it was necessary to set up a completely new system of registration, having more in common with the existing title system than with the system of registering deeds. It was envisaged that the system should make use of local offices linked to a central computer. The computer would hold a summary of the information relating to a specific plot, its index number, the owner's name and a reference to the description of the interests in it. The local offices would have terminals linked to the central computer. Descriptions of the interests and copies of the original documents would be available on microfilm in the local offices. Registration of interests would be filed with the local offices which would transmit a warning to the central computer which would show against any print-out of an entry relating to the plot in question, pending transmission by post of the details of the change to the central computer for permanent up-dating of the central records.

A feature of the Ontario report is a detailed costing of the introduction of a computerized system as against the costs of introducing a new manual system. By limiting the mapping work to that necessary for the production of adequate index maps, it is envisaged that 85 per cent of the plots in the province could be entered into the system within a period of five years, if the legally easy ones are put in first. On the basis of the figures in the consultants' report, which were not wholly accepted by the Commission, the new computerized system would begin to show a discounted cost/benefit advantage

[7] Cp. Newhook, 'Computerizing the New Zealand Land Registry Office', 1971 *Auckland University L.R.*, 1.
[8] See, further, Report on Land Registration by Ontario Law Reform Commission (1971).

over a new manual system by the end of the fifth year of operation, with a break-even point at the end of the seventh year. This analysis also makes it clear that the direct cost to the government of the provision of a computerized system is greater, but that the savings for lawyers are very much more than commensurate, so it is not unreasonable to suppose that lawyers could hold their charges to clients constant while still paying higher search fees to the government. The computerized system would break even with the cost of continuing the present system in about thirteen years, whereas the break-even point for a new manual system against the present manual system would be delayed long beyond that, and could not even be forecasted with any reliability. As a byproduct of the introduction of a new system it is recommended that Ontario should adopt a code numbering system based on geographical coordinates.

Land registration in Sweden[9]
By parliamentary resolutions of 1968 and 1970 Sweden decided to set up two new registers, one a register of real estate, and the other of rights in real estate, to replace the existing registers. As a pilot study for this work, a trial data-base has been established for Uppsala County making extensive use of modern computer technology. This data-base relates to about 38,000 plots, but because of duplication of notation systems, amounts to about 60,000 notations. One system is designed to convert searches under any existing notation into the new notation being introduced as part of the rationalization. The main aim of the pilot study is to permit the use of the most advanced electronic aids, in particular video terminals, for the compilation, up-dating and searching of the registers. The register of population based upon real estate units already existed on magnetic tape, and this was used to create the new electronic register of real estate, subject to amendment by comparison with the conventional bound volumes of the existing register of real estate. Elaborate suites of programmes have been devised to handle compilation, up-dating and searching of both the main registers. In the case of the register of rights in real estate there are four basic programmes covering notification of rights, allocation of a daybook number, up-dating of the register, and approval of up-dating. The last operation requires authorization by an approved official and is effected by the removal

[9] See, further, Alpsten, 'ADP System for a Data Bank for Real Estate', mimeograph, Stockholm (1971).

of a warning symbol which is automatically inserted against the entry at the notification stage.

The search routines are flexible, and designed to permit browsing by the user. This might seem unnecessary in a land registration system, but it must be remembered that in Sweden such registers are also used for a large number of environmental planning purposes, in addition to their normal legal uses. The browsing routines work on the basis of units calculated in terms of screens of text. The main search routine allows ten screens each of twelve lines with eighty positions to be browsed at a time. There are separate routines for searching by way of either the old notation, or the new notation, or by street address. If the last is employed the programmes anticipate that there may be some variation and uncertainty, and a truncation facility is provided permitting retrieval of all addresses showing the first three initial letters. This seems very expansive to one used to the English form of addresses, but perhaps styles are different in Sweden. There are further special facilities for tracing the history of a particular plot through previous designations, until a point is reached at which more than one predecessor is revealed, at which stage the enquirer is informed, and must choose whether, and if so how, to continue.

3 FUTURE POSSIBILITIES

It is suggested that in both the Swedish and to a lesser extent the Ontario systems a feature is the integration of other governmental interests with the registration of land. In Sweden land is regarded as a prime unit to which many other activities are related. Thus it is used to measure population, and to assess taxes. The Swedes also plan to use the land data banks, which contain much more information than those in other countries including much that in Great Britain would be held by the Census Office, for purposes of economic forecasting and general social organization. It is for them a prime source of social statistics, and the hinge upon which all planning dependent upon such statistics turns.

This is perhaps further than many countries would be prepared to go. But it clearly is sensible to marry some other governmental functions with land registration systems, if only to avoid wasteful duplication of effort. Thus if accurate mapping is to be carried out for land registration purposes, as recommended in the Ontario Report, these maps should be made available for all governmental purposes. Similarly if, as in many countries, taxation is raised upon the ownership or occupation of, or dealing with, land, the registration records should be integrated with those of the revenue departments. Indeed it would be relatively simple to devise automatic addressing and assessment routines which would reduce delays in notification and collection, while at the same time cutting out unnecessary clerical activity.

Finally there are planning and land use activities. These depend quite fundamentally upon access to accurate information about the current use being made of land in the country. Since some government regulations and activities, central and local, have to be considered during any conveyancing transaction, it is sensible to integrate information about these into any computerized land registration system. It must not be forgotten that the main advantage of a computerized system, as of the computer itself, lies in its versatility. Information which is entered in one form for one purpose can be made freely available in other forms for other purposes, and the costs of initial entry and the establishment of the system spread over a large number of uses. The development of ever-larger computers, and better terminal links, should enable such integration to take place on an increasing scale.[10]

It is thus possible to look forward to a time when information about and for all central and local governmental activities touching land and land registration will be handled by one large data centre. This should improve efficiency and control in two ways : the activities of the governmental bodies should be capable of operating more efficiently, and in particular should be better able to restrict the evasion of obligations by individuals, but at the same time individuals should be able to discover more information about governmental activities more easily, and be in a better position to expose errors and control abuse.

[10] For a description of a computer simulation of the operation of such an interactive system conducted at the Harvard Law School, see Degnon and Haar, 'Computer Simulation in Urban Legal Studies', 23 *Journal of Legal Education*, 353 (1970).

SELECT BIBLIOGRAPHY

This bibliography has been selected so as to guide the reader into the field, not as a survey of every blade of grass to be found in it. It is divided into a general section, and sections dealing with special topics. Where a general work includes sections referring to special topics it is not separately mentioned under these topics. It is heavily biased towards works in English.

GENERAL

Books

    Computers and the Law (ed. Bigelow, 2nd ed. 1969).

    Cases and Material on Computers and the Law (ed. Freed, 3rd ed. 1971).

    Proceedings of the Computers and Law Conference 1968 (ed. Johnston, Queen's University, Kingston, Ont. 1969).

    The Law of Computers (ed. Holmes and Norville, 1971).

    Computers and the Lawyer (University of Sydney, 1968).

Reports

    Computers for Lawyers (Aitken, Campbell and Morgan for Scottish Legal Computer Research Trust, 1972).

    Computers and the Profession (Slayton for Department of Communications of the Government of Canada, 1972).

    Das Juristische Informationssystem (Herausgegeben von Bundesministerium der Justiz, 1972).

Journals

    Jurimetrics Journal (formerly *Modern Uses of Logic in Law*) (American Bar Association).

Law and Computer Technology (World Peace Through Law).
Rutgers Journal of Computers and Law (Rutgers University).
Systema (University of Turin).
Datenverarbeitung im Recht (Bonn).

Special Numbers of Journals

Themis, 1971, no. 1 (Montreal); especially strong on developments in the French-speaking part of Canada.

Law and Contemporary Problems, 1963, no. 1.

AF – JAG Law Review, 1966, no. 6; mainly describes the LITE system.

Law Library Journal, 1971, no. 2; mainly describes library applications.

EVIDENCE

The best accounts are to be found in the general works, especially those edited by Bigelow and Freed, and the University of Sydney symposium.

PRIVACY

Books

Westin, *Privacy and Freedom* (1967).
Westin, *Data Banks in a Free Society* (1972).
Warner and Stone, *The Data Bank Society* (1970).
Miller, *Assault on Privacy* (1971).

Reports

Ontario Law Commission : Report on the Protection of Privacy in Ontario (1968).

JUSTICE Privacy and the Law (1970).

Royal Commission on Privacy (Ch. Sir Kenneth Younger) Cmnd 5012 (1972).

Articles

Warren and Brandeis, 'The Right to Privacy', 4 *Harvard L.R.*, 193 (1890).

Westin, 'Legal Safeguards to Insure Privacy in a Computer Society', 10 *Communications of A.C.M.*, 553 (1967).

Fried, 'Privacy', 77 *Yale L.J.*, 475 (1968).

Miller, 'Personal Privacy in the Computer Age', 67 *Michigan L.R.*, 1091 (1969).

LEGISLATION

Reports

Elkins, Survey of the Use of EDP by State Legislatures (2nd ed. 1971).

Statute Law Society, Statute Law Deficiencies (1970).

Articles

Horty *et al.*, 'An Information Retrieval Language for Legal Studies', 4 *Journal of ACM*, 380 (1961).

Chartrand, 'Application of ADP in Legal Information Handling', Library of Congress Legislative Reference Service (1966).

Caldwell, 'Legislative Record Keeping in a Computer Journal', 5 *Harvard J. of Legislation*, 1 (1957).

Skelley, 'Computers and the Law', 33 *Saskatchewan L.R.*, 167 (1968); 'The Computer and Legal Information Retrieval', 3 *Ottawa L.R.*, 433 (1969).

Niblett and Price, 'The Status Project', UK-AEA Research Paper CLM-R101 (1969).

CASE LAW

Reports

Fraenkel, Legal Information Retrieval, 9, *Advances in Computers*, 113 (1968).

Tapper, Feasibility Study on Retrieving Legal Information from Two Types of Natural Language Text, OSTI Research Report 5062 (1969).

Canadian Department of Justice, Operation Compulex (1972).

Articles

Wilson, 'Computer Retrieval of Case Law', 16 *Southwestern L.J.*, 409 (1962).

Link, 'RIRA – A Legal Information System in the IRS', 43 *Taxes*, 321 (1965).

Kayton, 'Retrieving Case Law by Computer : Fact, Fiction and Future', 35 *George Washington L.R.*, 1 (1966).

Fraenkel, 'Full text Document Retrieval', Proceedings of ACM

Symposium on Information Storage and Retrieval Applications (1971).

LITIGATION

Most of the recent documentation is to be found in *'Judicature'*.

Report
'Recording Court Proceedings', Lord Chancellor's Office (1972).

PREDICTION

Books
Schubert (ed.), *Judicial Decision Making* (1963); (ed.) *Judicial Behaviour* (1964); *The Judicial Mind* (1965).

Special Number of Periodical
Harvard Law Review, 1966, no. 8.
These sources give a wide cross-section of approaches to this topic which has stimulated an enormous amount of writing, much of it description of applications to various courts.

INTERNATIONAL LAW

Book
Sprudzs, *Treaty Sources in Legal and Political Research* (1971).

Article
Rohn, 'United Nations Treaty Series Project', *XII International Studies Quarterly,* 174 (1968).

LAND REGISTRATION

Articles
Whalen, 'Electronic Computer Technology and the Torrens System', 40 *Australian L.J.,* 413 (1967).
Cook, 'Land Law Reform: A Modern Computerized System of Land Records', 38 *Univ. of Cincinnati L.R.,* 385 (1969).
Ruoff, 'A Computer for the Land Charges Department', 67 *Law Society's Gazette,* 115, 545 (1970).

General Index

Index of Names